The Beast Was Out There
The 28th Infantry Black Lions and the Battle of Ông Thanh
Vietnam, October 1967

On the morning of October 17, 1967, the 2nd Battalion of the 1st Infantry Division's 28th Regiment ("Black Lions") initiated contact with the 271st Viet Cong Regiment near the jungle stream of Ông Thanh, some fifty miles north of Saigon. The ensuing clash quickly escalated into a full-scale battle that saw the VC gaining fire superiority over the Americans, attacking their attackers with skill and ferocity, inflicting 134 casualties—including 57 killed—by the time the fighting had ended.

There were many extraordinary acts of heroism that day by the men of the Black Lions, which made the unexpected outcome all the more shocking. An experienced, combat-tested unit, the 2-28 was nevertheless badly mauled by an enemy it had actively pursued and with whom it had aggressively initiated battle, in the fullest confidence that it would prevail. How and why did this happen?

The Beast Was Out There is the product of a decades-long effort by James Shelton, the 2-28's former operations officer, to answer that question. In what is both an historical narrative and a personal memoir, the author reconstructs the chain of events leading up to the violent encounter with the VC regiment, and describes in gripping detail the battle's tragic and disastrous unfolding. In doing so he reveals aspects of fighting often neglected by historians and provides a new vision of the war in Vietnam and, in a larger context, perhaps why the United States' effort was not successful.

More Praise for The Beast Was Out There

"I started reading it over the holidays and could not put it down. It brought back many memories of my own time in Vietnam as an infantry battalion S3—memories that I had long since forgotten…. The candor in this book is what I would expect from the Jim Shelton I knew when we served together as lieutenants in the 82nd Airborne Division….[the story] is an enormous legacy to thousands of young warriors yet to come."

Lieutenant General James H. Johnson Jr., U.S. Army (Ret.)

"I was immediately hooked…and read your [book] from beginning to end. You did a great job…. Your description of infantry operations in jungle terrain was most accurate, and I could almost smell the foliage…. Your discussion of foxhole strength at company level was on target."

Brigadier General Grail L. Brookshire, U.S. Army (Ret.)
Former commander 2nd Squadron, 11th Armored Cavalry Regiment,
"The Blackhorse Regiment," with service in Vietnam

"It was a sad day of course for [the] 2/28 and the division but through your writing it was clear how professional the division was. Also how much everyone cared for their soldiers…. Congratulations on a great book."

Major General Calvert P. Benedict, U.S. Army (Ret.)
Former commander 1/16 Infantry, 1st Infantry Division at the
Battle of Ông Thanh; former commander 1st Infantry Division

"I read it, relived it, and enjoyed it…. Your book should be used at the Infantry School and CGSC—preferably in a 'case study' mode…. Our folks are not good at after-action and historical lessons. We STILL seem to make the same mistakes again and again."

Lieutenant General Robert Haldane, U.S. Army (Ret.)
Former commander 1/28 Infantry, 1st Infantry Division, in Vietnam

"[Major General James] Vaught's chief of staff when he was at Fort Stewart was a man who would have been played by John Wayne if his life had been made into a movie. James Shelton was cut from the same cloth as Vaught...and he was the same kind of straight talker and soldier's soldier that his boss was." [*The Beast Was Out There*] is a story of guilt, disappointment, tragedy, valor, anxiety, anger and humor. But most of all, it is what I would have expected of Shelton: a realistic picture of what the military and war are like."

Elijah Gosier, columnist for the *St. Petersburg Times* in his article
"A Deserving Leader of Men, " December 24, 2002

The Beast Was Out There "...is already unique in my mind because it actually deals with a tactical battle which we lost. That was needed. Jim Shelton is a superb soldier and a very fine human being and he is to be thanked and congratulated for this contribution to history."

Lieutenant General DeWitt Smith, U.S. Army (Ret.)
Former commandant, U.S. Army War College

The Beast Was Out There

Cantigny Military History Series
John F. Votaw, General Editor
Steven Weingartner, Editor
John M. Lindley, Editor

The Cantigny Military History Series is sponsored by the Cantigny First Division Foundation. The series presents conferences and related publications that address issues consonant with the foundation's mission to preserve and promote the history of the 1st Infantry Division of the U.S. Army within the context of America's military history.

The conferences are hosted by the First Division Museum at Cantigny, the estate of the late Colonel Robert R. McCormick. Cantigny is located in Wheaton, Illinois, approximately thirty-five miles from Chicago.

Other Cantigny Military History Series Books:
Blood and Sacrifice
The History of the 16th Infantry Regiment
From the Civil War Through the Gulf War
By Steven E. Clay

In the Wake of the Storm
Gulf War Commanders Discuss Desert Storm
Edited by Steven Weingartner

The Greatest Thing We Have Ever Attempted
Historical Perspectives on the Normandy Campaign
Edited by Steven Weingartner

A Weekend With the Great War
Proceedings of the Fourth Annual Great War Interconference Seminar
16-18 September 1995
Edited by Steven Weingartner

Blue Spaders
The 26th Infantry Regiment, 1917-1967

No Mission Too Difficult!
Old Buddies of the 1st Infantry Division Tell All About World War II
By Blythe Foote Finke

Cantigny at Seventy-Five
A Professional Discussion
May 28-29, 1993
Edited by Steven Weingartner

Cantigny Military History Series

The Beast Was Out There
The 28th Infantry Black Lions
and the Battle of Ông Thanh
Vietnam, October 1967

Brig. Gen. James E. Shelton, USA (Ret.)

Foreword by David Maraniss

Cantigny First Division Foundation
Chicago, IL
2002

Printed in the United States of America

ISBN: 0-7394-3662-7

The Cantigny First Division Foundation
151 S. Winfield Road
Wheaton, IL 60187
630/668-5185

This book is dedicated to Specialist Fourth Class
Ray Neal Gribble US 55891439, U.S. Army,
killed in action on October 17, 1967,
while serving as a member of Company A, 2nd Battalion,
28th Infantry Black Lions, 1st Infantry Division,
Republic of Vietnam

Contents

List of Maps and Photographs

Foreword

On the afternoon of January 22, 2000, I sent a note to Jim Shelton introducing myself and asking him whether he would be willing to talk to me for a book I was beginning to research that would deal in part with the battle of Ông Thanh on October 17, 1967. I knew nothing about Shelton except that until a few weeks before the battle he had been the operations officer of the Black Lions battalion and that, in the years afterward, he rose up the ranks to retire as a general. He could have told me that he had no interest in helping me because he had been working on his own book about the battle for more than a decade. Or he could have said that he saw little use in talking to someone who had not served in the military and therefore would never understand how it was in Vietnam. Or he might simply have ignored me. Instead, he responded quickly and with unbridled enthusiasm. "Tell me when and where we should start," he wrote back. Then he proposed that we start on the golf course down where he lived in Englewood, Florida.

As I would discover to my everlasting delight, and as readers of Jim's fascinating book will readily see, that was typical Shelton. He is a remarkably welcoming and generous man, always thinking about something and eager to discuss it. He tells things exactly the way he sees them, yet is unusually open-minded. He can talk about anything, and b.s. his way if he has to, yet he has none of the arbitrariness of a know-it-all general. A one-time lineman at the University of Delaware, he is a big, burly, tough guy with a resonant voice and an authoritative bearing, yet he has one of the softest hearts I have ever encountered. Just ask the three daughters of Terry Allen Jr., who lost their father in that long ago October battle, then found a new father when Big Jim came into their lives, even though he already had eight kids of his own. He is in no way a saint, but something better than that, a full-bodied character out of some Irish novel, overflowing with life, the friend you want to have around and on your side.

Shelton accepts people as they come to him, with no concern for rank and status. That was true even when he was in the army, where rank has its privileges, and it has become ever more evident since. During the last twelve years, an odd and marvelous little gang has developed around some of the veterans who survived the October 17 battle. They gather for what they call the November Nightmare, a misnomer not worth explaining except to say that they convene at West Point for a football weekend that usually falls in early November. Most of the guys were privates back in 1967 and never got close to then-Major Shelton. A former lieutenant in the group knew him but was scared to death of him. Now they all call him "Fearless Leader," at once showing him respect and mocking him. Just visit the November Nightmare for a few hours and it becomes obvious that General Shelton loves being one of the guys and would rather hang out in a hell-hole CP in a roadside motel on the edge of Highland Falls drinking and snoring and laughing and telling tales with Doc and Goody and Woody and Joe and LT, and wolfing down his brother Pete's mayo-dripping hoagies, than sipping evening cocktails with fellow brass at a gated-community country club.

The Vietnam that Shelton brings to life in this book strikes me as the real deal, free of excessive romance or cynicism. He has some of the ironic eye of Joseph Heller, seeing the zaniness in daily life in the war zone. He and his compatriots in the Big Red One were real-life characters with human flaws. He is not reluctant to talk about the human shit sticking to the shoes of an unwitting general. He sees errors of tactics and strategy made by the American military and is not hesitant to point them out. Yet what shines through every page of this book is respect. Not the easy rhetoric of duty and honor and patriotism, not the political arguments about whether the war was right or wrong, but something deeper and more meaningful. *The Beast Was Out There* in the end is not just about the beast, not just about the awfulness of one October battle, but about the hearts of men like Jim Shelton who worked so hard, day after difficult day, and the love that arose out of fear and courage and blood and death and sweat.

David Maraniss
Washington, D.C.
March 30, 2002

Preface

T his volume in the Cantigny Military History Series provides a first-person account of an historic, if little known, action in the Vietnam War, the Battle of Ông Thanh. Fought on October 17, 1967, it was a confrontation between two formidable adversaries, the 2-28 Infantry (Black Lions) of the 1st Infantry Division and the 271st Regiment of 9th Viet Cong Division. It took place in a remote jungle tract just west of Highway 13 near Chon Thanh, an area that had never been penetrated by U.S. Army forces. The Black Lions went there looking for trouble, and trouble is what they found: the Viet Cong formation turned on them like a cornered animal, mauling the American battalion that had been hunting them.

From his post at division headquarters then-Major James Shelton, formerly the 2-28's operations officer, monitored the battle over the radio, listening with growing alarm, then horror, as the battalion's losses mounted. By nightfall, when the battle ended, U.S. forces had suffered 134 casualties, including 57 killed. Among the dead was the 2nd Battalion commander, Lieutenant Colonel Terry Allen Jr., a friend and mentor of Shelton's whose father, Terry de la Mesa Allen, had commanded the 1st Division in North Africa and Sicily in World War II. Also killed were Major Don Holleder, a former All-American football player at West Point, and Second Lieutenant Harold B. Durham Jr., who was subsequently awarded the Medal of Honor for gallantry in action.

The Black Lions fought valiantly that day, but their valor proved unavailing. Traditional notions of what constituted success and failure in battle are not easily applied to the conflict in Vietnam, and the Battle of Ông Thanh is no exception—in this clash, as in so many others, the confused nature of the fighting is reflected in different judgments about its outcome. But where wire service accounts reported it as a victory, accounts by many veterans of the 2-28—including Shelton—count it as a tactical defeat.

Now a retired brigadier general, Shelton has long sought to reconstruct what happened at Ông Thanh and thus discover how and why the battle took such an ill-fated turn for the 2-28. To that end he has drawn on a range of sources, including official records, the recollections of fellow soldiers and, not least, his own experience of jungle warfare in Vietnam. The result is a compelling narrative of combat in Vietnam. Shelton pulls no punches; his analyses and assessments are blunt, unsparingly honest, and fair. Mistakes and mischances are fully chronicled; so, too, are the many courageous deeds that the young officers and men of the Black Lions performed at Ông Thanh.

But this is more than the anatomy of a defeat. Writing with insight and passion, Shelton vividly portrays the harshly oppressive character and brutal complexities of jungle warfare in Vietnam, and the problems of command attendant to these circumstances. His analysis of these problems and the methods by which various commanders dealt with them should prove instructive for junior officers and noncommissioned officers trying to develop their own approach to leading men in stressful conditions.

Shelton also reveals aspects of the fighting often neglected by historians of the war and provides a new vision of the conflict that goes far in explaining why, in a larger context, the United States did not win it. What emerges is a clear picture of how tactical defeat at Ông Thanh and strategic defeat in Southeast Asia were in many ways related. But there is another lesson to be learned from this book. The Ông Thanh battle was notable not only because it was a defeat, but also because such defeats were rare: in the main, the Black Lions and the 1st Infantry Division in particular, and the U.S. ground forces in general, achieved success in their operations and encounters with the enemy. Shelton helps us understand why this was so in Vietnam, and how it can and should be the case in wars present and future.

John F. Votaw, Lt. Col., USA (Ret.)
General Editor, Cantigny Military History Series
September 2002

Author's Preface

Regardless of the effort made, any attempt to chronicle real experiences of human endeavor is fraught with well-meaning, but superficial, analysis. What happened and why it happened is awash in human motivation, which is a function of many uncontrolled and inexplicable variables, studied after the fact. This chronicle is not the real truth—we will never know that! This is only a human and imperfect perspective. If someone should think, however, that this is an effort to denigrate anyone who participated in these momentous efforts, they are wrong. I am still alive, but I left part of myself in Vietnam. I will never recover what I lost in that country; I will never forget those who did not return.

As Lord Byron so aptly wrote in his historical drama *Marino Faliero:*

> They never fail who die in a great cause: the block may soak their gore, their heads may sodden in the sun; their limbs be strung to city gates and castle walls—but still their spirit walks abroad. Though years elapse, and others share as dark a doom, they but augment the deep and sweeping thoughts which overpower all others, and conduct the world at last to freedom.

Much has been said and written about the purpose for existence of mankind. I believe each human being exists for a reason. Although we don't think about it very much, our reason and our ego tell us that we are not just chunks of protoplasm that somehow came together, and after some finite time period just turn to dust.

In the final analysis, what really gives meaning to our lives is mankind; that is where we fit in with others like ourselves. I believe that the "master plan" for every human being is to relate the purpose of his or her existence—individual oneness and individual uniqueness to a totality that is called mankind. (Every human being that ever lived is unique.)

Our purpose in life is to contribute to mankind. The way we live our lives either uplifts or degrades mankind, and during the course of our individual lifetimes, we all do a little of both. But when the final balance sheet is focused on our lives, where will we come down on it? Did we give more or take more?

Ray Neal Gribble, to whom this book is dedicated, and other men like him, did not want to die at age twenty-four in the middle of a hostile jungle. But at a critical point in time, he made a decision to place himself in harm's way on behalf of his fellow soldiers. It was a very conscious decision, with an understanding of the possible consequences. He did it. He assured that a purpose was given to his life. His selfless act is an uplifting example to all of us. He fulfilled the purpose of his existence: to use his life to inspire the lives of others in the best interests of mankind. Ray Gribble's actions added to the nobility of mankind; his act made him immortal. As we look forward to our own eventual demise, will we be able to say the same?

*

I wish to acknowledge the help, assistance, and encouragement, first, of my hard-working editors, Steve Weingartner and John Lindley. Particular thanks goes out to John F. Votaw, general editor of the Cantigny Military History Series and executive director of the Cantigny First Division Museum in Wheaton, Illinois. Other organizations that have helped me were the Muncie, Indiana, *Morning Star* and *Evening Press,* and the library of the United States Military Academy, West Point, New York. Individuals who have helped me in many ways are the daughters of Terry de la Mesa Allen Jr.: Consuelo, Bebe, and Mary Frances; Brian Baldy; Tom Baldy; Dave Berry; Martin Blumenson; Ed Burke; John Cash; Dick Cavazos; Joe Costello; Eric Davidson; Mike Dinkins; Bill Erwin; Fred Gantzler; Jim George; Bob Gillard; Steve Goodman; Paul Gorman; Tom Grady; Eileen Gribble; Mike and Vicki Gribble; Joe Griffin; Gerry Grosso; Tom Hinger; Bill Jackson; Jim Kasik; Don Kovach; Bob Loomis; Mike Lude; Bob Mager; Mike Mahler; Pam Gribble Mahoney; Mike Malone; David Maraniss; George MacGarrigle; Billy Murphy; George "Buck" Newman; Roger Nye; David Osborne; Bill Ostlund; Charles Robinson; Sandy Rocheleau; Bill Rosson; Ed Scribner; Frank Serio; Anne Sliker; Ed Smith; Harry Summers; Jim Swink; Gwendolyn Tetlow; Heath Twitchell; Sam Vaughan; and Clark Welch.

A special acknowledgement must be made for the title of this book. Among many others quoted in this book I asked Captain Jim Kasik, who commanded B Company during the battle, to give me his remembrances. In the course of his story he said, "The Beast was out there–and the beast was hungry." I thought that it was an apt description. John Lindley, my first line editor, suggested we use it for the book title. Consensus was reached rapidly between myself and the senior editors. Many thanks to my old comrade, Jim Kasik, for originating the title.

Finally, and especially, I thank my wife, Joan, and the children she raised, Peggy, Patty, Terry, Mac, Paul, Kathleen, Terry Allen, and Sarah; my mom and dad, Helen and Bob Shelton Sr.; my brothers, Bob, Pete, and Ned; and my "band of brothers," the Black Lions.

Any and all errors in this book are my responsibility alone.

Jim Shelton
September, 2002

Note: There are a number of quotations in this book that make up this story, but they are not verbatim quotations. In most cases where quotations are used, the reader should understand that they are to be accompanied by the expression "or words to that effect."

Maps

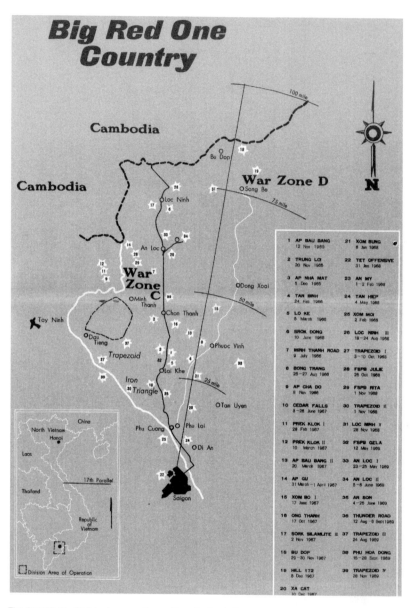

Big Red One Country

Cambodia

Cambodia

War Zone D

N

100 mile

Bu Dop

Loc Ninh

Song Be

75 mile

An Loc

War Zone C

Dong Xoai

50 mile

Minh Thanh

Chon Thanh

Tay Ninh

Dau Tieng

Trapezoid

Phuoc Vinh

Lai Khe

25 mile

Iron Triangle

Tan Uyen

China

North Vietnam
Hanoi

Laos

Phu Cuong

Phu Loi

Di An

17th Parallel

Thailand

Republic of Vietnam

Saigon

Division Area of Operation

No.	Battle	Date	No.	Battle	Date
1	AP BAU BANG	12 Nov 1965	21	XOM BUNG	8 Jan 1968
2	TRUNG LOI	20 Nov 1965	22	TET OFFENSIVE	31 Jan 1968
3	AP NHA MAT	5 Dec 1965	23	AN MY	1–2 Feb 1968
4	TAN BINH	24 Feb 1966	24	TAN HIEP	4 May 1968
5	LO KE	5 March 1966	25	XOM MOI	2 Feb 1968
6	SROK DONG	10 June 1966	26	LOC NINH III	18–24 Aug 1968
7	MINH THANH ROAD	9 July 1966	27	TRAPEZOID I	3–10 Oct 1968
8	BONG TRANG	25–27 Aug 1966	28	FSPB JULIE	26 Oct 1968
9	AP CHA DO	8 Nov 1966	29	FSPB RITA	1 Nov 1968
10	CEDAR FALLS	8–26 June 1967	30	TRAPEZOID II	1 Nov 1968
11	PREK KLOK I	28 Feb 1967	31	LOC NINH V	28 Nov 1968
12	PREK KLOK II	10 March 1967	32	FSPB GELA	12 May 1969
13	AP BAU BANG II	20 March 1967	33	AN LOC I	23–25 May 1969
14	AP GU	31 March–1 April 1967	34	AN LOC II	5–6 June 1969
15	XOM BO I	17 June 1967	35	AN SON	4–25 June 1969
16	ONG THANH	17 Oct 1967	36	THUNDER ROAD	12 Aug–8 Sept 1969
17	SORK SILAMLITE III	2 Nov 1967	37	TRAPEZOID III	24 Aug 1969
18	BU DOP	29–30 Nov 1967	38	PHU HOA DONG	15–28 Sept 1969
19	HILL 172	8 Dec 1967	39	TRAPEZOID IV	28 Nov 1969
20	XA CAT	10 Dec 1967			

The 1st Infantry Division's area of operations in South Vietnam, III Corps, War Zones C and D. The battle of Ông Thanh (No. 16) is incorrectly located east of Route 13 (Saigon-Loc Ninh road); it should be west of the road between Minh Thanh and Chon Thanh. (1st Infantry Division)

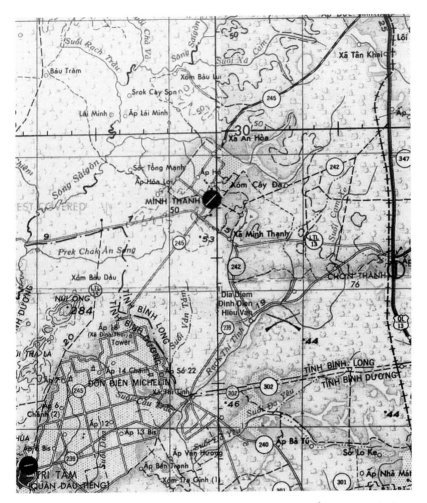

Tactical map of Black Lions area of operations in mid-October 1967, with Ông Thanh battle site marked by the crossed rifles at map coordinates XT684579. (Govt. Printing Office/Paul Gorman)

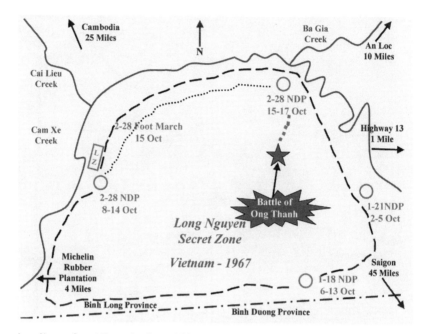

Long Nguyen Secret Zone, showing activities leading up to the October 17, 1967 action. To our knowledge, no U.S. units had entered this area previously. (James Shelton/William Ostlund)

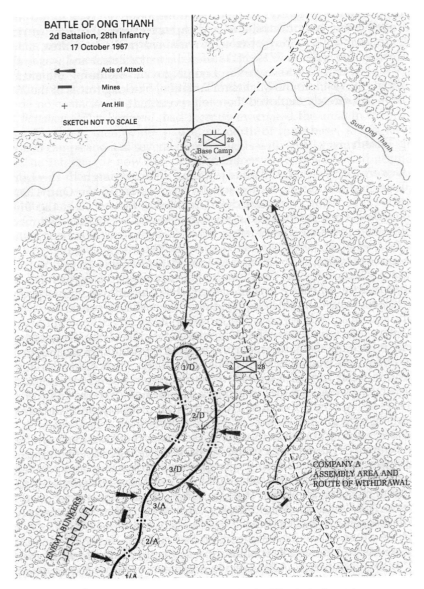

BATTLE OF ÔNG THANH
2d Battalion, 28th Infantry
17 October 1967

← Axis of Attack
— Mines
+ Ant Hill

SKETCH NOT TO SCALE

Suoi Ong Thanh

2 ⊠ 28
Base Camp

1/D
2 ⊠ 28

2/D

3/D

COMPANY A
ASSEMBLY AREA AND
ROUTE OF WITHDRAWAL

3/A

ENEMY BUNKERS

2/A

1/A

This map of the Ông Thanh battle site appeared in *Taking the Offensive* by George L. MacGarrigle (Washington, 1998). Courtesy of U.S. Army Center of Military History.

Threat of Cong attack on Saigon nipped in jungle

From Our Wire Services

SAIGON—American bombers and artillery blasted suspected enemy hideouts yesterday after a raging jungle battle between U.S. and Viet Cong infantrymen took a heavy toll on both sides but helped smash Communist strategy for a double-prong attack on Saigon.

Lt. Gen. Fred C. Weyand said the Viet Cong 271st Regiment, which clashed with troops of the 1st Infantry Division northwest of the capital, was the spearhead of a division which planned to attack the city from the north.

"This regiment is as close to destruction as it has ever been," the commander of II Field Force declared.

FROM THE EAST

The other assault was to come from the east. But Weyand said the seizure of a huge stockpile of Communist weapons 30 miles east of Saigon had ended the threat from that direction.

The veteran 271st Regiment, hunted by soldiers of the Big Red One (1st Infantry) since late September turned on two American companies and a battalion command detail Tuesday in what the generals called a "meeting engagement" but what the GI's who were there described as an ambush.

Two widely known officers—Lt. Col. Terry Allen Jr., 38, and Maj. Don W. Holleder, 32—were among the American dead in Tuesday's action.

Allen's father commanded the Big Red One, in Tunisia and Sicily in World War II.

Holleder, who starred at West Point as an end and

Maj. Donald Holleder
Grid star killed

Lt. Col. Terry Allen Jr.
Dad was a soldier too

quarterback, was voted the most valuable player on the Army's 1955 football team.

The struggle erupted in the Iron Triangle sanctuary 41 miles north of Saigon. The victory, in which the Americans fought out of the trap, was costly. Fifty-eight U.S. soldiers were killed, and 61

(Please turn to Page 12)

Cong repulsed

(Continued from Page One)

wounded. But at least 103 Communists died.

"It was a typical "L" shaped ambush," said 1st Sgt. Jose Valdez, 35, of Velarde, N.M., a 15-year veteran who took over one company when its commander was cut down by a Claymore mine.

Other Communists hid in trees, dropped grenades and fired automatic weapons as the Americans tried to pull back. The infantrymen lay on their backs and shot the Communists out of the trees.

At one point, the fighting was so heavy the infantrymen had to leave behind the bodies of 22 Americans. They were found yesterday among North Vietnamese bodies when the Americans returned to the battlefield at dawn.

Spec. 4 James Schultze, 19, of Ozone Park, Queens, N.Y., concurred with Valdez: "It was an ambush. They were just on all sides of us. I never heard so much fire in my life."

But Gen. William C. Westmoreland, commander of U.S. forces in Vietnam, who flew to the scene, said:

"I'm not aware of there being any ambush involved. To the best of my knowledge, this was a meeting engagement."

Maj. Gen. John Hay, commander of the 1st Division, nodded.

Westmoreland said: "I would say the enemy stood and fought with a greater degree than he has in recent weeks in this area," but he saw no change in enemy tactics.

"These are Viet Cong tactics," he said.

THREE RAIDS

Air Force B52 bombers flew three raids dumping hundreds of tons of bombs on routes where the Communist forces were believed to be withdrawing with more dead and their wounded.

The infantrymen were part of some 4,000 Americans involved in operation Shenandoah II, which swept into the area two weeks ago when a battalion of uniformed troops was spotted moving in from the Cambodian border.

Since the operation began, the Americans have killed 305 Communists in a series of sharp clashes.

A battalion intelligence officer and a platoon leader also were killed and two company commanders were wounded.

The air war over the north also heated up Tuesday, with American strikes again as close as 10 miles to Red China's frontier. Targets included the previously attacked Lang Son railroad bridge in that area and the Lang Giai railroad yards, 20 miles south of the border.

Four American planes were shot down and the pilots are missing. The U.S. command said the planes were three Air Force F105 Thunderchiefs and a Navy A4 Skyhawk. Announced plane losses over the North thus rose to 705.

This is a wire service account of the Battle of Ông Thanh that appeared in several U.S. newspapers during the period October 18–20, 1967. In the second column, under the pictures, there is the statement: "The victory, in which the Americans fought out of the trap, was costly. Fifty-eight U.S. soldiers were killed, and 61 wounded. But at least 103 Communists died."

The Battle of Ông Thanh was not a victory. This book is one account of what really took place, and why it happened, written in the interest of historical clarification.

"I stood there asking myself
the question I am sure
Roman legionnaires must
have asked in Gaul—
What the hell am I doing here?"

Captain Colin Powell upon his arrival in Vietnam, American Journey

Chapter 1
The Battle of Ông Thanh: A Perspective

My age of consciousness was probably 1940. I was five years old. I remember December 7, 1941, when the Japanese bombed Pearl Harbor. I didn't know where Pearl Harbor was, but I knew the United States was going to war. Soon we children were fighting the "Japs" and Nazis on the school grounds. If we held our arms out on both sides and started running around, we were fighter planes. We could strafe and bomb through the whole recess period in the fields outside the school. When school was over, we rushed home, changed our clothes, and headed for the nearby woods to dig in and establish machine-gun positions and ambushes.

The world was at war, and we were a big part of it. One or two nights a month there were air raid drills. We had to turn off all the lights in the house. An air raid warden would walk up and down the street checking to see if there were any lights still on. My brother Bob and I were always afraid the warden would catch us with a light on. That would be downright unpatriotic, and a Japanese or German bomber might zero in on our house as a target. We also had air raid drills at school.

Our lives were filled with war. Soldiers, sailors, marines, and airmen were in uniform everywhere we went. Food and gasoline were rationed. Occasionally my dad would get us all into the car in New Jersey, and we would drive to Brooklyn to see grandma. In the Cypress Hills section of Brooklyn, there were cemeteries everywhere.

I think everyone who had ever died in New York City was buried there. Just above Highland Park, which was a big green hill in Brooklyn, there was a reservoir. Around the reservoir sat a row of antiaircraft guns. They were sandbagged all around, and there were men standing by the guns with helmets on. We were at war, and war seemed to be the only thing that mattered. War penetrated our beings and occupied all of our time.

For children living then, war was a romantic notion. War meant death, but it also meant honor, and those who served were honored. My dad was too young for World War I and too old for World War II, but he was very aware of the war and tried to support it in many ways as a civilian. We were children of war. It was in our beings.

I have many memories of those times, but they are seemingly all about the war. I remember *Life* magazine: the war dominated its pages, too. Most of its advertisements, including the ones for ladies' underwear, have tie-ins with the war. In the movies we watched Robert Taylor and Anthony Quinn finally succumb to the Japanese soldiers with long bayonets at Bataan and Brian Donlevy as marine Major Devereaux finally overrun by those same Japanese on Wake Island. We saw Randolph Scott strike back with his Carlson's marine raiders on Makin Island in the movie *Gung Ho* and infantrymen Dana Andrews and Richard Conte take on the Germans in *A Walk in the Sun*. In another film, Paul Muni struck back against the Nazis in Norway in *Commandos Strike at Dawn*. The movie I remember best is *The Story of GI Joe*, which was based on a book by Ernie Pyle, the great war correspondent. The stars of this movie were Burgess Meredith as Pyle and Robert Mitchum as the captain/rifle company commander in Italy. We were inundated by war, and American infantrymen were my heroes.

By 1950 I was in high school. Football and the Korean War occupied my thoughts. With World War II still fresh in our minds and permanently dominating our subconscious, the much less romantic and downright ugly Korean War, which was being fought in a land so far away and so unknown, quickly became a reality. When I went to college in 1953, we registered for the draft and frozen Chosin (Korea) became a part of out lives. ROTC was mandatory at the University of Delaware for young men in their first two years, and the football coaches all strongly recommended that we take Advanced ROTC in our junior and senior years. After graduation, those who had gone through the ROTC program could get a commission in the army as an officer and serve their two years' obligation. The coaches said that ROTC tried to teach leadership and teamwork, just like they did. I didn't need much convincing; I had already been persuaded by Robert Mitchum, Randolph Scott, et al. This was also the time of Senator Joe McCarthy and the heightening of anticommunist sentiment in the United States. The Cold War with the Soviet Union was in the newspaper headlines, and in May 1954 Ho Chi Minh's forces defeated the French troops at Dien Bien Phu in Vietnam. Meanwhile, the U.S. government was providing aid and support to the anticommunist leaders of the Republic of South Vietnam in the southern part of that Asian country.

I grew up in the zinc-mining town of Franklin in northwest New Jersey. I believe the influences of World War II and football made the greatest impact on my psyche. Military operations with all of their complications and the game of football have amazing similarities. They provided endless challenges to the mind and body, and I was drawn to both. More than academics, football dominated my life in high school and college mostly because of those challenges. When I began the serious study of military tactics and strategy in ROTC in college, I was astounded by parallels with football. Teamwork and training ruled both activities.

I graduated from college in 1957 and was commissioned a second lieutenant of infantry in the army reserve. I knew that soon I would be called to active duty. That call came in October 1957. I received orders to report to Fort Benning, Georgia, for basic infantry officer training. My girlfriend all through college, Joan, and I decided to get married before I went into the army. Our honeymoon was a drive over the Blue Ridge Parkway to Fort Benning. Ten years and six children later in October 1967, I listened on the radio as my battalion, the 2nd Battalion, 28th Infantry, was chopped apart in a battle that has since had such a controlling influence over many of my conscious and unconscious hours.

After teaching weapons at Fort Benning, I served infantry tours of duty in the 1st Cavalry Division in Korea, the 82nd Airborne Division at Fort Bragg, North Carolina, and the Berlin Brigade in Germany. By the time I reached the Berlin Brigade in 1964, American military advisors were being killed in Vietnam. I volunteered for Vietnam in 1966, and after a brief stint at Fort Ord, California, helping to beef up the infantry training base there, I departed for Vietnam in July 1967. I thought I was prepared for this assignment. My goal was to get to an infantry battalion. I had been promoted to major, so I would seek to be a battalion operations officer (S3) or battalion executive officer.

While I was at Fort Bragg in 1961, I had the opportunity to read some intelligence reports about Vietnam. At the time Fidel Castro and Soviet missiles were our major focus of attention, but the Vietnam intelligence reports were worrisome. The North Vietnamese, in violation of the Geneva peace accords of 1954, were infiltrating weapons, equipment, and personnel into South Vietnam, mostly by sea and waterways. The infiltration was extensive, and it seemed to me that the United States either had to stop that infiltration or accept the inevitable defeat of South Vietnam by the North. These reports were classified "secret" and were the most accurate information then available. As the U.S. naval presence along the coast of Vietnam increased in an effort to cut off the seaborne infiltration of the South, the forces in the North increased their use of the Ho Chi Minh trail that ran through Laos and Cambodia deep into South Vietnam. To me and to many American observers, the challenge in Vietnam was the same challenge we had faced in Berlin, Cuba, Korea, and all around the world. The communist system was challenging democracy, positioning itself to "bury" us, as Khrushchev had predicted in the early 1960s. Wars of national liberation were being fought to free mankind from the yoke of capitalism and impose the "bliss" of economic equality on the world.

To me, communism was a joke. I thought it failed to recognize human nature, but the challenges presented by the wars of national liberation that were carried out in its name were very real. And I was convinced that, in things human—in the world as it is—the weak do not inherit the earth. Further, to be dominated is equivalent to not living; it is merely existing. These views were the underpinnings of my belief that we must be prepared to meet force with force. Inasmuch as we had the wherewithal to defend ourselves and our beliefs, we could not stand by and watch as some other power thumbed its nose at us and proceeded to impose its will at our ultimate expense. I believed, and still believe, that what we did in Vietnam was right. Much of the righteousness of our stand as a nation was, however, severely undercut by death and destruction, stupidity, overkill, arrogance, lack of resolve, excess, impatience, and wanting to keep more of our own plenty.

I arrived at Bien Hoa air base in early July 1967. My choices for assignment were to join the 173rd Airborne Brigade, the 1st Brigade of the 101st Airborne Division, and the 1st Infantry Division, in that order. Service in an airborne unit meant an extra $110 per month in jump pay, and I knew my dear wife and six "ankle biters" could use the money. As I might have known, I was assigned to the Big Red One.

A division is a big unit with over seventeen thousand men. I wanted to be in an infantry battalion. There are probably fifty or sixty majors in a division, but only eighteen majors, two each, in its nine battalions. The division personnel officer (G1) told me there was only one battalion S3 vacancy, in the 2nd Battalion, 28th Infantry Black Lions. I got the job. After one night in Di An, the division's base camp north of Saigon, I loaded into a CV-2 Caribou with several other men and flew to Lai Khe, the base camp of the 3rd Brigade. As we approached Lai Khe, I saw lush tropical greenery and rows of rubber trees surrounding the dirt airstrip. It was a serene view that masked the blood, sweat, red dirt, grime, and anguish that were to come. Three battalions called Lai Khe their home: the 1st Battalion, 16th Infantry; the 2nd Battalion, 2nd Infantry (Mechanized); and the 2nd Battalion, 28th Infantry Black Lions.

The battle of Ông Thanh occurred on October 17, 1967, about one hundred days after my arrival in South Vietnam. The battle was named for a small stream, Suoi Ông Thanh, whose waters eventually flow into the Saigon River near the Michelin Rubber Plantation some fifty miles north of Saigon. The major adversaries in this battle were the 2nd Battalion, 28th Infantry, 1st Infantry Division, United States Army; and the 271st Regiment, 9th Viet Cong Division, National Front for the Liberation of South Vietnam (NFLSV). Aside from a military analysis, the Battle of Ông Thanh was not of particular significance to the overall outcome of the Vietnam conflict.

To some degree, the fighting at Ông Thanh may have represented a departure in strategy on the part of the Viet Cong insofar as they deliberately stood their ground long enough to conduct a pitched battle, and on their terms. Up to this time in the war and in this particular area (Military Region III), large Viet Cong (VC) forces had typically avoided pitched battles against all U.S. forces in general and against the 1st Infantry Division in particular. In fact, the 1st Infantry Division forced this battle, as U.S. forces had generally done in nearly all major battles prior to October 1967. Since the 1st Division's deployment to South Vietnam in 1965, big battles involving the division had come about because U.S. forces either penetrated VC base camps or took up positions that forced VC units to attack, if they were to maintain their main lines of communications.

However, subsequent battles, such as the Battle of Loc Ninh and the Military Region II battle at Dak To in November 1967, may have indicated a change in VC strategy. The enemy's Tet Offensive in January 1968, approximately three months later, manifested this need to "make something happen." The objective here is not to analyze Viet Cong strategy but to recount how the 1st Infantry Division forced the VC to stand and fight a tactical battle at Ông Thanh.*

---

*For a definition of the term "division" and other military terms and acronyms used in this book, see the Glossary on page 316.

"No mission too difficult, no sacrifice too great— duty first."

Motto of the U.S. 1st Infantry Division

Chapter 2
The Big Red One: History

The 1st Infantry Division was, and is, a very proud U.S. Army division. Popularly known as "The Big Red One," it traces its origin back to 1917, when it became the first U.S. Army division to be organized after America entered World War I. Subsequently deployed to France, the division won the first American victory in that conflict when its 28th Infantry Regiment attacked and seized the French village of Cantigny on May 28, 1918. In honor of this achievement the regiment was dubbed "The Black Lions of Cantigny." The 2nd Battalion, 28th Infantry "Black Lions," which fought the Battle of Ông Thanh some fifty years later on October 17, 1967, was the lineal descendant of that regiment.

As a result of the Cantigny battle and other actions, the Big Red One gained a reputation for efficiency and aggressiveness, prompting this tribute from General John J. Pershing, commander of the American Expeditionary Forces in World War I: "The Commander-in-Chief has noted in this division a special pride of service and a high state of morale, never broken by hardship nor battle."

In World War II the 1st Infantry Division was among the first American units committed to battle when, on November 8, 1942, it landed in Algeria near Oran as part of Operation Torch, the invasion of North Africa. After a harsh learning period culminating in the Battle of Kasserine Pass in mid-February 1943, the division matured into a superior formation, lauded for its combat effectiveness. The men of the Big Red One accordingly came to think of themselves as something special, developing a unique esprit that was inspired and encouraged in no small measure by their colorful and charismatic leader, Major General Terry de La Mesa Allen.

Much has been said and written about General Terry Allen. I have personally heard two highly decorated and respected World War II battalion commanders, who later became general officers, state unequivocally, "Terry Allen was the greatest division commander—ever." Testimony to his leadership abilities, and to the excellence of the division he commanded and molded in the North African campaign, can be found in the demand made by General George S. Patton Jr. to include the Big Red One in the assault force used in the Allied invasion of Sicily on July 9-10, 1943. Evidently Patton, when appointed to command the U.S. component of the invasion, would not take the job until he had been assured of the 1st Division's involvement. Patton's confidence in the division was justified by its heroic stand against the counterattacking Hermann Göring Panzer Division at Gela beach on the second day of the invasion. In stopping this elite German unit, the Big Red One prevented the American beachhead from being overrun, thus ensuring the success of the landings.

At the end of the Sicily campaign, however, Allen was relieved of his command of the 1st Infantry Division and sent back to the United States. The reason for his relief remains unclear and a subject of dispute. Allen was then among the most respected division commanders. His image had appeared on the cover of *Time* magazine and A.J. Liebling, a highly regarded journalist and war correspondent, had written about him in glowing terms. In their memoirs both Patton and General Omar Bradley claimed to have relieved Allen, and both indicated that they found the task distasteful. Allen himself never admitted to having been relieved. In a letter to his wife, Mary Frances, he wrote that Patton had told him that he (Allen) had been chosen to organize and train a new division for the forthcoming invasion of Northwest Europe. Subsequent to his return to the United States, Allen was indeed given command of a new division, the 104th "Timberwolves." Arriving in France shortly after the Normandy invasion, the 104th served with distinction through the end of the war, compiling an impressive combat record under Allen's leadership. That division's excellent performance, and Allen's characteristic élan and ability in leading it, further deepens the mystery of his forced departure from the Big Red One. The question as to why he was relieved continues to be asked, and a definitive answer continues to elude it.

In any event, Allen became a legendary figure in U.S. Army annals. His reputation was further burnished by a study in leadership, written at the U.S. Army Command and General Staff College at Fort Leavenworth, Kansas, that compared his manifestly successful leadership style to the equally successful but radically different leadership style of Allen's successor, Major General Clarence R. Huebner.

After Allen's relief in Sicily, the 1st Infantry Division continued to acquit itself admirably, first on Omaha Beach, D-Day, June 6, 1944, and subsequently in the fighting across France and into Germany until the end of the war. Although the 1st Division did not fight in Korea, its reputation did not diminish during occupation duty in Germany during the Korean War. The division returned to the United States in 1955 and remained at Fort Riley, Kansas, until its deployment to Vietnam in 1965. Not insignificantly, the commander of the 2nd Battalion, 28th Infantry, at the Battle of Ông Thanh was Lieutenant Colonel Terry de La Mesa Allen Jr., the only child of Major General (retired) Terry and Mary Frances Allen of El Paso, Texas.

"The generals worried much less about the enemy's strength than about his traditional reluctance to stand and fight."

Robert M. Utley commenting on the U.S. Army before the Battle of the Little Big Horn, Frontier Regulars

Chapter 3
The Big Red One: Vietnam

L et us now return to the 1st Infantry Division in Vietnam. Although historical designations in the U.S. Army may remain unchanged, and the history and esprit of a division lives on, people and circumstances do change. By the time the division fought the Battle of Ông Thanh in October 1967, it had gone through three distinct periods of change. Some might even say that by October 1967, three different divisions had worn the same shoulder patch. Initially there was the division that deployed in July 1965 under the command of Major General Jonathan O. Seaman. This force established the division's three major base camps at Bear Cat, Di An, and Phouc Vinh. The men of the division wore the standard U.S. Army cotton fatigues, leather boots, and carried the 7.62mm M-14 rifle, which was accurate at long range but cumbersome, unwieldy, and heavy. Seaman's command tour in Vietnam was largely characterized by getting settled in, establishing bases and areas of division responsibility, and feeling out the capabilities of the enemy.

By March 1966, the 1st Division was ready to increase its level of operations against the enemy. It began its second distinct period in Vietnam when the feisty, controversial, energetic, and incisive Major General William E. DePuy took charge. Known by some as "Mighty Mouse," General DePuy lit a fire under the Big Red One. He commanded with presence and style. An acerbic wit, quick to anger, and impatient with those of perceived slow intellect, DePuy was a demanding taskmaster, known for relieving battalion commanders who tried to learn on the job. DePuy had little time for a commander who was not ready to lead from his first day in his new assignment. There was a good bit of fear on the part of aspiring lieutenant colonel battalion commanders who may not have been totally confident of their own abilities after being assigned to the 1st Division.

In contrast to the acerbic DePuy was the assistant division commander, the incomparable "John Wayne" of Vietnam, Brigadier General James F. Hollingsworth, or "Holly" to all who knew him. Where DePuy commanded the soldiers around him with intellect and perspicacity, Hollingsworth was earthy, profane, and lovable. The 1st Division had not seen a more two-fisted approach to command of the division since the days of Terry de La Mesa Allen and his colorful assistant, Brigadier General Teddy Roosevelt Jr., in World War II.

As a battle commander, DePuy was an innovator and an opportunist. When planning an attack, he made extensive use of maneuver (in the form of helicopters), speed, surprise, and firepower. His keen mind allowed him to orchestrate a battle and to make quick decisions. Caution was not one of his watchwords. He believed in fast and decisive action in maneuver, and woe to subordinates who were not up to his speed—and very few were. When his forces were on the defensive, DePuy believed in extreme preparation. Thus he demanded that his troops dig in every night, to include constructing overhead cover. This insistence on defensive cover led to the development of the innovative "DePuy bunker," essentially a two-man foxhole with overhead cover, firing ports at the front corners, and a large berm in the middle front to bury the impact of the VC's dreaded RPG (rocket propelled grenade). Use of these DePuy bunkers was standard throughout the division. A company or battalion-sized NDP (night defensive position) was prepared with two concentric circles of DePuy bunkers. Frontal bunkers (the outer circle) were covered by the firing ports of rear bunkers (the inner circle). The scheme was effective: No NDP so configured was ever penetrated by a VC or North Vietnamese Army (NVA) attack. What's more, enemy attacks on these fortified positions practically guaranteed a big kill for the defenders with minimal friendly losses.

In some ways, DePuy was the U.S. Army's equivalent in Vietnam to Fredrick the Great. He was not loved, but he was respected, and his insight and intellect left a lasting impression on the 1st Infantry Division. By the time DePuy left the division for his next assignment, all the men were wearing the army's new lightweight jungle fatigue uniforms and jungle boots, and were armed with the new, lightweight M-16 rifle.

The man who replaced General DePuy in February 1967 and began the third distinctive period in the 1st Division's stay in Vietnam was Major General John H. Hay. When Hay took command of the 1st Division, he knew he had a big pair of boots to fill. John H. Hay was the division commander during the Battle of Ông Thanh. A native of Montana and a graduate of Montana State University, he started his career in World War II as a member of the unique 10th Mountain Division, which had been formed initially from skiers from the western states, including Montana, Colorado, Washington, and Minnesota. John Hay was one of the few men in the U.S. Army who could still wear the red, white, and blue patch with crossed bayonets beneath the word "MOUNTAIN" on his right shoulder, signifying combat experience with that unit in World War II. Hay was also a senior parachutist, having served as a peacetime battle group commander in the 101st Airborne Division.

He was an impressive figure. Hay was called "Handsome John," but not to his face: tall and erect with chiseled features, black wavy hair, white teeth, and an athlete's build, he could have been a cover man for *Esquire* or a movie star of the Robert Taylor ilk. His impeccable appearance was his most unique characteristic, and he was not unaware of it.

Affable and intelligent, John Hay's leadership approach differed from the bombastic style of the DePuy/Hollingsworth tandem. Shortly after Hay joined the division, Brigadier General Bernard C. Rogers was brought in to replace Hollingsworth as assistant division commander. Rogers was a more DePuy-like general who would later become chief of staff of the army in the late 1970s and subsequently served as the Supreme Commander, Allied Forces, Europe (SACEUR) into the late 1980s. Hay's other assistant division commander was Brigadier General William S. Coleman, a down-to-earth South Carolinian with a good feel for the troops and a keen tactical sense. Coleman actively participated in the Battle of Ông Thanh, but Rogers had departed the division prior to the battle and was not involved.

Subsequent to Hay's assumption of command, the 1st Division conducted Operations Junction City I and II (February 22-April 15, 1967) and Manhatten (April 23-May 11). Planned and executed largely by staff and commanders selected by DePuy, these operations were named for towns in Kansas, the stateside home (Fort Riley) of the Big Red One; the towns were also near the Kansas City home of the division's assistant chief of staff, or G3 (Operations, Plans, and Training), Lieutenant Colonel Elmer D. Pendleton. Pendleton was an old hand in Vietnam, having served as a district senior advisor in the U.S. Military Assistance Command, Vietnam (MACV) prior to assignment to the 1st Division. He had also been a battalion commander during the reign of DePuy, commanding the 2nd Battalion, 28th Infantry Black Lions in 1966. He was equal to both tasks and was the most knowledgeable senior officer in the 1st Division. Pendleton quickly became, by virtue of his ability, experience, and position, Hay's right-hand man.

With Hay in command, the division began conducting Operation Billings (June 12-26), a name with a particular Montana ring to it—which perhaps signified that the DePuy era was over. For those who are unaccustomed to changes in military commanders, it can be easy to underestimate the significance of a new commander taking over from a particularly strong personality like William DePuy. When I arrived in the 1st Division in July 1967, I could clearly sense an attitude of resentment toward General Hay on the part of those who had served under General DePuy. This resentment was not necessarily a result of anything Hay had done poorly. Most old timers simply felt that DePuy could not be replaced, and they resented the man who was trying. This is not an uncommon phenomenon under similar circumstances in any military unit.

Although Operation Billings was called a success, U.S. casualties were 47 killed and 197 wounded. Enemy killed were reported as 347. Regardless of the reported number of enemy killed, which was always suspect, the American death toll was the division's largest for a single operation, including Junction City, up to that time. The men who participated in Operation Billings, most of whom were veterans of the war, did not consider it a victory. Moreover, in July 1967, General Hay was faced with a turnover rate of perhaps 80 percent in the soldiers in the combat units of the division. Since the division had arrived in Vietnam in July 1965, there had been a wholesale turnover of combat personnel in July 1966, and again in July 1967. The division might have been able to more readily overcome either the combat losses from Operation Billings or the turnover of experienced personnel in the division if these circumstances had existed in isolation from each other and from U.S. policy regarding the typical length for a tour of duty in Vietnam.

A one-year tour of duty had been established for all U.S. personnel in Vietnam, causing the turnover phenomenon, and very few men would volunteer to extend. This was not surprising. The tempo of operations in the 1st Infantry Division was phenomenal, and the work was both physically and mentally exhausting. A soldier who spent a year there, particularly in an infantry battalion, was typically worn out by the end of his tour. There were exceptions to this, but the grueling pace in a demanding environment took its toll on the stamina of all men. It is difficult to put this into perspective. For men assigned to combat units, sleep normally came from exhaustion; and many nights were as exhausting as the days. The oppressive heat and boredom of army food did not help. Men did not eat nourishing, complete meals with regularity. Hot food was normally delivered in mermite cans (insulated food containers) in the early evening by helicopter. Many men were so tired that they didn't bother to eat. A can of C ration fruit, usually peaches, pears, or fruit cocktail, would eliminate stomach gnawing. If a soldier did take hot chow, he could usually count on the rain to drown his mess kit or paper plate while going through a jungle chow line.

In my case, I joined the 2nd Battalion, 28th Infantry on June 20, 1967, weighing approximately 215 pounds. When I left the battalion on October 3, 1967, some one hundred days later, I weighed 167. Most people who knew me then (and now) would say a forty-eight-pound weight loss in one hundred days probably was good for me. I may have been overweight, but I had played varsity college football at two hundred pounds in the 1950s. I also know that because of the heat, heavy daily physical exertion requires three good meals a day. And few men in infantry battalions got them.

Additionally, on Wednesday of each week every man was required to take a malaria tablet. This was not a pill. It was about the size of a penny in diameter and about four or five pennies thick. Everyone hated them. Imagine for a moment swallowing something like that—and we really enforced it. We should have enforced the three square meals a day as firmly as we enforced the taking of malaria tablets. For the combat soldier, the food was available, but men were generally averse to eating much, and the malaria tablets didn't help. Three or four hours after taking a malaria tablet, your intestines would start to knot. These stomach cramps were then followed by an overpowering churning of the bowels. In many cases, nature would work faster than the time it took to drop your pants and squat. Fortunately, we wore no underwear; we would just hang on until the next rain (six or seven times a day in the wet season), then pull our pants off and wash them. Unfortunately, it was not over. Diarrhea could normally be counted on for up to twenty-four hours after taking a malaria pill. In spite of friendly camaraderie, it was always embarrassing to drop your pants within everyone's eye-view and squat like a dog with a problem.

On the plus side, the consequences of taking malaria pills helped to keep officers in infantry battalions from being too officious. There was something leveling about the process.

As long as I'm on that subject, I should point out that we also used latrines and cat holes in the field. As time permitted during the construction of our DePuy bunkers and command post bunkers, we usually managed to dig a hole in the center of our perimeters. When our resupply came in at night by chopper, you could normally count on the battalion supply crew to include a two-hole box along with ammo, water, sandbags, food (mermite cans with evening chow), and sufficient C rations (canned food) for breakfast and lunch the next day. The two-holer box was ceremoniously placed on the latrine hole to the accompaniment of mild cheering. This latrine represented, to some extent, our acknowledgment that after all we were *Homo sapiens,* the highest species in the animal kingdom—the species that could distinguish right from wrong and whose individual members normally exercised modesty in the performance of their bodily functions.

Actually, the latrine was never really used that much. Cat holes were easier, and squatting in front of your peers became acceptable practice. In addition, at night, no one liked to move from his position. From time to time, leaders might move about to check on their men, but roaming around the perimeter in the black of night looking for the latrine was no one's idea of fun. I did it once or twice because using the latrine seemed somehow civilized. In addition I wanted to sit, not squat, and let my mind wander as nature took its course. One night while in this position a sniper decided to throw a few rounds in our direction. Fear immediately dominated the scene. As I crouched down behind the two-holer box with my feet in the hole while also contemplating placing the rest of my body in the hole if the firing increased, I imagined the telegram to my wife: "Dear Mrs. Shelton. The Secretary of the Army regrets to inform you that your husband was killed in action while hiding behind the battalion two-holer. He was last found cringing in a pile of shit donated by himself and his fellow soldiers."

I think this was the last time I used the two-holer.

"A 'modern' infantry may ride
sky vehicles into combat,
fire and sense its weapons
through instrumentation,
employ devices of frightening
lethality in the future,
but it must also be old-fashioned
enough to be iron-hard,
poised for instant obedience,
and prepared to die in the mud."

T. R. Fehrenbach, This Kind of War

Chapter 4
Life in an Infantry Battalion in 1967

Starting in the fall of 1967 American units began what was called the "infusion" program, which transferred certain selected soldiers, primarily officers and noncommissioned officers, between units in order to reduce the annual heavy turnover that had resulted from entire army units being deployed en masse to Vietnam on a particular date. By July 1967, before the "infusion" program got underway, the Big Red One had already lost through turnover practically all of its combat veterans and, in particular, its experienced commanders. When I joined the 2nd Battalion, 28th Infantry, every line commander (four companies and the battalion commander) was new, give or take thirty days. As battalion operations officer, I was also new. By the end of July there were very few veterans around to call us FNGs—"fucking new guys."

The turnover situation meant that General Hay had to conduct what turned out to be a less-than-successful initial operation (Billings) with all us FNGs, the soldiers who were there to fill the holes left by those who had completed their tours of duty and moved on to assignments in places other than Vietnam. Without underscoring his concerns in this area, he began a series of quasi-combat operations that were centered on helicopter assaults, limited search and destroy missions, and heliborne extractions into areas not known for heavy concentrations of enemy. I joined the battalion after it had made a heliborne assault into an area just north of the Dong Nai River, less than ten miles north of Bien Hoa air base. Since the enemy had launched some rocket attacks on Bien Hoa quite recently, this assault had a flavor of combat realism, and each new battalion took its turn going in, using standard tactical air and artillery preparation followed by waves of troop-carrying "Huey" (UH-1) helicopters, also called "slicks." Five slicks at a time, called a "flight of five," would put approximately forty men on the ground simultaneously. Each flight of five took from one to two minutes to unload on a five-ship landing zone. If a battalion was fortunate enough to have thirty helicopters for the assault, six flights of five could put 240 men, or two understrength rifle companies of 120 men each, on their landing zones in ten to twelve minutes.

This was a maneuver that required extreme speed and surprise. It was carefully planned and timed, starting with the tactical air strikes, normally using a combination of cluster bomb units (CBU) and napalm. Just as the air force planes were finishing up their runs (perhaps a total of ten minutes), the artillery (105mm and 155mm) would take over and direct heavy fire on the periphery of the landing zone for two to five minutes. As the last artillery rounds were on their way to the target, the first flight of five slicks was on its final approach to touchdown accompanied by helicopter gunships. The timing of the arrival of the gunships was critical because in the event there were enemy forces near the landing zone (LZ), the friendly troops could be on ground and the slicks taking off before the enemy soldiers could recover from the intensive air and artillery prep. The accompanying helicopter gunships normally hosed the flanks of the LZ with machine-gun, 40mm cannon, and 2.75-inch rocket fire for the first flight in. If we were taking fire, the LZ was called "hot." We never knew if a LZ was going to be hot or not, but the prep was always reassuring.

The standard operating procedure (SOP) in the Big Red One under General Hay was that every airmobile assault would be preceded by a prep. A number of people questioned this tactic because they felt it compromised surprise. I favored the tactic, perhaps because I liked the thought of firepower. If enemy forces were near the LZ, they weren't going anywhere during the prep; they were in their foxholes. The surprise came from the prep itself, and at least the enemy would be somewhat disorganized and confused as the slicks were landing.

Although I have read accounts of many hot LZs in Vietnam, in the Big Red One I remember few. Hot LZs were definitely not desirable places to land troops, because the helicopters were most vulnerable to enemy fire as they left their unloading hover to pick up forward air speed along a predictable flight path. A downed helicopter in the middle of a LZ could really screw up a carefully planned operation. An airmobile assault in the Big Red One was a carefully planned and executed operation, and it was normally scrutinized carefully by one of the general officers of the division, and later critiqued intensely after the operation. Many battalion commanders dreaded those critiques more than a hot LZ.

The post-combat critique was another custom of the 1st Infantry Division in Vietnam worth describing. By that time in my military career, this was the fourth tactical unit with which I had served. I had been a platoon leader and company commander in the 1st Cavalry Division in Korea in the late 1950s, a company commander and assistant operations officer in the 82nd Airborne Division at Fort Bragg, North Carolina, and an operations officer in the Berlin Brigade in Germany. I was accustomed to rough talk and criticism. The 1st Infantry Division in Vietnam was, however, the "ass-chewingest" organization I have ever seen in my twenty-seven years in the army. Maybe it was combat that made the difference. I also think that General DePuy's influence had much to do with it. Praise was a rare commodity. Normally it was saved for "donging" ceremonies where awards and decorations were presented ("dongs" were medals). Ass chewing was the name of the game; everyone did it, seemingly, all the time—in person, on the radio, and on the telephone. It was SOP. After awhile, you grew to expect it. On several occasions I remember my battalion commander being reamed on the radio by someone above him in the chain of command, and he just grinned. We were usually prone to grin even more when someone else was getting it, and the rest of us were monitoring the transmission. Eventually, an ass chewing was something combat leaders looked forward to, with a sort of masochistic pleasure, as something that went with the turf.

A really bad habit in the Big Red One was the overuse and abuse of FM radio communications protocol. Since FM radio was the standard means of communication, this was a serious breach of professionalism. Actually, the problem went beyond overuse and abuse. For ten years in the army prior to Vietnam, I hated, but used, standard army radio/telephone procedure. We had to authenticate, communicate with brevity, encode, use proper call signs, and frequently change call signs and codes to avoid enemy monitoring, decryption, and deception. In my experience prior to Vietnam, most tactical units were not good at communications security, but they worked at it and knew when they had erred and why. It was a discipline that had to be practiced and mastered. In Vietnam, however, we totally ignored it. It was so much easier to talk in the clear, except for map coordinates, and we never changed call signs—never. The rationale was that the tempo of operations was so fast that the enemy couldn't react even if he heard it. But as we were to learn later in the 1970s, after overrunning an enemy communications bunker deep in War Zone C, we gave away for free exceedingly large amounts of intelligence and order of battle information by not following standard communications protocol and changing call signs.

The call signs were a fetish. The division commander's call sign was Danger 77, and nobody called him General Hay, even in casual conversation. He was called 77. Every key person in every unit was referred to by his call sign. A typical conversation during chow might go like this: "Man, Ole 77 was fired up yesterday. He got Daring 6 on the horn and really reamed him, and when 77 spit him out, 78 took over. At one point Daring 6's Romeo broke in to tell 78 that Daring 6 had to leave the radio; and 78 went berserk and reamed the Romeo [radio/telephone operator]. Then 78 got on Devil 6's frequency (push) and reamed him because Daring 6 had left the radio. Great day!"

Nobody had a name; only a call sign. For one hundred days I was Dauntless 3 (operations officer, 2nd Battalion, 28th Infantry). When I left the battalion and went to division headquarters, I became Danger 76H (operations officer, G3, 1st Infantry Division). In the battalion, the battalion commander called me "3," and I called him "6." We called the executive officer (XO) "5," and company commanders were Alpha 6, Bravo 6, Charlie 6, and Delta 6.

Here's a typical conversation:

"6, did you hear Charlie 6 call you on the command push?"

"No, 3, what did he say?"

"He said 5 was at his location and wanted to know if you wanted him to go to Alpha 6 position next or to your location."

"3, tell 5 to leave his Romeo at Charlie 6's location, come here, and then return there."

This was not over the radio; this was normal conversation between two people eyeballing each other!

"So this is combat. I've only had one day of it. How does a man stand it, day in and day out?"

Lieutenant Paul Boesch after his first day of combat in Germany, Road to Huertgen: Forest in Hell

Chapter 5
Living and Learning

After arriving by chopper in the battalion position north of the Dong Nai River, I reported to the battalion commander, who had been in command approximately one week. He struck me as extremely nervous, and, as it was getting near dusk, he didn't have much time for me. He wanted to check the perimeter. He introduced me to the S3 (battalion operations officer) I was to replace, Lieutenant Colonel (formerly Major) Terry de la Mesa Allen Jr. Because he was introduced to me as "Terry," I didn't realize at the time who he was. Later that night, when I asked him if he was related to General Terry Allen, he told me, "Yes, I'm his son."

I liked Terry from the moment I met him. He immediately introduced me to those in the area, including the radio/telephone operators. I liked that touch. He treated them with respect, as members of the team and not merely his subordinates. I decided right then that I liked Terry Allen.

He asked me what experience I had, and I related my previous assignments. As majors were judged in the division at that time, I believe I had had a good bit of tactical experience, including being assistant operations officer of a battle group in the 82nd Airborne Division. I was familiar with airmobile operations, and I believe Terry felt I could become a decent "3" to replace him. He told me he would stay with me a day or so and that I should pick his brain for information about division SOPs and the battalion.

Having just been promoted to lieutenant colonel, he was due to go to division headquarters to a staff job. He had served as the battalion S3 under the previous battalion commander and was very familiar with division operations. During the next two days, we developed a close rapport. He was full of helpful hints, and he willingly passed on to me everything he knew: pitfalls, what to do, how to answer the radio, how to plan operations, and what to watch for.

That first night with the battalion was unforgettable. It was raining; we were lying in shallow holes in the mud with no lights, no cover except ponchos. Occasionally, a friendly artillery concentration would land in the jungle nearby. These were "DEFCONS," that is, defensive concentrations. Although they landed at least five hundred meters from our positions, they were deafening, screaming in and landing with a jarring crunch. Additionally, 175mm "Long Toms" were firing harassing and interdictory fires over our positions into War Zone D. The rounds sounded like elevated trains going above us through the night's total blackness. Many men in the battalion slept well that night, despite the mud, and the rain, and the noise, and the blackness. I was a "FNG," so I barely slept at all.

The next few days were spent conducting search operations on the ground. Each day we would send two companies out into the jungle while the third company secured the night defensive position (NDP). We made no contact with the enemy. After about two days, Terry Allen told me he was leaving. He reminded me of some of the basic principles to keep in mind: (1) battalion commanders and S3s fight the war on the radio; (2) always have an LZ for a medevac picked out—always; (3) don't let aviators push me around. They have their job; I have mine; (4) keep my artillery liaison officer (LNO) close enough to touch him at all times; (5) always take the battalion command (BN CMD) and operations (OPS) net radios (PRC-25) into choppers with me. Don't count on chopper radios; and (6) don't give higher headquarters the idea that I'm not in control. Always have a "pat" sitrep (situation report) ready to give; otherwise someone will try to take over. He also briefed me on the techniques of a battalion-sized airmobile extraction. He then left by chopper, following a firm handshake and a "good luck."

The extraction ran something like the assault—only in reverse. The helicopters would come in five at a time, and hovered in a formation we called a "Christmas tree" or "staggered trail." The pickup zone was called the PZ, and we normally marked the spots where we wanted the choppers to land with a sandbag. Then groups of eight men each would wait, normally concealed in the bush close to their sandbag. Five choppers at a time meant you could pick up forty men. In the field a battalion of three rifle companies, its headquarters, and supporting elements numbered between four hundred and four hundred fifty men. If there were a total of twenty choppers, each flight of five would have to do three turnarounds. A flight of five would go in, pick up forty men, take them to a secured landing zone, and then go back for another pickup.

An extraction didn't take very long, but it was more cumbersome and complicated than the assault. When planning for an extraction, I always assumed that an enemy force would try to attack while we were withdrawing. Thus the effectiveness of the extraction plan depended on excellent timing and fire support. Although we wanted to ensure all-around security throughout the extraction, we also wanted our men in groups of eight ready to rush into the choppers as they came in. Consequently we always positioned ourselves in a circle or perimeter, with each rifle company securing one third of the circle, keeping some men in security positions while moving others to the pickup points.

In the 2nd Battalion, 28th Infantry, we attached the three squads of the battalion reconnaissance platoon to each of the rifle companies. The recon platoon would be the last element of the battalion to be picked up. The recon platoon leader would exercise unity of command over the last elements, and he made sure that everyone was extracted. Before the extraction started, the members of the recon platoon would lay a circle of claymore mines facing outward from the perimeter along likely avenues of enemy approach. They also laid an inner circle of claymore mines just outside the chopper pickup points. As the recon platoon withdrew toward the PZ, they would blow these claymores to impede any enemy from coming to the edge of the PZ and firing on them as the extraction was being completed. We also placed tactical air strikes, artillery fire, and helicopter gunship suppressive fires along the outside edges of the PZ. The battalion or brigade commander, who was flying in a command and control (C&C) helicopter that bored circles in the sky at about one thousand feet, sometimes higher, sometimes lower, controlled these artillery and aviation fires.

During this extraction following Terry Allen's departure from the battalion, I was sitting in the open door of the C&C, next to Captain Nick Halley, our artillery liaison officer. Nick was controlling the artillery fires. The battalion commander was sitting looking out the other side of the chopper.

Suddenly, Nick said to me, "Knock it off."

I said, "What?"

He said, "You punched me."

I said, "No way."

He looked down on the floor of the chopper and picked up a shrapnel shard about ten inches long. It must have weighed a pound, and it was still hot. It had apparently expended its force, but came right in the open door of the chopper. I quickly told the pilot I thought we were a bit close to the artillery blocking fires.

Other than this encounter with a piece of shrapnel, there were no particular mishaps during the extraction. The battalion commander kept complaining that the men were moving too slowly. I reminded him that we were at one thousand feet, and the men were, in some cases, up to their knees in water and mud and were carrying thirty or forty pounds of equipment. He kept hollering that the men moved too slowly, and right during the extraction he said to me over the intercom, "I want PT when we get back to base camp." I didn't argue with him, since I figured he'd forget about it later. I knew he was nervous because this was his "graduation" exercise in airmobile extractions, and he was waiting for the ever-present critique that would be conducted by one of the generals shortly afterward. (The expected ass chewing did not transpire, however.)

We landed in Di An, the 2nd Brigade base camp. Our base camp was in Lai Khe, about twenty miles north. We were told to occupy barracks of the 2nd Battalion, 18th Infantry, which was out fighting somewhere else. It seemed like a battalion of the Big Red One was never in its own base camp; it was always just passing through the nearest base camp on the way to the next operation. Our battalion had been out in the bush for about ten days, and everyone was exhausted. Nevertheless, the battalion commander called me to his makeshift office that night and told me he wanted the line companies to do physical training (PT) first thing in the morning. I told him I didn't think that was a good idea. I told him that the men had not been slow, but they had appeared slow because of the water, being weighed down, being tired, and the fact that we were watching their movement from one thousand feet above. He was adamant, saying something like, "Just execute my orders, don't question them." I had only known this man about five days, and he was my battalion commander, and I owed him loyalty. But I was also beginning to think he had a crazy streak in him.

I then assembled the company commanders and told them, "We will have PT at 0700 in the morning." They nearly went crazy. Ed Burke, who commanded C Company, was a captain who had seen a good bit of combat and was almost ready to leave. I was a major. He said to me, "Are you nuts? My men are beat, and now you want to run them around. That's crazy." Mel Adams, a first lieutenant who commanded B Company, just looked at me and shook his head. They were both right. Nevertheless, I told them, "Your asses better be on that road at 0700 tomorrow." And they were.

"Everything is very simple in war, but the simplest thing is very difficult. The difficulties accumulate and produce a friction which no man can imagine exactly who has not seen war."

Carl von Clausewitz, On War

Chapter 6
Seal of Dog Leg Village

We did PT just that one day. The next day we were ordered to conduct a "seal" on a village about ten miles north of Di An called Dog Leg Village. The actual name was Chanh Long, and the "seal" was just that, an operation in which we would surround and seal off all escape routes. The village was shaped like the back leg of a dog, at least on the map; thus our name for it.

Practically every Vietnamese village was surrounded by a berm, a mound of dirt normally six to eight feet high, which encompassed all the huts of the village. The dirt was normally overgrown with grass. Some berms had entrances cut in them, but we could normally just climb over a berm like we would a small hill. It was not really an obstacle, although it might provide cover (shielding from direct fire). The orders called for our battalion (2-28 Infantry) to seal the west side of the village while another battalion (2-16 Infantry) sealed the east side. The 2nd Brigade would be our higher headquarters for the operation. Both battalions would move north about eight miles by truck to Phu Loi, which was the Big Red One's base camp for the aviation battalion. From Phu Loi each battalion would move its separate way on foot to the village about three to four miles north of Phu Loi. The seal was to be in place prior to daylight at 0500. Naturally we did not want the enemy to find out about the seal.

Our intelligence indicated that some wounded VC Main Force guerrillas had been moved to Dog Leg Village for medical treatment.

We hoped to surprise the guerrillas in the village, sealing it off, and capturing them. At daylight a helicopter with a loudspeaker mounted in it would fly low over the village announcing that it was sealed and about to be entered by a search party. The latter normally consisted of South Vietnamese soldiers and police, with the U.S. soldiers establishing the seal around the village.

Our deception plan was simple. Our battalion moved outside the perimeter of Phu Loi base camp about two miles and dug in. At dusk we built fires and continued digging in. It looked like we were going to spend the night in our NDP. Around 2300 we began to move our men out of the NDP, leaving the fires going and a few soldiers to tend them. Then we advanced quietly, in single file, through the flooded rice paddies on the two- to three-mile march to the village. At the same time, the 2-16 Infantry was doing essentially the same thing some two miles to our east.

It was slow going. The water in the rice paddies was up to our knees. As men moved along, the walls of the rice paddies became slick, and some soldiers fell into the paddies. Then it began to rain. It was a blinding, driving rain. We could not even see the man immediately ahead, so we tried to hold on to his webbed suspenders to avoid getting separated. All were laden with weapons, ammo, and light packs. Muffled cursing could be heard when a soldier went down, and others would reach to help him up.

At midnight, word was sent up to the front to halt. Imagine some four hundred men in single file having to come to a stop with a minimum of noise in the rain and the darkness. The battalion commander asked me where we were in relation to the village. I gave him my best guess and also told him I would move forward to confer with Lieutenant Mel Adams, the B Company commander, who was in the lead. It seemed to take hours getting to the front of the column.

"Mel, do you know where the hell you are?" I asked.

"Well sir, we've been following this compass azimuth like a dog's rear end, and I think the village is about a one thousand meters off to our right front."

We could see nothing in the rain, but I figured that Mel was right, based on the distance we had covered. I told him that when he got the word to move, he should advance another one thousand meters on this azimuth, then stop, and be prepared to execute a flanking movement to the east.

I moved back down the column and told the battalion commander what I had done. He said, "Okay, let's go." We began to move again, and the rain subsided. We still could see nothing. Suddenly, toward the front of the column, but right in our midst, there was a flash and an explosion. We crouched, but forward of us, men had screamed and dived into the rice paddies.

My first thought was ambush, but no firing followed. My second thought was that someone had stepped on a mine or booby trap. I also figured that if anyone was in the village, they must have heard the explosion and the shouts. I moved quickly forward to where I heard loud groaning. I found a soldier lying on the bank of the rice paddy. We stuffed a rag into his mouth to muffle his cries, and I asked what had happened. A nearby trooper told me that this man had stumbled while carrying an M-79 grenade launcher. The launcher had fired its 40mm round into the man's leg. The unexploded round was lodged under the skin in the fleshy part of his inside right thigh. I couldn't believe it! Normally an M-79 round becomes armed twenty to thirty feet after leaving the muzzle of the grenade launcher. Here was a man squirming in the mud with a live M-79 round embedded in his leg.

I told the men who were nearby to keep him immobile and quiet, and that we would dust him off (medevac by chopper) after the seal was put on the village. He wasn't going to bleed to death, and as long as the round didn't go off, he wasn't in any danger, only pain. The seal came first.

Our estimates of where we were had been right on the money. Mel Adams reported seeing the northwest end of the berm, and he was moving his company into position to link up with the leading elements of the 2-16 Infantry at the north of the village. Our A and C companies covered the west side and south side with C Company linking up with 2-16 on the south. Everything looked good.

At very first light, although it was still dark, a helicopter with loudspeaker flew over the village jabbering Vietnamese. As the chopper cleared the area, a noise from inside the village was followed by four rapid shots fired from the village. Two U.S. infantry battalions, loaded for bear and facing each other with the village in between them, thought the VC were about to attack. All hell broke loose. Automatic weapons fire kicked up dirt all around me, tracers crisscrossed our positions, and 40mm grenade rounds began to crunch around us. The same thing was happening to the 2-16 Infantry on the other side of the village. Using radios, we finally got the firing stopped. We had suffered no casualties—a miracle. It was the biggest firefight our battalion was to have until the Battle of Ông Thanh, and this one had been with the friendlies.

We conducted a search of the village, but found nothing significant. I went into the village, and in one location we found eight to ten sets of black pajamas that were covered with blood that had not dried. Obviously a number of VC casualties had been in the village, but they had either been evacuated before the seal was established, or they had been taken to an underground tunnel, and we could not find the entrance. Although this operation had not been successful in terms of results, it provided the battalion with a good training exercise.

As we waited for our next orders, the battalion commander and I evaluated how we had done. It was the first good conversation I had had with him, except that, during the conversation, he told me that he knew he "had not been wanted" in the 1st Division, that his assignment as battalion commander had been "force-fed," and that he expected to be relieved. I told him I thought that that was a crazy idea. I said that I didn't think that General Hay played those kind of games, and that he should get those kind of thoughts out of his mind and concentrate on doing what he thought was right, not in worrying about who was going to second guess him. In spite of his negative thoughts, it was a good conversation, and I felt we had at least developed a dialogue. That feeling was to be short-lived.

"And I will show you something
different from either
Your shadow at morning
striding behind you
Or your shadow at evening
rising to meet you;
I will show you fear
in a handful of dust."

T. S. Eliot, "The Waste Land"

Chapter 7
Phouc Vinh

W e moved from the seal of Dog Leg Village on foot back
to Phu Loi. We had barely gotten inside the gate of Phu
Loi when we were told that Phouc Vinh, the 1st
Brigade base camp to the north, had received a heavy 122mm rocket attack the night before with some thirty or so friendly casualties.
None of the battalions assigned to the 1st Brigade (1-26 Infantry,
1-28 Infantry, 1-2 Infantry) were at the base camp. As usual, they
were scattered somewhere in the division's TAOR (tactical area of
responsibility), as we were. Division was anticipating a ground attack
at Phouc Vinh that night, and our mission was to fly in to Phouc Vinh
by chopper and assume perimeter security for the base camp.

After we assembled our battalion and passed out a quick frag
(fragmentary) order, I jumped aboard a chopper with one or two others and flew to Phouc Vinh to make a hasty reconnaissance and find
out what the situation was on-site. By this time it was dusk, and the
bulk of the battalion would not arrive until after dark. This type of
operation typified the majority of the missions our battalion was
given during the one hundred days I spent as a battalion operations
officer.

Although we conducted one or two planned operations, the
large majority were really ad hoc, reaction-type operations in which
we had little or no intelligence, and sometimes no map sheets of the
area. A kind of helter-skelter methodology dominated planning so
that we never knew where we would be the next day. The name of

the game for leaders was: "MAKE ORDER OUT OF CONTINU-OUS CHAOS." Every time we were scheduled to get some rest time, an emergency operation would materialize, and off we went. This is not a complaint. It was just the way it was. In the 2-28 Infantry, there was little or no rest, continuous and changed operations, and a new chain of command (bouncing from brigade to brigade on a continuing basis) every day. Unlike what I had heard about the life of front-line soldiers in World War I, World War II, and the Korean War, there was little or no boredom in an infantry battalion in Vietnam.

When I arrived at Phouc Vinh, I was appalled. The senior man in this division base camp was a captain, and he was in a state of high anxiety. This captain was an infantry officer, who apparently had not had much experience. He had been present during the rocket attack the night before and had spent the entire day evacuating casualties and trying to restore some order. From what I could gather, there were only about thirty able-bodied soldiers scattered throughout the base camp, and most of these were either new arrivals or those getting ready to leave. I asked the captain whether he had anyone who could show me the positions along the perimeter of the base camp that were manned. He called a heavy-set sergeant forward. The sergeant told me that his primary job was working with the radios in the base camp operations center, but he had been around the perimeter in daylight.

Originally the defensive perimeter had been prepared so that it might be defended by as many as three infantry battalions, the three battalions under the operational control of the 1st Brigade. The battalions rarely, if ever, got to their base camps. Consequently only a small rear detachment could be found at the camp. It normally consisted of a resupply team of perhaps eight men who ensured that ammunition, rations, water, sandbags, and any other required equipment got out to the battalion in the field. This crew was normally made up of men who had spent time in the field. They were dependable for two reasons. First, they knew what it was like in the bush, and they felt sorry for the guys out there. They knew the battalion depended on them. Second, they liked their jobs, at least relatively. The chances of being blown away seemed to be a lot less in base camp than out with the battalion. Others in the rear included cooks, clerks, and people coming and going. Typically, the battalion executive officer (XO) stayed in the base camp to make sure that all the "ash and trash jobs" got done and that the battalion in the field had what it needed. Our battalion XO was Major Bob Gillard, one of the finest soldiers I have known. He was second in command of our battalion and, by the tables of organization, he was my boss.

The XO of a battalion is a very important man. A battalion has only three field-grade officers: the commander (a lieutenant colonel), the XO (a major), and the S3 or operations officer (a major). Everyone in the battalion looks to them for command and control. In an infantry battalion, very little is done without counting on someone else for something, such as for flank security, for resupply, or for other forms of support. The three field-grade officers are there to see to it that everyone is working together to achieve the mission of the battalion. Bob Gillard's job was to make sure we were supported in the field, and that's what he did. He was my senior in rank and experience, and he was my boss (my rating officer); yet he never interfered with my relationship with the battalion commander. Because I was in the field with the commander, calling many of the operational shots for the battalion, Bob could very easily have resented my position and made things difficult for me. He never did. He was a mature pro who worried about the battalion as a whole and could always be counted on for sympathy and support. Bob was an experienced special forces officer and did not have a great amount of time in a regular infantry battalion, but he knew soldiers. He knew that people were counting on him, and he never let us down.

Unfortunately, when I arrived in Phouc Vinh that night, there were no battalion XOs to be found. There was only the captain whose cage had been rattled. The sergeant also informed me that Phouc Vinh had formerly been a French base camp, and there were a number of old French minefields around the perimeter. There were no maps, but most of the areas outside the perimeter believed to contain French mines were overgrown, and barbed wire (now covered by undergrowth) surrounded them.

The sergeant and I went on a quick tour of the perimeter. It consisted of built-up, sandbagged bunkers connected by communications trenches. They were not in a good state of repair, but they were protection. Beyond the perimeter, there were barbed-wire fences, old but relatively formidable. As we were making this quick reconnaissance, the men from my battalion began to arrive.

I rushed back to the landing zone because at this point the companies had no idea where they were going, and it was dark. As each company commander arrived, I asked him to put his men into assembly areas, and I would issue a frag order to all company commanders in five minutes. The commanders assembled in a bunker illuminated by one electric light, and I drew them a quick sketch of the Phouc Vinh base camp on a piece of cardboard covered with acetate that I carried with me. A picture truly is worth a thousand words! I assigned areas of responsibility for each company, and we put the mortar platoons (three 81mm mortars per company) in a battery firing position (all together). I told the company commanders to move out and that I would be around to check their positions. I then went to find the battalion commander. He was located at the "hooch" (living quarters) of the commander of the 1st Battalion, 28th Infantry, who probably hadn't been in the place since he assumed command of his battalion. It did, however, have two bunks with mosquito nets draped around them and an overhead fan that kept the air moving. All in all, this was not too shabby.

The battalion commander was lying on his bunk with his forearm over his eyes. I told him the instructions I had given to the line companies and that I was now going out to check the positions. Suddenly he threw his legs off the bunk and sat up.

He said, "What about the ambush patrols?"

The division had a standing SOP that each battalion would send out three ambush patrols per night, one from each rifle company.

I told the CO, "Sir, I don't think we should do that tonight. The men have had no time to prepare, no rest, and we don't really have any intelligence. Also, I've been told there are old, unmarked French minefields out around here. I don't think we should do it."

He said, "What makes you think you have the authority to change the division SOP? If the general were to come in here tonight or tomorrow morning and ask me about our ambush patrols, what would I tell him? I want three ambush patrols out tonight."

I then said, "Sir, that is absolutely crazy. The division SOP is not a replacement for common sense. Putting ambush patrols out here under the circumstances doesn't make any sense!"

He said, "Goddammit, 3, are you going to do what I tell you or not? Every time I tell you something you have a better idea. Now execute my orders."

"Yes, sir!" I was furious, literally in a rage. I went to each rifle company commander and told him to have an ambush patrol ready to go out in one hour. Each one in turn told me I was crazy, and I, in turn, hammered each one of them saying basically, "Shut up and do it."

I then went and found the sergeant who had earlier shown me around the perimeter positions. I asked him, "Do you know how to get out through the barbed wire around the perimeter? We have three ambush patrols that have to go out."

"What?" he said. "Sir, are you crazy? You can't send ambush

patrols out through here tonight."

I said, "Look sergeant, I don't need advice. What I need is someone to show me a way out through the wire. Can you help me?"

He said, "I've never been out through there, but there is a path. I'll try."

I said, "Great, meet me here at 2145, and we'll give it a shot."

At 2145 the three ambush patrols, one from each company, each with five men commanded by a sergeant, were standing by waiting for instructions. They were loaded down with claymores, ammo, grenades, and one machine gun per patrol. I showed each patrol leader where I wanted his patrol located. They had to be far enough apart so they wouldn't come in conflict with each other in the event that an ambush was sprung.

In general, I thought ambush patrols as SOP were a good idea. With the men properly rested and prepared, they were an excellent tactical tool, adding security, keeping the enemy off balance, and giving us some of the initiative. But not tonight. The whole situation made me so mad I couldn't think straight, and the patrol leaders just weren't mentally ready to do the job. I told them I would lead them out through the wire. I didn't tell them that I had no idea how to get out myself. I introduced them to the sergeant, adding that the sergeant knew the area, which he did not. We moved out between the bunker lines.

There was enough ambient light to silhouette the bunker line to our rear and the pickets holding the barbed wire to our front. When we reached the wire, I was ready to go into shock. It was covered with kudzu and other vines. The sergeant whispered to me that he had found the path. I moved to his position, and he pointed to two pickets, "I think that's the way out. Just follow this line of pickets, and I think that's the safe lane." I turned to the lead patrol leader and told him, "Pass it on: move slow, quiet, single file. When we get through the wire, I'll count each patrol off. Follow me."

I started to move slowly down through the line of pickets with fifteen men behind me. I was scared to death. I had always tried to picture myself as a heroic figure. Now I was there, and I didn't feel heroic. Every small sound was intensified one hundred times. My throat and mouth were so dry I couldn't swallow, and every muscle in my body was tense. I was like a slowly moving, coiled spring. When I was about halfway through the wire and the last man was just entering the wire, I moved my leg forward, and then I felt what seemed to be a trip wire go "pop," like an explosive sound. A cry rushed from my dry throat: "AWWW!"

Every man went down in unison. I knew I was dead. Suddenly, a bright light flashed out in the wire, blinding us. This was a familiar sight: I had popped a trip flare intended to give warning in case the enemy tried to come up through the safe lane. I went to my knees and just stared at the light. I was absolutely drenched in sweat and, as I turned, I saw the sweat on the faces of the men behind me gleaming in the bright light. Here we were in the middle of a minefield in Vietnam at ten o'clock at night. I felt naked—as if I had been caught naked in the street. But I also began to breathe again. As the bright light of the flare suddenly subsided, I became conscious of my own breathing, and I took several deep breaths.

I wondered how many VC had seen us standing out there in the minefield with our asses hanging out. I was sure that every VC within a hundred miles had seen us and was laughing at us right now. "Stupid Americans. Can't even get through their own minefield without setting off their own trip flares. Well shit, let's go ambush them now."

We continued to move out through the wire till it ended. As each patrol leader came to me, I pointed out the direction of his ambush site. I told each that we would be ready with mortar fire if they needed it, to report in every thirty minutes, to start back in at first light, and not to ambush each other. I wanted to kiss them goodbye. You poor bastards, I thought. Somebody is sending you out here to sweat it out all night in no man's land. I was sure none of them knew the name of this place, Phouc Vinh, why they were there, or what we were trying to accomplish. All they knew was they were on an ambush patrol in Vietnam. They also knew that if they didn't pop the ambush, they might get back through the wire alive. If the enemy gets in the kill zone, they knew they had to pop the ambush and hope for the best. Then it would be just keep shooting and hoping all the VC are either laying in a pile so we can count them, or running like hell in the other direction and never coming back. If the two forces became intermingled in the blackness, it would be a nightmare.

A case in point is what happened to Captain Jim George, who would play a major role in the Battle of Ông Thanh as the lead company commander. Severely wounded in that battle, George was hospitalized in Japan, subsequently returning to the 2-28 Infantry to command B Company. One night in the spring of 1968 he accompanied an ambush patrol, which was not something we really wanted company commanders to do; but I guess Jim George always figured the Lord would protect him. He had a great and abiding faith in God, which seemed to keep him calm and smiling in good or bad times.

At any rate, according to Jim, the patrol he accompanied popped its ambush, and suddenly his men were intermingled with the enemy in the blackness. He thought the patrol was moving to a new position. With shooting and confusion all around him, he followed the man next to him for twenty or thirty meters, then grabbed the man by the shoulder to stop him. As the man turned, Jim saw he wore no helmet. We normally wore helmets on ambush patrols. The man wore a soft cap and carried what looked like an AK-47. Jim suddenly realized that he had been following a VC, and the VC thought he was a VC. Jim is not, and never was, a vicious man. He is one of the nicest, friendliest guys I have ever known. But when he told me this he was smiling.

I said, "What did you do?"

He said, "Man, I just pulled up my CAR-15 [a submachine gun version of the AR-15] and emptied the whole magazine into him on automatic. The muzzle was against his belly."

That was the kind of story that always seemed to come out of ambush patrols, such as this one, that popped a wild and woolly night. Even those patrols that were not popped by an enemy probe or something else that was unexpected came back exhausted mentally and physically after a night of fear in the dark. Either way, the men who had been on an ambush patrol would never be the same again. Those kinds of experiences leave an indelible mark on a man's psyche. No, it doesn't make him a raving maniac. But I know experiences like these forever change a soldier in ways he may never fully understand. Just like in Herman Melville's novel, *Moby-Dick,* when Ahab's hair suddenly got a streak of white in it after his encounter with the white whale. A night on an ambush patrol can bring out strong emotions such as fear, incomprehension, incredulity, and other involuntary responses that go ricocheting through each man's brain and body and soul, whatever that is.

As the last ambush patrol moved out, I turned and headed back through the wire, full of hate. Hating myself for being so scared, hating that son of a bitch battalion commander who had sent us out here, hating the bastards who had sent us to Phouc Vinh with no orientation or preparation time, hating Vietnam, and hating the night. Then suddenly, I stopped hating. I realized that I'd better start thinking. I hoped my own men on the perimeter wouldn't decide that I was a bad guy. Fortunately, the sergeant who showed us the safe lane had a red flashlight, and he'd made a prearranged signal with the guys manning the perimeter. Nothing like being with a thinking sergeant, especially when you're an enraged major who hadn't really been thinking clearly since the battalion commander's decision on the ambush patrols.

I normally slept with the battalion commander, either on the ground next to him or on a bunk near him. On this night I went to the TOC (tactical operations center) where all the radios were.

"Do we have contact with brigade, division, battalion rear, all the companies, and the ambush patrols?" I asked the radio operator.

"Yes."

"Any new intelligence?"

"No."

"Okay, wake me if anything happens."

Then I lay down on the floor and went to sleep. There was no enemy activity that night. The following day we were assigned to a new operation because 1st Brigade had elements coming in to assume defense of the camp's perimeter. I was glad to get out of Phouc Vinh. I would rather be in my own NDP in the jungle than in a base camp where you might be shot by friendlies whom you didn't even know.

"They were numerous, united, confident, superbly led, emotionally charged to defend their homeland and freedom, and able, through design or good fortune, to catch their adversary in unfavorable tactical situations."

Robert M. Utley commenting on the military capabilities of the Indians at the Battle of the Little Big Horn, Frontier Regulars

Chapter 8
Playboy, Ambush, and Retribution

Our mission would be to establish an NDP near a village called Tanh Phu Kahn, which was known to us as Playboy's Palace. We were to be under operational control of 2nd Brigade, and our job was to search out the area in the vicinity of Tanh Phu Kanh and a nearby leper colony. Sounded like fun. We choppered back into Phu Loi that day, spent the night there, and then moved out on foot. It was about a five-mile march. While the battalion moved on foot, I took an H-13 Light Observation Helicopter (LOH) and flew to meet the village chief, nicknamed "Playboy," in the village of Tanh Phu Kanh. He was set up in a two-story stone building in the center of the village, much like a Mexican bandit. His soldiers, dressed in a mixed bag of civilian clothes, uniforms, and black pajamas, lay around the building like sacks of flour. Weapons and ammo were carelessly lying about. The smell of noucmam, a hot pickled fish sauce, and buffalo dung permeated the building.

Playboy was squatting in the middle of the room smoking a cigarette with a cigarette holder and grinning so that his many gold-trimmed teeth showed. I squatted down, we shook hands, and I spread my map in front of him. With an interpreter close at hand, I began:

"This Playboy's Village. Tanh Phu Kanh," pointing. "U.S. Army go here. Stay maybe three, four days." I pointed to the spot we had picked, about a mile north of the village in an open field but near enough to a patch of jungle from which we could cut logs for overhead cover. Playboy grinned, shaking his head up and down.

I then said, "Nighttime, we ambush VC. What place we ambush VC?"

The interpreter interpreted.

Playboy brought his hands together like a monk, smiling, head bobbing up and down, making clucking sounds in his throat. He pointed to a spot just outside the village at the north end with his bony finger jabbing at the map up and down.

The interpreter said to me, "Tonight, you kill VC here. You see. You come; wait. VC come tonight. Here."

Hot damn! Real live intelligence. I shook Playboy's hand and left some mementos that included a cigarette lighter with the battalion crest on it, some cigarettes, and a case of C rations. Pointing at the map, I told him we would ambush VC tonight. He kept shaking his head and smiling. I had been told he was trustworthy and that the VC had a price on his head. He didn't mind our battalion being around his area at all. I flew back to the spot we had chosen for an NDP, over-flying our battalion's foot movement to the spot. I did several 360s over the site to get a feel for the lay of the land, including the ambush site Playboy had pointed out.

I could clearly see a footpath coming out of the jungle heading toward the village. It went through a cluster of burial mounds, including what looked like some headstones, and then on through a cut in the village berm. The ambush site would be in the cluster of burial mounds. I then landed at the NDP site, where the first company was just closing in. It was about noon, and the digging of our perimeter bunkers began in earnest. I was anxious to brief an ambush patrol. I called the A Company commander and asked him to send me a patrol leader, which he did. I briefed the sergeant (E-5) on the site and told him to begin preparations. I also briefed the company commander and told him the ambush patrol would be under his command, not the battalion's. Digging in, cutting down trees for overhead cover, and security patrolling all occupied the remainder of the day. After dark, A Company reported that the five-man ambush patrol had gone outside the perimeter. We settled into our new home.

The battalion command post/operations center was set up in the center of the NDP. There a large hole, about eight feet in diameter, had been dug, over which we had mounted a hex tent. The men had also dug a connecting trench to a bunker immediately adjacent. This bunker had overhead cover, but the hole and hex tent did not. In the event of incoming indirect fire, we would crawl into the bunker. Otherwise, we operated in the hole with the hex tent over us. It was a tight, but relatively secure, arrangement. Another hex tent was placed near the TOC and adjacent bunker. This was where the battalion commander and I would sleep on canvas cots, legs dug in so that we were only inches above the ground. We sandbagged the hex tent walls so we could roll off the cots and crawl into the bunker if mortar rounds started coming in.

That night just after dark three ambush patrols departed our NDP. One went to the location where Playboy had told us to go. The night was uneventful until about 2300. Suddenly we heard several explosions and automatic weapons fire. The ambush position was less than a mile from our NDP. We called the ambush patrol leader. His voice was excited and high, "We're running out of ammo. We need help."

I told him, "Hang on. We'll send a platoon out to back you up. Don't fire them up."

He replied, "Roger." I turned to those in the TOC and said, "Who should we send?" The consensus seemed to be that we didn't know what leader to send out. Because the company commander of A Company had just taken command of the company that day, we agreed that he wouldn't know either. I looked at my S3 Air, First Lieutenant Billy Murphy. Murphy had been a rifle platoon leader and had already won two Silver Stars. He was a bona fide hero and had three weeks left to go in Vietnam.

I said, "Murphy, you're the man. You can do it!"

Murphy shook his head, "Aw, sir, I've only got three weeks. I don't want to get my ass shot off."

I said, "Murphy they need you."

He said, "Okay, let me get my shit together."

I called A Company and told them to have a platoon ready to move out, now, to reinforce the ambush patrol. Murphy was back in an instant. I took the map and showed him where the patrol was located. I told him, "Move directly through the open field. I'll start dropping mortar rounds along the wood line to your left. You can use the explosions to muffle your movement and guide on."

I shook his hand, and he moved out. He called in to report that he had twenty men and was moving out of our perimeter. Suddenly, I heard a large explosion—a claymore—right where Murphy and his makeshift platoon should have been leaving. I called, "Murphy. You okay?"

A stuttering voice, choked with fear replied, "Goddamn. Goddamn. We hit a trip wire and blew off one of our own claymores. Goddamn." After a few moments, the platoon moved out.

We dropped the mortar rounds along the wood line. In about forty minutes Murphy called, "We got 'em all okay, and we got one dead VC with an M-16 rifle. We're coming back in."

Hallelujah! No casualties and we got one of theirs. As far as I could recall, the division hadn't had a confirmed kill in a month. They'd had lots of reported kills, possibles. But we had a body and a rifle. We were jubilant.

The next morning General Hay arrived at our NDP. He congratulated us for doing a good job and pinned a silver star on the ambush patrol leader's chest. He examined the M-16 rifle that the VC had been carrying. The name "REBEL" had been carved into the hard vinyl-polymer stock. We had no idea where it had come from, except that at that time no South Vietnamese forces were carrying M-16s. He must have gotten it from an American. When we handed the body over to Playboy, we didn't feel too much sympathy for the dead VC. We were told Playboy hung him up by his heels in the village marketplace. We wouldn't have done that, but we didn't care much, either. Our battalion was on a high.

For the next two days we conducted company-sized search and destroy operations without much success. One company found an old tunnel complex, but it didn't appear to have been used recently. When I got to the tunnel entrance several of the troops said, "Go on down there, sir. See what it's like." I really didn't want to go down. I had grown up in a mining town and had been a mile under the earth. I also had crawled through a few mangy caves as a kid. But, I really didn't want to go down.

Nevertheless, I threw my leg onto the makeshift ladder and climbed down into the dark. A soldier was standing at the bottom of the ladder with a flashlight. He told me to get down on my knees and crawl on all fours. I crawled for about ten feet, and the tunnel emptied into a room. The ceiling of the room was rounded, like a dome, and hundreds of large black spiders were clinging to the dirt roof, which had been turned black from the carbon of torches. I sat on the floor of the room, and as my eyes became more accustomed to the relative darkness, it looked like the room could hold about twenty people. Also, there were two tunnels leading out on the other side of the room. I was amazed. The rooms and tunnels were simply dug out of the dirt. There was no revetment—no nothing—just dirt.

I started to crawl through one of the other tunnels when it hit me: claustrophobia. I had started down the tunnel when suddenly I felt like I was going to throw up. I told the man behind me, "Back up." I then retraced my crawl back to the first room, turned around, and crawled through the tunnel I had originally entered. I got to the ladder and went up, never missing a beat. Emerging from the hole at the top of the ladder, I must have looked like a missile coming out of a silo.

One man said to me, "What's it like, sir?"

I said, "Great. Really great. Well, I'll see you guys later. Good hunting." It was then I decided that, although I would be very glad about every tunnel we found, I had just conducted my last visitation to one of those rat holes. The experience also increased my grudging admiration for the enemy. Living in those holes was not what human beings were meant to do, but they did it. I thought, what a motivation must be driving these people.

As I moved back into the NDP that afternoon, I noticed that several Vietnamese villagers were in the fields near our NDP. Although I did not find the Vietnamese people at all repulsive—as a matter of fact I marveled at their exquisite bone structure that seemed so fragile and delicate—I did not like to see them near our NDP. Some of them could easily be casing the joint. I told our observation posts to chase the Vietnamese away.

Late that afternoon I had a normal meeting with the company commanders, who by this time were all FNGs, except for First Lieutenant Mel Adams of B Company. At the meeting we discussed preparations for the night and some tentative plans for the following day. I told them, "Tonight, I want you to put out two listening posts (LPs) per platoon." (We normally put out one per platoon). This elicited a chorus of groans. Nobody liked listening posts, especially those who had to man them.

Normally we put LPs out so that they would be within seeing distance from the NDP, but spending the night in one of them was no fun. The security of a bunker was a lot more comforting than lying fifty or so meters outside the NDP with another man, listening for any sounds that might announce an attempted enemy approach. We normally used sound-powered TA-1 telephones or PRC-25 radios at our listening posts. The radios could make noise, however, and the sound-powered telephones were better. If an LP heard something, it would give an immediate warning. Normally LPs also had claymore mines facing the enemy, ready to detonate, so that if they were in danger of being overrun, the men could pop the claymore and run for the NDP.

One problem we always had with LPs was that both soldiers would go to sleep, regardless of the danger. When this happened, and it seemed to happen every night, it was one of our most aggravating experiences because it meant we had lost communications with an LP. Then someone, usually a sergeant or platoon leader, would have to crawl out to check on the LP. It was a court-martial offense to be caught sleeping on guard on an LP. But no one was ever court-martialed. Sometimes it was impossible to stay awake. Exhaustion seemed to be the normal cause of falling asleep in an LP, and it was more than physical exhaustion. It was also lack of eating properly, the heat, the rain, the sweat, the dirt, and the fear—a nagging gut-wrenching feeling that you could be surprised by a mine, a booby trap, or a VC, at any time. There was also fear of the friendlies: careless handling of weapons, explosives, and also friendly mortar or artillery fire. There were many apparent dangers, and they all took a toll on stamina. So sleeping LPs were chastised, told to stay awake and report in every thirty minutes, and left out. It was not enjoyable duty.

After our meeting, the company commanders returned to their respective pieces of the pie that made up our NDP perimeter. About an hour later, I decided to take a walk around the perimeter. Dusk begun to settle over the field and the NDP; the nearby jungle was silhouetted against the sky. When I got to the first platoon of A Company, I met with the platoon sergeant, asking him, "Where are your LPs?"

He said, "Sir, we only have one LP, and it's right out by those bushes."

"What," I said. "I told your company commander two LPs per platoon!"

"I don't know anything about that," he replied.

I rushed to find the company commander and said, "You only have one LP per platoon. What the hell is going on?"

He said, "Sir, we asked the battalion commander if we could keep it at one, and he said okay."

Now I was really wound up. I said, "Did he know that I had told you to put two LPs out? Goddamn it, those VC are going to try to get revenge for that ambush the other night. I saw some bastards casing us this afternoon. And it's not jungle. It's out in an open field. Goddamn it. I'll get back to you later."

I went charging for the battalion CP. I think I was as mad as I have ever been in my life. The battalion commander was in his hex tent, actually our hex tent, since we shared it. He had his shirt off and was washing up.

I said, "Sir, I told the companies to put out two listening posts tonight. When I checked them, I found they only have one. They told me you said one was okay. Is that true?"

He didn't look at me. He just said, "They came and asked me. Everybody's tired. One is enough."

I said, "Sir, you can't do that to me. If I put an order out—and I thought I had that authority—I would think we should at least discuss it before you countermanded my order. These guys won't listen to me at all if they think you will countermand me. I realize you have that authority, but we can't work as a team that way."

He realized that I was infuriated. He smiled and said, "3, take it easy. You're getting this all out of proportion. Sit down, have a cup of coffee. We're doing okay."

This was a new twist. In the past it had always been me trying to get him to lighten up. I sat down on the bunk. I thought, am I cracking up? A voice inside me said, "No. He's wrong. Hang in there." I calmed down somewhat, and then asked him for permission to speak. I said, "Sir, I thought I had good reason to increase the number of LPs. I know we did not discuss it, but I absolutely resent your changing my order without discussing it with me first."

He said, "Okay. Let it go."

I left the tent and went over to the berm around the TOC bunker and sat in the dirt. I was still angry. I was also frustrated. I didn't know how much longer I could cope with this relationship. I was deep in thought, and it was now dark. Abruptly, there were two huge flashes followed by deafening explosions. "Claymores," I said to myself. I dived to the ground and crawled toward the battalion commander's tent. Captain Nick Halley, our artillery liaison officer was also on the ground.

I said, "Nick, get artillery. Get some rounds on the ground."

He said, "Roger, request is in."

At the same time two automatic weapons began raking our perimeter. I could see the muzzle bursts and red tracers streaking everywhere. It didn't occur to me at the time that they were red tracers—American ammunition—as opposed to the green tracers that the enemy normally used. In other words, the VC were using our own ammo against us. The tracers ripped through the battalion commander's tent, kicking dirt in my face, and burning out in the weird way that tracers do, which looks like they are trying to burn a hole in the ground as though they were mad bees.

My radio with the brigade and battalion operations nets was inside the TOC bunker, and my RTO was monitoring it. I knew I had to get to the radios. Tracers were still flying everywhere. I pounded Nick on the back, "Where's the artillery? Goddamn it, Nick, artillery."

Nick was angry. He said, "It's coming. It's coming."

It came. Almost immediately the rounds came screaming in.

Next there was an explosion, which knocked the wind out of me and lifted me at least twelve inches off the ground. This experience was immediately repeated. I could hear shrapnel buzzing over my head. I had heard shrapnel before in training, but it sounded nothing like this.

"Nick," I screamed. "Short rounds. Short rounds."

Nick was already hollering into his radio, "Check fire! Check fire!"

I pounded Nick on the back. "You worthless bastards! Short rounds!"

He said, "It's not my fault. I'm lying here with you."

I told him, "No more artillery. You hear? No more artillery." I got up and headed for the TOC bunker. About ten feet away, another burst of tracers sprayed around me. I dived for the bunker entrance, and the adrenaline must have been really working. My head squarely matched up with the ten-inch-diameter log over the entrance to the bunker. Fortunately, my helmet hit the log, not my head, but I thought I had been blown up. I saw stars and collapsed into the hole. In the next moment the battalion communications officer, a salty old captain, dived on top of me. We looked at each other, and both started laughing hysterically. He then went for one of the radios. I lay there for a moment in the dark at the bottom of the hole. I looked up and saw a face glowing in the dark above. It was the face of my brother, Ned. He had been killed in an automobile accident in 1960, seven years before, when I was a lieutenant in Korea. His face was clear to me—glowing—and he was smiling. It was only for an instant.

The communications officer's voice on his radio broke my trance. I got on the battalion operations net and called the companies. I told them, "Open fire. Open fire. Don't just sit there. Open fire. Drop some rounds down the mortar tubes. Do something."

The enemy fire had ceased. It had only been about five minutes since the claymores had gone off. But no one inside our perimeter had fired a round. Here we were, a whole infantry battalion, locked and loaded, nine mortars ready to fire—and we hadn't fired one round in return fire. Unbelievable! And now, after I had called on the radio, still there was no fire. I didn't know what to do. I couldn't fire my .45-caliber pistol from the center of the perimeter.

I got on the brigade operations net. I called, "Dagger 3. Dagger 3. This is Dauntless 3, over."

The reply, "Dauntless 3, this is Dagger 6. Can you give us a sitrep?" It was Colonel Chuck Thebaud, the 2nd Brigade commander. I had worked for him in a past assignment, and it was good to hear his voice.

I said, "Dagger 6, Dauntless 3. We have been attacked by unknown size enemy force with claymores and automatic weapons. Request gunships and a flareship."

He asked me if we had casualties, and I told him I did not know, but I would call him back.

He told me, "Take it easy. Help is on the way."

I then received a report that one man had been killed and several wounded. I called back to Dagger 6 and asked him to send a dustoff (aeromedical evacuation chopper) to our location ASAP.

As I looked from my hole, I saw someone about fifty meters away holding up a large flashlight. I didn't think that was very smart. I ran over to the light and shouted, "Hey, you dumb bastard, shut that light out."

The reply came back, "Screw you. Who the hell are you?"

I replied, "I'm Major Shelton, Dauntless 3. Who are you?" He said, "I'm Captain Swink, the battalion surgeon, and I need the light."

I said, "Okay," and went back to the radio. I had never met the battalion surgeon, Jim Swink. After this battle I was to learn that he was the same Jim Swink who was an All-American tailback at Texas

Christian University in the early 1950s when I was playing in college at Delaware. His picture had been on the cover of every football magazine in the country. He had gone to medical school after TCU and was serving his time in the army when he was sent to Vietnam. Swink had immediately gone to treat the wounded after the attack had begun and had been hit by small arms fire in the shoulder. He continued to treat the wounded despite his own wound, and when I had called to him, he was bleeding from his own injury. Swink received a Silver Star for his cool actions that night, working with the wounded though wounded himself.

I then heard the battalion commander calling me. "3. 3. Where the hell are you? What are you doing?"

I had returned to the bunker and the radio. I told him I had talked to Dagger 6 and requested gunships, a flareship, and a dustoff.

He said, "Okay."

Then the dustoff aircraft came up on our operations net, "Dauntless 3, this is Dustoff. What is your situation?"

I told him, "We have one kilo [KIA], seven WIA. Receiving no fire. I will put a strobe out to mark LZ."

"This is Dustoff, roger. I'm about five minutes from your position, out."

I got my strobe light out and moved to a position inside the perimeter near the wounded. The dead man was wrapped in a poncho. I laid the strobe light on the ground and pressed the "on" button. The strobe began flashing. I saw the dustoff chopper on his approach, headlight on. Only he went right over the strobe and landed outside the perimeter. I ran to the chopper. The door was open, and the crew chief leaned out the door.

"Back on the strobe," I shouted. "Land on the strobe." I was screaming at the top of my lungs, and I couldn't imagine why he hadn't landed on the strobe.

Slowly the chopper rose, peeled over to its right, and circled to land on the strobe. I ran back to the strobe, and this time the dustoff came in at the right spot. As his skids settled on the ground, the wounded were helped aboard. There was a lot of noise from both the chopper and the wounded men. We stacked the wounded in, making sure that we recorded each man's name. Then the dustoff started to rev-up for takeoff.

I looked down and saw the poncho with what was left of the dead man. He had taken the full blast of the first claymore, and he was in pieces. I grabbed the poncho with both arms and swung the package up to the crew chief. As the chopper started to take off, a gusher of blood sloshed out of the poncho, hitting me flush in the face, right in my open mouth. I swallowed some of the blood, as it splashed off my face and went down my chest. The dustoff moved off into the night, and I went down on all fours and started to retch. I was there like a dog—on all fours—for about a minute, puking and retching. I got my canteen out, took a gulp of water, swirled it around in my mouth, and spit it out. Then I did it again. I wiped my face with the long front tails of my jungle fatigues and stumbled over to the TOC bunker. I went into the hole, and that was the last thing I can remember about that night.

"The men of the battalion came to know him, liked what they saw, and respected his abilities."

From the eulogy for Lieutenant Colonel Terry Allen Jr., West Point magazine Assembly *(December 1975)*

Chapter 9
New Commander

I woke the next morning with a terrible taste in my mouth. And as I got up, I could feel the dried blood caked on my body hair from my chest right into my crotch. Several people thought I had been hit. I found a water can and, using a wet towel, got most of the blood off. Shortly after breakfast we received a terse order from brigade: "Disestablish NDP at present location, move on foot to new NDP position. VIC XT (coordinates). Move ASAP."

We disestablished our NDP, which was no small feat. It required emptying every sandbag (about fifty-five thousand were used in a battalion NDP), salvaging the bags, and filling in the bunkers. After a careful police to ensure we had everything, we started to move out. I think we were all glad to get out of there, and there was little horseplay during the march. We were heading due north to establish an NDP north of old Dog Leg Village.

As we walked along, I couldn't get our failure to return fire out of my mind. I was bound and determined to come up with a scheme that would keep the enemy from crawling in on us again and to loosen up our trigger fingers.

We arrived at our new location early in the afternoon. I gave instructions that there were to be two listening posts per platoon, and each listening post was to install five claymores. Three rifle companies meant nine rifle platoons, or eighteen listening posts. Each LP would set up five claymores. So our security forces would have ninety claymores facing the enemy. We devised a plan to fire the claymores randomly throughout the night. This would help keep the LP's awake, and maybe give the enemy second thoughts about crawling in on them. We also established H&I (harassing and interdictory) fires with M-79 grenade launchers. The "thump guns," as we called them, fired a 40mm grenade a good three hundred meters outside our position, and using them periodically throughout the night put us in an active, as opposed to a reactive, mode. I was not too happy with our past reactive performance.

When our NDP preparations were well underway, we received a call that Danger 77, General Hay, and Dagger 6, Colonel Thebaud, were en route to our new location, each in his own chopper. The battalion commander met the two choppers as they landed and then, along with Thebaud, he climbed aboard Hay's chopper. After conferring for about five minutes he emerged from the chopper and said to me, "3, get Jones to pack my gear and throw it on Dagger 6's aircraft. I've been relieved of command."

I was stunned. It seemed so sudden. For no reason, I began to cry. He said, "Forget it. Good luck to you, Jim." Then he shook my hand and got on the chopper.

Dagger 6, Colonel Thebaud, came over to me. He said, "Jim, take command of the battalion. Someone will be coming out later."

I said, "Yes sir." Within another hour Major Bob Gillard arrived. He told me he had been told to take command. I told him, "great," and briefed him on our tactical dispositions, including the new SOPs on H&I. He wholeheartedly agreed. As we were eating C rations before dark, another chopper arrived. It was Terry Allen. He told us he was taking command of the battalion, and that Bob Gillard should take his chopper back to our base camp at Lai Khe. I was elated! I thought Terry Allen would be a great battalion commander.

After Bob Gillard left, Terry called me aside by the TOC bunker. He said, "Jim, I want to say a few words to you about this battalion. You are a great S3, and I know you are doing a great job, but remember this: I am the battalion commander and you are the S3. I'll run the battalion; you help me pick up the pieces. You got it?" I smiled. "Yes, sir. I got it." I knew what he was saying. The former battalion commander let me run the show subject to his whims. I wasn't used to that kind of an arrangement, but I could fill vacuums. According to Terry, as I read it, he wasn't planning on allowing any vacuums—and he didn't. I was doubly happy to have him as my commander. It was the last week in July 1967.

Terry Allen assumed command that night in late July in an NDP north of Dog Leg Village. We took a few VC mortar rounds during the night but nothing more. The next day we received orders by radio telling us to disestablish the NDP and move by foot to Phu Loi. We went through the arduous task of destroying all the work (bunkers) we had done the day before. A Chinook helicopter (CH-47) soon arrived to take away the equipment we needed but could not carry on our backs—mortar shells, extra ammo, tents, two-holer latrines, water cans, sandbags, and so forth. We referred to these items collectively as our "shit"; hence, the Chinook's nickname, "shithook." Sometimes this equipment could be brought in by a Huey with a sling load, but normally, on the first night we had too much of it for a Huey; and, always, when we disestablished an NDP with all its sandbags, we needed a CH-47 to retrieve it.

It was only after the CH-47 had flown off with our equipment that we started the trek to Phu Loi. In addition to carrying my own gear and weapon, I carried two pairs of jungle boots around my neck, and two cans of 7.62mm machine gun ammo that someone had neglected to load aboard the CH-47. The ammo was great because it kept me balanced as I walked through the tepid rice paddy water. This explains how infantrymen got their nickname "knuckle draggers": if you carried ammo cans long enough, your arms would stretch. Then after they had unloaded the ammo, they could just walk around the area with their knuckles dragging on the ground.

The area that we were walking through was west of Dog Leg Village. It was basically the same area we had come through in the rain and pitch black on the seal of Dog Leg, but now we could readily see that it was absolutely wide open. Because it was wide open, we were spread out, which was a far cry from holding on to each other in single file as we had on that night in the rain. As we trudged along, it occurred to me that a VC 82mm mortar round had a bursting radius of approximately thirty meters. That meant there was a ninety percent probability that anyone within thirty meters of where the round hit would be a casualty. When I watched soldiers moving in the open, I always thought of that, and I was the crabby son-of-a-bitch who was constantly on the radio hollering, "Spread out, goddammit, spread out."

In situations such as this I would also make believe I was a VC with an RPD (a Soviet machine gun) or a BAR (a U.S. Browning Automatic Rifle) who was hidden out to our front, or our flank, or even our rear, and then I tried to see how the lines of our men would be in enfilade fire from the most likely automatic weapons positions. Enfilade fire is where the line of our troops would coincide with the long axis of the area where fired rounds would land. (The textbook definition of enfilade fire is when the long axis of the target coincides with the long axis of the beaten zone. The beaten zone is where the fired rounds land.) A gunner really gets his money's worth with enfilade fire. I would keep hollering at our people to stagger themselves with reference to those suspected VC locations so the enemy could not have enfilade fire. I don't think our guys ever knew what I was talking about, and it always seemed like there wasn't enough time to explain. All I know is that when I was moving with troops in the open, I was a worrywart over what might happen, and therefore, I was a real pain-in-the-ass on the radio and as far as I could holler.

The walk we made that day was a tough one. Terribly hot, moving at high noon, no shade, carrying too much, and short on drinking water. Mostly we were walking through shallow rice paddies. The water was actually hot, and the sun reflected off it. Everyone seemed to be staggering and stumbling, and we were only about half way to Phu Loi. I figured that if the enemy had started shooting at us now, everyone would just lie down. We would get no maneuver. No one would be able to move.

Fortunately, we got no fire from the enemy. But we did have one or two men go down from heat exhaustion, and Terry Allen got his first ass chewing compliments of Brigadier General Rogers (Ole Danger 78). Rogers just couldn't figure out how a soldier could get heat exhaustion if his leaders were taking care of him. The men had to be medevaced by chopper (dustoff) and the general tore Terry's butt. Terry was philosophical about it, but he felt bad, and he really could not argue about it. (According to the "Book": A commander is responsible for everything his men do or fail to do.)

General Rogers was really good at ass chewing. I guess that was his way of helping. I never remember him ever doing anything that I would consider helping. I always thought that a large part of a senior officer's job, especially if the officer was an assistant division commander, was to help. If General Rogers's definition of help was ass chewing, then he gave everybody lots of help.

In any event, about the time our lead elements were reaching the Phu Loi perimeter, a Huey buzzed low over us, and the pilot asked us to halt. We halted, and he landed. It was Major Herb Sink, commander of the "Robin Hoods," the Field Force helicopter lift company stationed in Lai Khe. Herb was a good guy. He told us we were going to get a mission momentarily to conduct an airmobile assault into a village east of Di An that was called Tan Hiep and located along the Dong Nai River. He showed us the village on his map because we didn't have maps with us that covered this particular area. Terry told me to get the battalion assembled for pick up (in other words, form a PZ), while he got more info from Herb. Sure enough, Herb had the right dope. While I was gathering the troops, a message came over the brigade command net to assemble the battalion and prepare for pick up. We made our plans quickly, and the lift aircraft called to tell us they were five minutes out.

We decided to put A Company in immediately in three locations right in the village and then to block with B and C Companies. Our frag order to the battalion went something like this: "Intel has hot report of VC with weapons in Tan Hiep. A Co lands in three locations and conducts immediate search of village. B Co will go in on north, C Co on south. Establish blocking positions." And then we executed the plan. Within twenty minutes after we had received our initial information, we were on our way; fifteen minutes later A Company was on the ground.

I vividly recall two incidents during this operation. First, we were flying in the C&C (command and control) chopper and I was watching the main body of A Company approaching the village. Suddenly, it seemed like every man in the company dived into the rice paddies with huge splashes. Then I heard the gunfire. Obviously men were moving faster than the speed of sound. Second, a while later I was up in an H-13 Light Observation Helicopter following the action. I noticed that one squad from A Company was clearly disoriented and moving through a small area that would lead them nowhere. I told the pilot to land near the squad. I got out, told the squad leader to go back and to the left, then I ran back to the H-13 and climbed in. As we took off, almost straight up, which had the little H-13 shaking with vibration, the pilot let out a yelp and goosed the engine full bore. I asked him on the intercom what was happening. He told me, "Somebody is shooting at us." He went crazy with that little chopper, flying all over the sky. I never saw a thing. He said a burst of tracers had gone under us. I never saw anything, but from the look on his face, he was sure we were going to get a face full. Fortunately, we got out of there without a hit. The Tan Hiep operation was a success. We captured five or six suspected VC, along with several automatic weapons and a weapons cache. A Company, with Captain Jim George in command, had done all the work, but the whole battalion savored its first success with Terry Allen in command.

"Well, my interest in Heaven
may not be much,
but such as it is,
I would be willing
to give it all for
a piece of artillery."

A veteran Civil War soldier, William R. Trotter, Bushwackers

Chapter 10
Securing Firebases

D uring the month of August, the 2-28 Infantry Black Lions were involved in a number of varied operations. The first operation was a firebase security mission along the Dong Nai River some fifteen miles northeast of Bien Hoa air base. Our battalion's job was to ensure enemy forces did not overrun four artillery batteries that were supporting operations to our south. In addition to our battalion, a company of South Vietnamese marines was also assigned part of the firebase perimeter security. I believe the firebase had been established to support a Vietnamese marine operation. We did meet two U.S. Marines who were advisors to the Vietnamese marines, but our job was to dig in and secure the firebase.

Because there were no trees in the vicinity, we could not build overhead cover for our bunkers. To solve this problem, division provided us with steel pickets that were normally used for erecting a barbed-wire fence. We used these steel pickets in lieu of logs, and they worked out quite well. The only problem came later when we tried to collect the pickets at the time we were disestablishing the firebase. The word had been passed that we were to evacuate everything, and burn any refuse we didn't want to evacuate. The Vietnamese marines somehow got the wrong word. When we went to get the pickets, we found that the marines were burning them in a huge bonfire! Obviously the pickets were not going to burn. Nor could we place them in a sling load to be carried out, as they were white hot. To salvage these metal posts, we had to wet them down with water, using our steel helmets as buckets. We never figured out why the Vietnamese marines had tried to burn these posts, and the incident did make us worry about marines in general.

Another incident that took place at that firebase was the crash of a U.S. helicopter lift ship (slick) into the Dong Nai River. The aircraft sank into the deep, fast-flowing water. Divers found the lift ship, and a huge CH-54 Skycrane helicopter was brought in to pull it. Our firebase was immediately adjacent to the recovery operation. An enormous chain was attached to the Skycrane, and divers went into the river to fasten the chain to the submerged aircraft. It was a risky operation. At one point the Skycrane was hovering over our positions with the chain dangling from its hook. It was chow time, and mermite cans (insulated food containers) and a huge stack of paper plates were sitting in a row waiting for men to start through the line. Suddenly, someone aboard the Skycrane jettisoned the dangling chain, right over our chow line. This chain, with links that must have been two inches wide and perhaps two hundred feet long, came crashing down out of the blue sky like a dead boa constrictor. It landed right on our chow line and crushed the aluminum mermite cans like eggshells. At the same time, the stack of paper plates was catapulted into the air, and hundreds of individual plates were caught in the downdraft of the helicopter. The paper plates looked like flying saucers, hundreds of white flying saucers. Miraculously no one was hit by the chain. The incident reminded me that there were many ways of being killed in Vietnam. Again I could see the first line of the telegram to my wife: "Dear Mrs. Shelton,..." and so forth.

The only other incident I recall at that weird firebase, which contained two 105mm batteries and two 155mm batteries (twenty-four tubes in all), was a visit from Ole Danger 78 (General Rogers). During his turn over the NDP in his command and control helicopter, he noticed a loose poncho lying beside a bunker. Over the radio he told Terry Allen that loose ponchos would not be tolerated in the Big Red One. We thought we had done a good job at establishing positions and securing this large firebase and that we had represented the Big Red One well in support of the Vietnamese marines. We had! But Brigadier General Rogers reminded us of our weaknesses. He was a difficult man to please, and I don't believe anyone looked forward to his visits. I believe he was trying to do his job the very best that he knew how. He just wasn't very long on encouragement.

Finally we extracted from that remote firebase and headed back to Lai Khe. Once we arrived there, we were immediately alerted for another operation. Plans called for this operation to be a two-battalion search of an area only about five miles north and slightly west of Lai Khe. Our job was to secure a position for a two-battery firebase. The placement of this firebase (I believe it was named Sicily I) would allow the 1-18 Infantry (Dogface) to conduct search operations beyond the 105mm fan (ten thousand meters) provided by the artillery batteries in Lai Khe.

The 105mm fan rule requires some explanation. Ordinarily, no units of the Big Red One were allowed to operate on the ground unless that ground could be hit by 105mm artillery fire. That meant that on an operations map a planner would draw a circle around any 105mm artillery battery in firing position. The radius of the circle was ten thousand meters, and thus troops were allowed to operate within that circle. Consequently the position of the 105mm batteries controlled the area in which any unit of the Big Red One could maneuver. Artillery and firebases were like solid gold. An infantry unit had to have them in order to move. If an infantry battalion or brigade commander wanted to conduct an operation somewhere, then he had to ensure that he had 105mm coverage. The only man with authority to move 105mm batteries was the division commander, who in our case was Major General Hay (Ole 77). General Hay was a stickler about this rule. On occasion infantry commanders would try to conduct maneuvers outside the 105mm fan, only to incur his wrath.

The maneuver plan was relatively simple. Our battalion, the 2-28 Infantry (Dauntless) would conduct an airmobile assault into the area selected for the firebase and secure it. Then CH-47 Chinooks would bring in the 105mm tubes and ammo. As soon as the batteries were ready to fire, the 1-18 Infantry (Dogface) would conduct an airmobile assault into the new ten thousand-meter fan created by the positioning of the new batteries.

I am still in awe of the precision and perfection with which these operations were conducted. Many of my memories of Vietnam are ugly, involving waste of material, lives, and effort. However, the precision with which we conducted airmobile assaults, particularly when a firebase was being established, was phenomenal. I marveled at the split-second timing involved in coordinating a prep (air strikes and artillery), with the maneuver of the lift ships, the speed with which security and communications were established, and then the efficiency with which our artillery units were able to mount their tubes. It was only a matter of minutes from the time the CH-47 brought in the sling-loaded 105mm tubes with piggybacked ammunition until the tube was firing. I am convinced that at that time our artillerymen in the Big Red One were as good as any artillerymen have ever been. That does not mean that artillery fire was always as effective as it might have been, given the limitations imposed by safety requirements or by a lack of coordination and agreement between the maneuver commanders in the field and the artillery command-and-control apparatus. Nevertheless, the gunners were superbly drilled, and they had very high standards of precision and excellence. To watch a 105mm towed artillery battery being set up as part of an airmobile assault and a hastily built firebase was a thrill. Seeing motivated men who knew what they were doing work as a team was absolutely great. I never wanted to be an artilleryman. The job just never computed for me. But a well-trained 105mm artillery battery in action is a sight to behold, a well-oiled machine.

I recall our briefing for the brigade and division commanders prior to this operation. Terry Allen and I briefed first for the 2-28 Infantry (Dauntless) and then Dick Cavazos and his S3, Jim Tucker, briefed for the 1-18 Infantry (Dogface). I thought we had done a particularly good job. I had white sheets of cardboard covered with acetate, and I had drawn sketches of our landing zone (LZ) plan, security plan, and final unit dispositions. But then Dick Cavazos got up. He tore a dog-eared piece of cardboard off a C ration box, drew some sketches on it, and then did his briefing. With his simple presentation, he exuded so much confidence and magnetism that the big wheels forgot all about us. Dick Cavazos had the ability to capture people's imaginations—at least he had mine.

The following day we were airborne, en route to the objective. Watching the prep as we approached the landing zone was always a thrill. The artillery was right on target, walking 105 and 155 rounds down the edges of the LZ perfectly. Our battalion command group was in the second lift of five aircraft, meaning that a platoon (forty men) would be on the ground when we landed. We wanted the battalion command element in early, and we had a goal of erecting a three-sectioned RC-292 antenna within one minute after touching down. The idea was to move from the LZ as rapidly as possible, get the 292 out of its case, and have it hooked up to the radio, even as the mast was being assembled and erected. The 292 antenna greatly enhanced communications, and we challenged all battalion elements to get these antennas up as quickly as possible.

As we approached the LZ, the butterflies were flying in my stomach. They always did on assaults because you always expected a hot LZ. As the first platoon landed, we got a report that the LZ was hot. My heart went into my throat. Fortunately, it was an erroneous report. Someone had seen one or two VC fleeing the prep area, but we received no enemy fire. The report did, however, briefly increase the excitement.

Using thirty lift ships, we had the bulk of our battalion on the ground fifteen minutes after the prep had ceased. The brigade commander, Colonel Bill Caldwell, and his S3, Major Don Holleder, came in with the last lift of five. They had just debarked from their C&C helicopter when the CH-47 with the artillery tubes came rolling in, and they both got caught in the downwash of one CH-47. It knocked them down and sent them rolling over several times. They were both big men, but they looked like rag dolls. Neither was hurt, but they were pissed. Terry and I rushed over to them, and then we all started laughing.

This was the first time I had worked with the 1st Brigade, but I thought both Caldwell and Holleder were pros, and they certainly did not get excessively involved in supervising our operation, as most senior officers in the division seemed to do. The artillerymen took only minutes before they had the first 105 tube barking out rounds. The speed of the artillery work was amazing as they fired the prep for the 1-18 Infantry (Dogface), which was going in to the west of our position using the same lift ships that we had used. All in all it was a very successful airmobile assault. Both infantry battalions were on the ground, and the artillery was already beginning to stock up its ammunition to two thousand rounds per battery.*

We spent all day digging in and preparing fields of fire. I believe this was the best NDP we ever established while I was in the 2-28 Infantry, because we were located at a high enough elevation that no positions were in water and we did a great job of cutting fields of fire.

---

*See Appendix 3 for the 1st Infantry Division booklet, *Fundamentals of Artillery,* which spells out the artillery SOP in the Big Red One.

Some two days after we went in, I viewed the NDP from a light observation helicopter at an altitude of about five thousand feet. It looked like a geometric design: the fields of fire were cut thoroughly and with great precision to a distance of about three hundred meters from the frontal bunker line, with the crisscrossing patterns of interlocking fires clearly delineated.

Unfortunately, neither our battalion nor the 1-18 Infantry achieved much during this operation. There were plenty of signs of enemy activity, but no concentration of enemy forces. I did, however, get a chance to direct an air strike against an enemy bunker complex. On the third day of the operation, I was flying an LOH to the southwest of our position when I saw movement on the ground. A closer look revealed a large bunker complex, and I saw at least ten chickens running around on the ground. I fired at the chickens with my CAR-15, hoping that a VC would come out to police up the dead birds. Then I called for an air strike. Almost immediately a forward air controller (FAC) appeared in an L-19 Birddog (a fixed-wing single-engine aircraft) and asked me where I wanted the strike. I circled the LOH, went down low, and dropped a smoke grenade right on top of the bunker complex. I heard the FAC talking to the fighter aircraft. I moved out of the way, and the FAC dived in and placed two white phosphorus marking rockets on top of my smoke. The first jet aircraft, I believe it was an F-100, came in and dropped a napalm can smack on the spot. Fried chicken! The second aircraft came in with either a 250- or a 500-pound bomb. The only problem was, he let it go too late. I watched this bomb floating through the air, way past the target area. It landed in the area where the 1-18 Infantry (Dogface) was conducting a search, at least one thousand meters from the cloud of black smoke that was rising where the napalm had landed. I heard the huge explosion as the bomb detonated, and our little LOH trembled in the sky from the shock wave.

My God, I thought. What if Dogface guys are there? And even

if they aren't, if Cavazos finds out I had anything to do with this fiasco, he'll cut my throat. I called to the FAC and screamed, "What the hell are you guys doing?"

He said, "No sweat. Don't worry about it. It just hung up on him a little."

I told the FAC, "No more passes," and headed out of there.

Fortunately, no Dogface guys were hit. But as far as I was concerned, so much for air force "surgical" strikes. They might hit the target, and they might not.

As long as I'm on the subject of air strikes, I must comment on my experience with them. I never heard of one air strike that helped while we were on offensive operations. When we were on the defensive and were in a static position, air strikes could be of great assistance. On the other hand, when we were moving, all air strikes did was slow us down and delay the action. They were of little help. Actually, they were a hindrance, and many times we had to shift effective artillery fires in order to put in the air strikes. Since fighter-bombers had a very limited loiter time over a target, we often had to interrupt what we were doing in order to employ their less-than-accurate support. The results may have been different in the Mekong Delta region, which was open and had easily definable ground features such as dike banks, rivers, and the like. Air strikes may also have been effective in the Vietnamese highlands, where there were discernable terrain features and reference points. But in heavily canopied jungle with no reference points except smoke, which drifted and mingled with fog and low clouds, air force tactical air support left a great deal to be desired.

Nevertheless, when the fighter-bombers arrived, we were obliged to try to put them in as quickly and as effectively as possible. Because tactical air strikes actually hindered most ground operations, they almost never happened when an infantry unit was on the offensive. There has got to be a better way!

"Watch therefore, for you know neither the day nor the hour...."

Matthew 25:13

Chapter 11
Uniontown

The firebase security mission lasted about five days, and then we returned to Lai Khe. It had been a good training operation, but there had been little or no enemy contact. Following the operation, we had a great party at Lai Khe. We ordered steaks and lobsters for everyone, and we were able to get them. We had dinner in the battalion headquarters, which was a French, red-tile-roofed, stuccoed building used on the rubber plantation. I'll never forget the large circular table, which had a rotating inner circle, like a lazy Susan. I think it was the only meal we ever ate at that table, which was loaded down with steaks, lobsters, and assorted delicacies. It was like a medieval feast.

We had invited 1st Brigade Commander, Colonel Bill Caldwell, and his S3, Don Holleder, to party with us. We had a great time. I know Don consumed at least five steaks. It was a night of camaraderie and debauchery, at least in the eating and drinking areas. There were no women present, which was probably for the best. Being in the army seemed to be fun again with Terry Allen as battalion commander. He liked to have a good time and didn't mind a few jokes being played on him. On several occasions during that party, I watched him enjoying the foolishness that goes on at a stag affair of this type. He really enjoyed it.

We spent perhaps two days in Lai Khe before we received orders for a road-clearing operation to the south. Road-clearing operations were absolutely no fun. I was not a road-clearing expert, but I became one. It was slow, tedious work, and the security requirements made it tough. Patrols had to sweep out on the flanks of the road ahead of the road-clearing teams. The road-clearing teams depended on mine detectors, which always seemed a bit temperamental. At any rate, coordinating the security teams with the sweep teams and the demolition teams was maddeningly difficult. It was also hard on the men. The minute someone relaxed, we could be in trouble. Many times the security teams ran into booby traps, and sweeping for and detecting mines was nerve-wracking work. I don't really remember which road we cleared. I only know I was glad when we came off of that mission.

Our battalion was beginning to jell. Captain Jim George had commanded Alpha Company for most of July and August. First Lieutenant Mel Adams still had Bravo Company, and Captain Al Ziegler was in charge of Charlie Company. Delta Company, under the command of First Lieutenant Al (Clark) Welch, was a newly reorganized fourth rifle company that was completing its advanced combat training at Lai Khe.

In late August we received notification that we would be detached from the Big Red One for approximately a month to conduct a II Field Force security mission in the Bien Hoa/Long Binh area north of Saigon. For this assignment, we would be attached to the 1st Brigade, 9th Infantry Division, which was the nearest tactical brigade headquarters to the area of operations. The mission, called "Uniontown," was rotated between the 9th, 25th, and 1st Infantry Divisions, and the 199th Light Infantry Brigade. It involved conducting extensive saturation patrolling mainly to the north and east of the Bien Hoa/Long Binh area. Our primary job was to keep large Main Force units from assembling in these unpopulated areas and to deter enemy rocket attacks against the Bien Hoa/Long Binh logistical sites. Uniontown was a huge mission covering thirty to forty square miles, and I believe it was expected to provide a deterrent to enemy operations in those critical areas. Naturally, we believed that we had been handpicked for this operation, to represent the Big Red One in protecting the guys at higher headquarters and the logistics people at Long Binh from trouble.

Being sent off on our own hook, especially after the amount of command supervision a battalion normally received from the headquarters of the Big Red One, was like being sent to heaven. Thus when the battalion rolled into the northern portion of the Long Binh complex to relieve the 1st Battalion, 27th Infantry (Wolfhounds) of the 25th Infantry Division for the Uniontown mission, we felt we were, as they say, "shit hot." At the time Lieutenant Colonel Ed Peter, a real pro who was more than ready to give up the mission and return to the 25th, his parent division, commanded the Wolfhounds. He later went on to be a three-star general. When we relieved his battalion, some of us could already see that Ed Peter would probably be a general some day, if he lived long enough—and he did.

Although I acknowledge here that the 1-27 Infantry was obviously an excellent unit, at the time we rolled in to take over the mission, with that Big Red One patch on our left shoulder, people in the Long Binh area stood up and took notice. You could almost hear them saying, "Hey guys, don't worry any more. The Black Lions of the Big Red One are in town to maintain law and order. Your asses are in good hands." The 1st Brigade of the 9th Division had to put up with some of our bravado. We figured that if we had enough time at Long Binh, we might be able to get them up to the standards of the Big Red One. We really thought we were hot stuff. No one did tighter airmobile operations than we did, and nobody knew how to dig like we did, and nobody was used to more ass chewing and excessive supervision than we were.

Looking back now, I can only say we were a cocky bunch. During the period of August 29 through September 19, we did a good job on the Uniontown mission, which included the period when the South Vietnamese government had their first real elections. No doubt we were somewhat overbearing to the gracious commander of the 1st Brigade, 9th Infantry Division, Colonel Don Seibert. He treated us well and put up with our puffery, and wrote us a nice letter of commendation when we left.

While we were on the Uniontown mission, division headquarters pressed our XO, Major Bob Gillard, into service as a task force commander. Bob took our Bravo and Delta companies to a Special Forces camp way to the north at a town called Dong Xoai. We had an artillery battery there supporting Special Forces operations. A not-too-trustworthy group of CIDG (Civilian Irregular Defense Group) troops were responsible for security at the camp. The artillery battery commander was afraid that the CIDG unit might turn on them and take the artillery tubes. So Bob Gillard took the two-company task force to Dong Xoai to put a perimeter inside the Dong Xoai perimeter. What a crazy war! Because Dong Xoai was in "Big Cong Country" and way off the beaten path, the concerns of the artillerymen were probably justified.

At any rate, we had little or no contact with Task Force Gillard until late September when we all came back together in Lai Khe after the Uniontown mission. We had done a good job on the separate missions, and we had not let the Big Red One down. The morale and esprit of the battalion then was as high as when we started that last week in September 1967. Little did we know that the battalion—our battalion, my battalion, Terry Allen's Black Lions—had about a month to live.

"Whereas you do not know
what will happen tomorrow.
For what is your life?
It is even a vapor
that appears for a little time
and then vanishes away."

James 4:14

Chapter 12
My Last Operation

While we were patting ourselves on the back over conducting a successful Uniontown mission, Division HQ was receiving more and more intelligence that VC Main Force units were on the move in the areas north of Lai Khe and west of Highway 13. Since the division's and II Field Force's plans called for opening up the former enemy sanctuaries that lay between South Vietnam's populated areas and the Cambodian border, the axis of the 1st Division's thrust was north along Highway 13 and its contiguous areas. Highway 13 started in the Saigon area and ran due north to the Cambodian border. The Big Red One decided that it would own that road, providing security for its few towns and villages and fanning out into the adjacent jungle to deny these areas to the VC as staging bases and logistical areas. Historically, we knew the VC used War Zones C and D as their major staging areas within Vietnam. Now signals intelligence was confirming what we already knew. The enemy was using these areas. After receiving some apparently very hot signals intelligence indicating that a battalion and large-sized VC headquarters were operating within fifteen miles of Lai Khe, division decided to put the 2-28 Infantry Black Lions into the center of the area where the enemy activity was the heaviest and see what would happen.

Our aim was to bait the enemy into attacking us. We would go into this jungle area, dig in, patrol during the day, and wait for the enemy to hit us at night. Ideally, after we had repulsed his first attack, the enemy would concentrate his forces and try again. We would counter by bringing in more battalions, and a big fight would ensue. A big fight was exactly what we were seeking, and what the VC had been avoiding. There was no question in our minds that we would be victorious in any large-scale battle with the VC.

It was the last week of September and, although I didn't realize it at the time, this was to be my final operation with the 2-28 Infantry Black Lions (Dauntless). It never entered my mind that I would soon be leaving. I was S3 of a first-class battalion, one of the best in the division. We had a reputation for doing the job well (at least we thought we did), and the division command was showing its confidence in us by sending us on these independent missions. This one was particularly exciting: the receipt of hot intelligence, followed by an air assault into previously untouched jungle, where we would dig in and try to get into a fight.

For this mission, we even had time to do a helicopter reconnaissance, a luxury we normally didn't get. After making our assault plans, we took our three company commanders (A, C, and D Companies) over the landing zone at a relatively high altitude to survey the LZ. (Because B Company had previously been detached and sent to a firebase security mission along Highway 13, it did not participate in this assignment.) Our reconnaissance flight showed that the area where we were headed was basically canopied jungle, and the LZ would be in a streambed about two hundred meters wide that was covered with elephant grass. We would land five slicks at a time into the elephant grass, charge into the surrounding jungle and establish security, and then build an NDP using the LZ as the center of the NDP. During the reconnaissance flight, we couldn't fly too low over the area or loiter and attract attention. We made one or two high passes and described the terrain. With our plans and the chopper recon flight, this was probably the most thorough planning job we had ever done.

The butterflies were really fluttering the evening before that assault, and it seemed like the night would never end. In the early morning hours the battalion began to assemble along the dirt strips among the rubber trees at Lai Khe that served as helicopter pickup zones. Cold and damp in the morning, by noon these dirt strips were cauldrons of swirling dust, unbearably hot—just pitiful places for human beings to be. Waiting at those miserable helicopter pickup strips was the bane of the infantry trooper in Vietnam, at least in terms of activities that did not involve being shot at.

The problem with this air assault was not that we didn't execute operations on time, but rather that we were, as always, over-anxious to be in position for the pickup—which led, inevitably, to playing the old game of hurry-up-and-wait. The plan called for everyone to wake at midnight for an 0800 pickup. In the eight-hour interim between waking and boarding the helicopters, we spent one hour in meaningful activity and seven hours flopping and sopping in an assembly area getting tired, wet, hot, dusty, and generally pissed off. This is the way of life of military organizations: there is never enough time to plan, or so much time that you waste a good bit of it with make-work activities. Since I was the operations officer, the S3, I would hasten to add that I was normally the primary culprit behind this sort of planning. But in my own defense, if I hadn't done it, the companies would have done it on their own. A bureaucracy boring itself into the ground with foolish, meaningless, and worry-producing activity while waiting to get started typically feels it is "really" doing something.

That morning Terry Allen, our two radio telephone operators who were carrying portable PRC-25 radios—one tuned in on the battalion command net and the other on the brigade command net—our artillery liaison officer, our command sergeant major, and I piled into a command and control helicopter and went airborne to control the operation. A command and control helicopter was basically a UH-1 with a console of radios mounted in it. It thus became an airborne command post. The portable radios we carried were for redundancy, and to provide instant and continuous communications after we landed for dismounted operations. In a very short time we were in the vicinity of the LZ, where the air force forward air controller (FAC) was already directing the first air strikes of the prep. A jet aircraft would come diving out of the sun to the east, belly down, and let loose a stream of CBU bomblets that would float down onto the LZ, where what looked like hundreds of explosions burst all through the trees. As the CBU runs ended, fighter-bombers then dropped four 250-pound bombs and made 20mm strafing passes. When these aircraft had finished their work, the artillerymen in a firebase along Highway 13, with a 105mm battery and a 155mm battery, went into action. There the section chief, on command, dropped his arm; the artillery-men yanked their lanyards, and instantly twelve artillery rounds tracked perhaps a five-second flight onto the same location, saturating it with steel. As the artillery prep continued, we could see the flights of helicopter lift ships approaching from the east, like a row of praying mantises about to pounce. When the artillery prep abruptly stopped, two waiting helicopter gunships immediately spewed 2.75-inch rockets, 40mm cannon fire, and 7.62mm machine gun fire on the flanks of the LZ as the first flight of five went in.

Almost immediately, I spotted trouble. As the lift ships hovered over the elephant grass, the downwash of the blades showed that underneath the grass was water, shining in the sun now that the grass was being beaten down. We knew it was a streambed, but we didn't know that the grass was growing in water. As men jumped from their choppers, they landed in water that was waist deep, and our imagined bolt of security forces for the protection of the jungle turned into forty troopers breast stroking for higher ground, loaded down with equipment and moving like ruptured frogs.

Fortunately, the LZ was not hot, and the landing was unopposed. Both Terry and I were anxious to get on the ground. We decided that one of us should stay airborne until most of the troops in lift ships had landed. So we dropped the C&C helo into the LZ, and I jumped out with my RTO, Specialist Fourth Class Pasquale Tizzio, to set up a temporary CP on the ground. Like everyone else, we were up to our waists in water. We moved toward the jungle, and the water became shallower as we got to the jungle's edge.

I got inside the jungle canopy and stopped to take a rest. Almost instantly something fell out of the trees and landed on my back. It was a large clump of black dirt filled with red ants. My neck, face, and my upper body were soon covered with red ants. They were stinging the hell out of me. I turned around, unsnapped my pistol belt and shoulder suspenders with all the junk hanging on them, jettisoned the impedimenta and my helmet, and started running back into the grass towards the center of the LZ. When I was waist deep in water, I dived into the grass and remained submerged, squirming and beating at my upper body and head. After about a minute in the water, the ants departed. My head and neck, and for that matter, my whole upper body burned like fire, but it wasn't unbearable. I made my way back to my pistol belt, suspenders, helmet, and weapon. So much for the John Wayne image I tried to cut; I looked more like a drenched rat. Everywhere around me, men were hooting and scratching.

I quickly realized that the prep had thrown portions of huge anthills up into the jungle canopy and, as men entered the jungle, they were bombarded by falling dirt debris and red ants. Having survived the attack of the ants, I started to make my way deeper into the jungle to get a feel for how thick the undergrowth was. It was quite thick near the edge of the meadow, but it thinned out a bit further in. I had only gone about twenty feet into the jungle when I saw something that looked like a vine moving back and forth in front of me. It was yellow and it was long, and it was moving from side to side in a wave-like motion, back and forth.

"Hell, man, that's a bamboo viper." I believe it was trying to hypnotize me and I seem to recall moving back and forth, too. This snake had just been through one of the Big Red One's finest preps, and I got the distinct impression that that skinny, yellow viper was pissed. Keeping my head and eyes completely still, I began slowly retracing my steps backward toward the meadow, but this time walking backwards. Finally, the snake threw itself back away from me. Right then I knew one thing, the battalion CP was not going to be near this location.

We began laying in our positions immediately. Each company, A, C, and D, picked up its share of the pie. Although most of the open area in the center of the NDP was waist deep in water, we managed to build up a resupply pad to receive supplies by CH-47, and we also built a pad for each company's three 81mm mortars, giving us a total of nine 81mm mortars in the NDP. Most of the frontal bunkers of the NDP were located in jungle, but in places where a company's area stretched across the elephant grass meadow and the stream, we had to build our bunkers up instead of down. We didn't want to do this since these sandbagged huts (that's what they looked like) made beautiful targets; however, we had no choice since we couldn't dig in water up to our waists. When all our bunkers were built, we had only about four of these hut-type bunkers, and we didn't think the VC would actually try to attack through the water.

We were really working hard. Security patrols sent out by each company had found fresh signs of enemy movements in the area. That lent a sense of greater urgency to our work. This was the deepest and thickest jungle I had been in. The deadfall (fallen trees) was thick, and we had to use chain saws and C-4 (plastic explosives) to cut fields of fire. Laying these positions in was very difficult because the jungle was so thick. Consequently the resulting fields of fire were actually tunnels of fire. This meant we couldn't see from position to position; yet we knew it was critical that the rear positions be sited to cover the frontal positions. Laying a Big Red One NDP out in the jungle required care and precision. Thus we didn't want anyone digging until we were sure that each position had been laid in properly. So while I was literally checking every position to ensure that it was tied in with the others, and particularly the boundaries between the companies, the troops cleared fields of fire. At the same time several patrols cloverleafed out from the perimeter to give us security.

The NDP was a beehive of activity. The VC surely knew that we were there. CH-47s were flying in with sling loads of sandbags, mortar ammo, and water. Chain saws were droning and screeching. Interspersed with all this noise and activity were shouts of "fire in the hole" and the subsequent blasts that came from exploding quarter-pound blocks of TNT as they blew down individual trees. On top of all that, axes chopped and shovels clanged. In short, we made a cacophony that must have resembled the building of the Panama Canal. We, however, had only a half day to get ready, to get everything all up tight and to be locked in and ready for Charlie. That's what we had come here for, and everyone knew it.

There was little or no need for motivational lectures or ass kicking. Everyone knew that we had to make the best use that we could of the time available. At the battalion CP, we didn't bother to put up hex tents as we normally did. We dug a bunker down, cut logs for the roof, and put two layers of sandbags on top. We must have had ten people in that bunker. These included the battalion commander, his two radio operators, me as S3, my two RTOs, the artillery liaison officer with his RTO, the sergeant major, and the battalion operations sergeant. None of us could stand up in this bunker; we could only kneel, sit, or lie prone. What a miserable hole. And it rained about six times that day.

We were able to register our 81mm mortars by firing down the streambed and elephant grass. At maximum elevation we could observe the rounds strike, but we could not observe them in any other direction. Consequently we knew our mortars would be of little use in the event of an attack because it was only about two hundred meters from the center of the NDP to the frontal bunkers. We would have to shoot practically straight up into the air to get rounds close to our perimeter.

The artillery DEFCONS were, however, another matter. We were only about six kilometers from our firebase on Highway 13, and at dusk we began firing them in. First we passed the warnings for everyone to get into their holes. While we were waiting, I noticed a Vietnamese Chieu Hoi (a VC who had surrendered) sitting near our CP. He had been a first lieutenant in the infamous Phu Loi battalion, a nemesis of the Big Red One since its arrival in Vietnam. He had been brought in by our new S2, Captain Jim Blackwell, to help us identify VC signs. Every unit from time to time used former VC to help interpret enemy signs in the jungle.

This guy was a mean-looking bugger. He had only one eye, lots of scars, and feet like elephant hide. He was squatting down, smoking a cigarette. I decided to ask him a few questions, using an interpreter.

"Did you fight against the Big Red One?" I began.

"Yes, several times." He replied.

"Were we any good?"

"Too slow; take too much time."

"Where will VC attack us? What place at this NDP?"

"Right here," he pointed. It was within fifty to seventy-five meters of our command bunker.

I said, "Why here?"

He said, "Here is battalion command post. Only seventy-five meters from jungle. Tonight, no attack. Maybe tomorrow. VC do reconnaissance. Find battalion command post. Use shortest route to overrun command post."

"Okay, baby, thanks a lot." I replied and turning around, shouted, "Whoa. Hey, arty LNO, See that area—right over there?" I pointed to where the former VC had pointed. "Lay me a DEFCON in, right there."

"Sir, you can't do that. It's only seventy-five meters. We can't shoot DEFCONS in less than three hundred meters."

"Okay buddy, you start shootin', and I'll tell you when to stop. That VC just told me that's where they're coming, and since I will be right over there, I want arty right over there."

We argued about it half the night. The DEFCONS that we fired in that night, one on each third of our perimeter, were the closest ones we'd ever had. It was scary to be calling your own artillery in that close. One minor error on the part of the artillery crew, or for that matter, the people who had made the ammo, and we could be on the receiving end of our own stuff. It scared the hell out of me, but when he told me he could not fire any closer, I still wanted it closer. I had visions of a hundred or so VC charging down that line of jungle toward our CP with only three or four of our bunkers able to shoot at them and our artillery shells landing behind them, which would only make the attackers run faster in our direction. The artillery said, however, "no more." Nevertheless I was glad I had talked to the VC Chieu Hoi. (Note: during the Tet Offensive some four months later in early 1968, that same Chieu Hoi was killed leading a group of NVA regulars toward Saigon south of Lai Khe. I guess he had joined us for a while to get a few good smokes.)

In spite of all the hard work that day, and plenty of visitors from brigade and division, there wasn't a great deal of sleeping that night. A new NDP was always like that. When night came, everything changed—everything looked different—especially on the first night. We had ringed ourselves in with listening posts, with four claymores controlled by each LP. The companies would notify us every twenty minutes or so that they were going to pop a claymore. We did this all through the night to discourage the VC from crawling in too close. We also fired the thump guns into open areas but not into the jungle. In the jungle the 40mm round might hit a tree or vine and bounce back in our lap. I believe we got a few sniper rounds the first night, enough to keep us awake, but no major activity.

The next day we sent a two-company search and destroy team out to the west of the perimeter. Terry Allen went out with them. They saw a lot of fresh signs but had no contact. Delta Company, which had stayed in to guard the NDP, did, however, get some action. Delta had security patrols out. Suddenly, one of Delta's security patrols walked right into a five- or six-man patrol of VC, who apparently had just arrived in the area, since they too were surprised. Both patrols started firing simultaneously. The Delta Company patrol leader, a sergeant, was surprised a second time when the first VC burst of fire struck his M-16 rifle, shattering the forearm grip as well as the vinyl stock. He found himself holding a barrel and a trigger-housing group. Undeterred by what had happened to his rifle, he still managed to kill two VC with what he had left. Two of our men were wounded in that engagement.

A sidebar to this action illustrates some of the over-control that always seemed to exist in the Big Red One at the time. Just as this action was taking place, the brigade commander (Duty 6) was flying over our position at a low level. He heard the shooting, and immediately called on the brigade net: "Dauntless, Dauntless, what's going on down there? Sitrep. Sitrep."

I had heard the same firing that he had heard, but at that instant I had no idea what was going on. I was waiting for a report from the company commander, First Lieutenant Clark Welch, who was on the ground with me but perhaps three hundred meters on the other side of the perimeter, and maybe another three hundred to four hundred meters from the security patrol.

I radioed back, "Duty 6, Dauntless 3. Roger. Getting Sitrep. Wait, out." Then I called on the battalion net. "Delta 6, Dauntless 3. Sitrep."

The next call was, however, again from brigade. "Dauntless 3, this is Duty 6. I want a sitrep, and I want it right now, over."

"This is Dauntless 3. Roger, wait, out."

Then I said, "Delta 6, this is Dauntless 3. I need a sitrep ASAP."

"This is Delta 6, goddammit. Wait, out."

I knew Clark Welch was pissed. He couldn't have cared less about giving me a sitrep. While we were talking on the radio, he was running through the jungle hoping he wouldn't find his security patrol in little pieces.

The brigade net again sounded. "Dauntless 3, this is Duty 6. What's going on? What is that shooting? I want an immediate sitrep, over."

"This is Dauntless 3," I responded. "If you'll wait a goddamned minute, I'll give you a goddamned sitrep as soon as I get the god-damned info. Out."

Clark Welch then called me with the pertinent information, and I passed it on to Duty 6. Strange. He didn't even land. I figured he was going to land and chomp my butt for insubordination, but he just went away. Good riddance!

I was not aware of it at the time, but this operation we were on was either the prelude to or the beginning of what the Big Red One was to call Operation Shenandoah II. Because we were south of the Binh Long/Binh Duong Province boundary, we were under the operational control of the 3rd Brigade (Duty). The 3rd Brigade, nicknamed the Iron Brigade, was the brigade our battalion was normally associated with. Its headquarters was in Lai Khe, and the three battalions in Lai Khe were the 2-28 Infantry Black Lions (Dauntless); the 1-16 Infantry Rangers (Devour), commanded by Lieutenant Colonel Cal Benedict and S3 Major Jim Sullivan; and the 2-2 Infantry (Mechanized) (Daring), commanded by Lieutenant Colonel Hank Davisson. At the time the 3rd Brigade commander was Colonel Frank Blazey and the S3 was Major Ed Trobaugh.

As mentioned, we had been put in this location as bait, and everybody was hoping we would be attacked. I had mixed emotions about that, but I didn't express them. Outwardly, everyone was saying, "Okay, you bastards, come and get it. We're ready. We're waiting." But inside, there was the gnawing doubt about whether we would cut the mustard when they did come. I think even General Hay felt that way deep down inside. I know he was mightily concerned about us. It took some inexperienced radio operators to make me find out how much he cared.

Just prior to this operation, at the end of our Uniontown mission, I had gotten a new RTO from A Company. RTOs were very special guys. Their job was difficult to describe—and absolutely critical. They had to do more than carry a radio. On many occasions they were called upon to give sitreps to higher headquarters. They had to be able to understand the situation and explain it concisely and clearly on a moment's notice. An RTO who could perform these tasks was worth his weight in gold. I had handpicked my RTO; his name was Ray Gribble, and he was a specialist fourth class from Muncie, Indiana. He had served in the same A Company squad for six months and was now the squad leader. Normally a squad leader had an enlisted rating of E-6, so Gribble was serving in a job that was two ranks higher than the rating he currently had. It was easy to see he was a good man. His squad was always squared away, with their weapons cleaned, and the men clean-shaven, with good morale. Although Gribble was a draftee, he was more mature than his peers. He was married, and he carried a Bible in his pack. He was obviously a brave man, a natural leader, a man of character. Captain Jim George did not want to let him go, but after some cajoling, he agreed that Gribble would do a good job for the battalion. When Gribble reported for duty as my RTO, he was reluctant to take the job, but within a few minutes, it was obvious that he was fully capable. He was mature beyond his years, and he had a grasp of the tactical situation from the battalion standpoint. He also knew the lingo, and very quickly became a superb RTO: knowledgeable, dependable, and savvy. I was really pleased to have picked this man. He made my job a helluvalot easier.

Then after about ten days on the job, Gribble came to me and said: "Sir, I'd like to go back to my squad."

I said, "Hey, Gribble, I need you here. The battalion needs you here. You were in a squad for a long time, and frankly, we need you more here in operations. Also, your chances of surviving this mess are a lot better as S3 RTO than down in a squad. You're not going anywhere!"

Tears welled up in his eyes. He was a handsome guy, taller than me at about six feet, two inches. He said to me: "Sir, I have to go back. My men need me. I visited them last night, and they are in bad shape. That's my squad. They need me. I've got to go back."

He was pleading with me to go back to the most difficult and dangerous job in the army: squad leader. He was a draftee. He hadn't been in the army more than perhaps a year, and he was teaching me what it was really all about. I don't think I have ever admired a man more in my life. I stuck my hand out, and he grabbed it.

"Okay, you can go back," I said.

"Thanks, sir."

We squeezed off a handshake, and he headed back to A Company. So this is why I am now out in the jungle on a "live bait" operation with an inexperienced RTO instead of Ray Gribble. We had settled in for the night, and we all expected an attack. We had gotten more familiar with our surroundings, and our confidence was up. Everyone was tired, however, and we were packed in that bunker like sardines. The RTOs took turns monitoring the radios at night. We had four RTOs plus the operations sergeant, and they monitored the radios on two-hour shifts. Sometime around midnight, A Company reported that a listening post thought they were in trouble. They reported that the enemy had turned their claymores around, and when they blew one, the LP was hit by fragments. This was a common report. LPs always saw and heard things that turned out to be false alarms. We had heard many reports that the VC tried to turn claymores around, but it was easier said than done.

The real problem was that we were all asleep, except for the new and inexperienced RTO. Because he didn't know better, he simply passed the information on to brigade in a matter-of-fact way, without telling anyone, and also wrote it in the battalion log. All us sleepers kept on sleeping.

His report, however, quickly produced consternation at brigade and then at division. The division headquarters, in contrast to our battalion, had three captains who monitored the division net for eight hours a crack, twenty-four hours a day. They were sharp, and normally they were always rested and alert when they came on shift. Thus while we are out in the jungle NDP, sleeping fat, dumb, and happy, a report came to division: "Dauntless reports unknown size VC force probing their position. Reports claymores have been turned around. A fired claymore has caused two casualties." General Hay, the division commander, was notified. Dauntless was in trouble. He paced the floor all night, worrying about this battalion that he put out for bait that was now being stalked by an unknown VC force, which was turning our claymores around. He probably wanted to call us on the radio and reassure us. But he didn't. He just stewed and worried, and hoped we are going to be okay.

Before first light, Hay called his assistant division commander, Brigadier General Bill Coleman, on the phone: "Bill, get out to Dauntless NDP and find out what is going on. I'm worried that the VC are going after them."

"Roger, sir, right away," was Coleman's response.

Thirty minutes later, as we are just waking up, cold and miserable, we received an urgent call on the radio: "Dauntless, Dauntless, this is Danger 79er, will arrive your location in 05." We looked at each other. "79er. Why in the hell is he coming in here at first light? Holy Cripes! Let's get squared away."

Nobody read the log. We couldn't possibly know why Ole 79er

was coming in this early in the morning. Terry was into his early morning shaving fetish, so I went to the clearing to meet 79er. We all liked 79er, Brigadier General Bill Coleman. He was easy to talk to, and he always had a smile and a word of encouragement.

Not this morning. I don't think he'd even had a cup of coffee. As I recall he jumped from his chopper and said: "3, what the hell is going on out here? Where are these guys who had the claymore turned around on them?"

"Jeez, sir, I don't know what you're talking about. We didn't have any claymore problems!"

"Goddammit, 3, the CG has been pacing the floor all night worrying about you guys. We had a report that you had some wounded men from a claymore that had been turned around."

"Jeez, sir. Are you sure it was us? I don't know anything about it. Can we go to the TOC bunker?"

We went to the TOC bunker. I looked at the log. Nobody said anything. There it was, in the log. Ole 79er was now really hacked off. Here the battalion was about to be attacked and neither the battalion commander nor the S3 knew anything about it.

"Where's that LP?" he hollered.

I said, "Over in A Company, sir. This way."

We headed out toward the A Company portion of the perimeter, where we were met by Captain Jim George, who was still scratching his butt, sleep still in his eyes.

79er said, "All right, captain, where're those wounded men and the turned-around claymores?"

George pointed, and we continued at a brisk pace through the mud and jungle, past the bunkers, out to the LP location. A sergeant was there.

"Sergeant, where was the claymore turned around?" 79er asked.

"Well, sir, what really happened was that the LP had put their claymore in front of an anthill. When they blew the claymore, the back-blast blew part of the anthill back into the LP. They thought someone had turned their claymore around. In the dark they thought they had been hit by fragments. Actually, there weren't any VC here last night."

Ole 79er was angry. "Let me see where it happened."

We walked out to the former LP site (it had been abandoned at first light). I looked down at the ground just in time to see 79er step in a huge pile of excrement that one of the men from the LP had deposited on the ground without using a cathole. 79er felt his foot sticking in something more than mud, and he looked down at his feet. By now the shit was oozing out of the waffle sole and up over the toe of his shiny jungle boot. 79er stopped. He said, "Goddamn."

I just looked at him. Thirty minutes ago I had been sleeping like a baby, and now I was standing at an LP site with an irate brigadier general who had human feces all over his boot. I don't remember 79er saying anything else. He just turned and started back toward his chopper. He stopped once or twice to try to wipe his boot in the elephant grass. He also stopped at the door of the chopper to ensure that he wasn't carrying any big chunks on board. I saluted. I don't remember whether he returned the salute or not. He got in and flew away.

After General Coleman left us that day, it was all downhill. We had been in this spot for about four days, and it didn't look like the VC were going after the bait. They knew we were there, but for one reason or another, they didn't come. At about noon that day General Hay and Colonel Pendleton, the division G3, came into our position for a visit. They told Terry Allen we would be extracting out of this position the next day, which meant there would be lots of prep-work. They also told him something else. I was to get on the general's chopper and return to Lai Khe, where I was to begin work as the division operations officer, G3, under Colonel Pendleton at division headquarters. A FNG—Major Jack Sloan—was to replace me as the S3, and he had arrived in the general's chopper. I was dumbfounded. I believe Terry was too. We were standing alone on the edge of the jungle in the NDP.

I couldn't believe it. I thought I was doing a good job. I had only been in the battalion since early July, about ninety days. I started to cry.

I said to Terry, "Sir, this isn't right. I belong here. This is my battalion."

He said, "Jim, he didn't ask me, he told me. No questions."

For a moment I thought I was going to go into shock. We stood in silence for what seemed like an eternity. Then I said, "Let me stay the night. You stayed with me for three days. At least let me stay one night with the new guy."

He said, "Let me see what I can do," and he moved toward the CG's chopper. I just stood there. A million things were going through my mind:

"Hey, man, you're lucky to be getting out of here. The law of averages always runs out."

"With only three months in the battalion as S3, people will think I was fired."

"Is this a promotion or a letdown?"

"You've got six kids at home, and the general is worried about the family."

"Who is this smart-ass who's trying to take my place?"

Terry came back with Jack Sloan. We shook hands. I hated him, thinking he didn't look ready to take my place. The general left in the chopper, and we started making plans for the extraction. It was a hairy place for an extraction, and we had to get a lot of stuff out of there. I didn't sleep much that night, and I don't remember if anything happened or not. I know I spent lots of time talking with Jack Sloan, trying to tell him everything I knew about being an S3 in the Big Red One in Vietnam.

Fortunately, most everything I knew I had learned from Terry Allen, and Terry was going to be around. The next day's extraction started off very smoothly. The PZ did present a problem if the aircraft landed from west to east (flying on an azimuth of 90°). The stream flowed out of the jungle from east to west. In the east the jungle formed closely along its banks. As the stream flowed west it began to delta out into a wider area. We had to land into the wind, and if it was blowing from the east we would be flying up into a narrowing cone formed by the jungle. We hoped that the winds would be blowing from the west, so that we could put the ships down in the LZ facing the wider portion of the streambed, and heading into the wind. That's the way we started.

Prior to the extraction, we had discovered a 250-pound bomb that had failed to go off during the prep some four days before. We hatched a diabolical scheme. We were quite sure the VC would move in quickly, either as we extracted, or right after we got out. We decided to put a demolition charge on the bomb, and have the recon platoon start a time fuse to go off about ten minutes after they were picked up. A nice little surprise for the scrounging VC, who always came in quickly to try to salvage anything we had left.

The extraction was going quite smoothly until the last full lift of a rifle company was all that was left. From somewhere deep in the jungle a lone VC—I always suspected that he was drunk—fired one burst from an automatic weapon at a helicopter gunship. The light fire team, two helicopter gunships that were flying shotgun for the lift ships, hosed the VC's location. Suddenly the brigade commander came up on the net and said, "I want an air strike on that VC position."

That was bad news. We didn't think we needed the air strike. It had been a long morning, and all we wanted to do was get our recon platoon out of there. We received a report that they had blown their outer ring of claymores, had armed the bomb, and were ready to go to their final position on the PZ. We could see the last five lift ships on final approach. The brigade commander told the lift ships to circle while the FAC put the air strike in. We asked the brigade commander to reconsider, but he was adamant. There had to be an air strike. Fortunately, jet aircraft were capping our extraction, and it only took about ten minutes to finish the air strike. But we were panicked. Finally, the last five lift ships touched down. Then the recon platoon leader reported, "We need another lift ship. We discovered two men on the ground who didn't make it out with the last company, and we've got too many guys."

Good God. We couldn't believe this. What had started out as a nice, smooth extraction was turning into a fire drill. We told the recon platoon leader to stay on the ground with the excess men, and we'd get another lift ship in. The rest of the platoon went out, and we told the air mission commander we needed one more slick. He had monitored the earlier transmission, and he told us one was on the way. Unfortunately, the aircraft was already loaded with about five people, and for some unknown reason the pilot landed from west to east. The last brave men loaded, giving him eight. Humidity was high that day, which meant his lift factor was low. Nevertheless he started up the narrow streambed, which kept getting narrower and narrower. It didn't look like he had enough air speed to lift the chopper sufficiently to clear the jungle. He was going to crash.

As our C&C chopper turned to try to give us better vision of the scene below, we lost sight of the struggling chopper between the jungle trees that lined the sides of the streambed. "My God, he's down," I thought. Then we saw his rotor blades coming seemingly right out of the jungle. With a last effort, he had made it out of that box canyon of jungle. We cheered!

Terry looked at me and said over the intercom of our C&C, "Thank God that's over."

I said back, "It's not over yet. We're still airborne and we're ten minutes from Lai Khe." Then we both laughed. Suddenly the 250-pound bomb went off, and we laughed again. "Hope fifty VC were standing around scratching their butts. Let's go home!" We made it safely back to Lai Khe. It was my last combat operation with the Black Lions.

"The omission loomed larger in hindsight than it did at the time."

Donald R. Morris commenting on the failure of the British Army to laager its wagons before the Battle of Isandhlwana, The Washing of the Spears

Chapter 13
Watching from Division

T RAGEDY SCENE: The Twilight Zone. It's a weekend, and it's Saturday morning. Your family, your wife and children and your parents, are driving to another city to spend the weekend with friends. The weather is not too good, and it's a hard drive, but the family has made the trip a number of times before. You've found yourself in this position before. You have to work this weekend, but you hope to be able to join the family before the weekend is over. You leave for work early in the morning. While at work, you receive a phone call: *There's been an accident. All in the car are either dead or seriously injured. Come to the morgue to identify the victims.*

*

I reported to division headquarters for duty the next day. The 2nd Battalion, 28th Infantry Black Lions base camp, our battalion headquarters, was located within five hundred meters of division headquarters. Lai Khe was a research facility for a French rubber plantation. It was a small plantation town with white, stuccoed buildings and red tile roofs, a pretty place before the war. The plantation, which had a large airstrip, was nestled in among a five-hundred-acre stand of rubber trees, and Highway 13 ran through the middle. It was in a rural area, about roughly half way between Saigon to the south and the Cambodian border to the north. It was the base camp of the 3rd Brigade, 1st Infantry Division, with three infantry battalions, and it had housed a forward command post of the 1st Infantry

Division since early 1967. In July 1967 it became the division main command post for operations. The division rear continued to operate farther to the south out of Di An.

During that first week in October, I was really busy learning my new job. The Black Lions had been designated Division Ready Reaction Force (RRF), which meant they were getting some rest time in Lai Khe. One night that week I was invited down to the Black Lions officers' club for a farewell party. We had a great time. The guys had worked up a number of crazy gifts to give me for my send-off. Jim Blackwell, the S2, had fashioned a large condom out of a plastic bag. I had more kids (six) at home than anyone in the battalion, and I think they were sending me this none-to-subtle message about family planning. I also believe that he had procured a Vietnamese lady for my old hooch that night. He kept prodding me to go over to my old living quarters, which I had never lived in. I didn't go because I didn't want to make a fool of myself. Anyway, the evening ended with the presentation of an engraved "Black Lions" cigarette lighter and some nice words from Terry Allen. Tears rolled down my cheeks as I said my few words of farewell.

My main job at division G3 was to know what was going on, where everything was, and planning the next day's support for approved operations. G3 operations handled everything the division was currently doing. We monitored all the division radio and telephone nets and kept operations maps and charts posted with the current situation, including all unit locations and capabilities. We were responsible to organize and conduct the evening briefings for the commanding general, and all briefings for visitors, which occurred daily. We also coordinated all artillery preparations and activities, all tactical air operations, all helicopter operations, and other transportation and communications. We operated the Division Tactical Operations Center (DTOC)—the nerve center of the division. It was an exciting, demanding, and interesting job.

Operation Shenandoah II had just begun, with the 1st Brigade operating north of the Binh Duong/Binh Long province boundary and generally west of Highway 13. The 3rd Brigade operated south from the province boundary to Lai Khe. The 2nd Brigade operated in the populated area south of Lai Khe. Just after the extraction of the Black Lions on the last week in September, the 1st Brigade intensified its operations north of the Binh Duong/Binh Long boundary.

The 1st Battalion, 2nd Infantry (call sign: Dracula) had gotten into a small fight just north of the area from which the Black Lions had extracted, and signals intelligence was indicating that major elements of the 9th VC Division were located in the Long Nugyen Secret Zone. Subsequently on October 5, the 1st Battalion, 18th Infantry (call sign: Dogface) conducted an air assault into the area south of the Secret Zone along the Binh Duong/Binh Long Province boundary. Over the next several days the Dogface battalion, commanded by Lieutenant Colonel Dick Cavazos, was to fight some major battles in an area only a few kilometers north of where the Black Lions had been extracted the week before. The Dogface battalion actions were later called the Battle of Dai Yeu, which is a story in itself.

The 1-18 Infantry was successful in both defensive and offensive operations. On October 6, they had just finished digging in when large-sized (platoon and company) enemy forces began probing their perimeter. The resulting battle, with elements of the VC 271st Regiment, lasted the entire night. Later reports from enemy prisoners indicated that as many as sixty VC were killed during those attacks, and another sixty wounded. U.S. artillery fire was later credited with driving off the determined enemy attackers. I vividly recall listening on the radio that night to Colonel Cavazos trying to get a dustoff in to save a wounded man. Helos then made several unsuccessful tries to reach the wounded man. The area was covered with fog, and it was raining. Visibility was terrible. Nevertheless, after several other attempts had failed, a dustoff from Cu Chi, some twenty miles to the south, tried again to get into the Dogface NDP. It crashed. The pilot, co-pilot, and attending medic were killed. It was a heroic and tragic effort. The soldier died in Dick Cavazos's arms.

The Dogface battalion stayed in the Dai Yeu area for approximately ten days, finally extracting from the area on October 13. The 1st Battalion, 28th Infantry Black Lions (call sign: Defiant), the sister battalion of the 2-28 Infantry (call sign: Dauntless), replaced the 1-18 Infantry there. Intelligence reports and the contacts that the 1-18 Infantry had made with enemy units told the division that it should position a force out to the west of Long Nugyen Secret Zone. Based on the information available, division planners had reason to believe an estimated two battalions of the 271st VC Regiment might be in the area and that some U.S. force should be positioned to block a possible VC escape to the west. By blocking this potential direction of withdrawal, the Long Nugyen Secret Zone could become a loose box with these major enemy forces in it. On October 8, the 2nd Battalion, 28th Infantry Black Lions, the Division Ready Reaction Force, air assaulted just west of the Long Nugyen Secret Zone. There was much excitement and apprehension about this assault because the men understood that they would be "closing the door" on the VC. If the division played its cards right, a major VC force, one that had bloodied the Big Red One in Operation Billings in June, would be boxed in.

The battles of Dogface at Dai Yeu had whetted the appetite of the press for a possible story. Consequently a mob of journalists accompanied the Black Lions in on this operation, hoping for a hot LZ. Among them was Italian journalist Oriana Fallaci, strikingly attired in a black jump suit. There were other famous journalists there, but the troops only remembered Oriana Fallaci.

The air assault that the Black Lions made that day may be compared with the British invasion of the Zululand. On that earlier occasion, journalists were also included in the invading force. Reading the description of the British invasion in the *Washing of the Spears* by Donald Morris is well worth the effort, and in a general sense, there are historical parallels between the Battle of Isandhlwana in Africa in 1879 (British vs. Zulus) and the Battle of Ông Thanh in Vietnam in 1967 (U.S. vs. Viet Cong). The U.S. air assault was, however, a big letdown for the journalists. They were looking for blood and action, and got neither. That night they left the battalion to return to Saigon, disappointed. Patience might have paid off, for nine days later they could have had plenty of both. But for journalists, nine days is a lifetime.

"They shouted loud
in some foreign tongue,
but no mercy was shown them.
We went over them like a wave,
and trampled them down
into the mud, for they were few,
and there was no end
to our numbers."

*Sir Arthur Conan Doyle in "Through the Veil" from Tales of Long Ago
describing Scottish Highlanders as they met a force of Roman legionnaries.*

Chapter 14
The Battle of Ông Thanh:
From My Perspective

In order to understand what happened in the Battle of Ông Thanh (October 17, 1967), I need to recount the trail of actions that led up to it, from October 8 through 16. Although these earlier actions had little direct influence on the outcome of the October 17 battle, they definitely had some general bearing on it.

At the time enemy forces occupied the center of the Long Nugyen Secret Zone, facing obstacles to their escape in nearly every direction. The 2-28 Infantry (Dauntless) was deployed two miles to their west, in an area that had already been heavily pummeled by B-52 strikes. The 1-2 Infantry (Dracula) was positioned three kilometers east of center, in the vicinity of Highway 13, a major north-south artery where U.S. military activity was heavy and constant. The 1-18 Infantry (Dogface) was deployed two-and-a-half kilometers to the south, where it had recently engaged and defeated elements of the VC 271st Regiment in what became known as the Battle of Da Yeu. Fought on October 6, this clash saw the VC initiating action with a violent attack, only to be beaten by a superbly led American force ably supported by well-executed artillery fires. No American forces were positioned to the north; however, enemy units attempting to escape in that direction would encounter the Cam Xe River, which flows west across the northern end of the Secret Zone before turning south, and which is flanked on either side by open ground some three to four hundred kilometers wide. In crossing that open ground the enemy units would find themselves perilously, perhaps fatally, exposed to attack by the U.S. aircraft and artillery.

The VC were boxed in, but the American cordon was by no means airtight. Why the 271st Regiment did not attempt to exfiltrate from the Secret Zone is a mystery.

Normally the VC would have moved out rapidly at night, most likely to the west and north, where there were no U.S. troops and the distance to the Cambodian border and relative safety from U.S. attack was only thirty kilometers. But for some reason they were in no hurry to leave the Long Nugyen Secret Zone. Looking back, it appears they remained in the Secret Zone more out of choice than because they felt trapped. Indecision may also have played a role. There's also the possibility the 271st had been told to stay put. The regiment's commanders would certainly do as they were told by their higher headquarters (the 9th VC Division). Nevertheless the VC's inability to overrun or otherwise discourage Dogface from remaining in the area would have been disconcerting to them.

Whatever the reason for the 271st staying in place, the VC soon found that the Dogface battalion was conducting reconnaissance-in-force operations in the south along the Binh Duong/Binh Long boundary and another U.S. battalion, Dauntless, had gone into the area to their west, following B-52 strikes. The 271st must have been feeling the pressure. From the west, Dauntless began to probe toward the center of the Secret Zone. Then, on October 11, the Dogface battalion also made a significant probe toward the center of the Secret Zone. The 271st tried to suck Cavazos into a "fire trap," but with the help of a scout dog and Cavazos's intuition, the 271st was instead mauled by U.S. artillery and helicopter gunships. Rather than engaging in a more even match of close-in infantry fighting, which favored the 271st and minimized the effect of U.S. air and artillery firepower, the 271st again found itself bloodied and thwarted.

Dauntless continued to probe the western periphery of the Secret Zone, moving in a northeasterly direction and keeping the

Cam Xe Creek to its rear. Dauntless's focus was toward the center of the Secret Zone. At this point, an outside observer might have begun to visualize a carefully coordinated operation on the part of the 1st Brigade or the division to ensnare the 271st.

From the G2 (intelligence) perspective, it probably was. In spite of this appearance however, it was not really a coordinated operation. Each infantry battalion operated independently. As a matter of fact, in Vietnam there was always a concern with getting friendly maneuver units on the ground intermingled. The conventional tactics of coordination with clearly defined tactical boundaries did not work well in this 360° warfare. In Vietnam most operations were circular rather than linear, and units operated out from their fixed NDP positions in a radial fashion rather than in the conventional linear configuration. This practice of conducting circular or radial operations was different from typical pre-Vietnam training routines and operational thinking, but U.S. infantry units adapted to it quite well. Even so, coordination between friendly units was always extremely problematic, which resulted in independent but "supporting" operations by battalions becoming the norm in an effort to minimize these problems.

As the Dauntless probes continued in a northeasterly direction, the battalion had to move its fixed NDP farther to the northeast. Thus, on October 15, the battalion relocated its NDP to the north of the Secret Zone, as opposed to the NDP it had previously established in the west. The battalion relocated its NDP primarily because it wanted to probe into the Secret Zone from the north and because its troopers had daily found more and more signs of fresh enemy activity. Although the 2-28 Infantry Black Lions (Dauntless) were wearing down physically, the imminence of contact with the enemy kept increasing. By mid-October the men had to be tired. Their initial air assault on the 8th had used up a lot of adrenaline even though their LZ hadn't been hot, and they had been beating the bush for seven days with no real results. Then they had to move their

NDP, which was a labor-intensive operation.

On October 16, in the afternoon, the Black Lions finally made a significant contact with the 271st, just to the south of their new NDP. Unfortunately, significant contacts made in the afternoon were not desirable from the Big Red One's perspective. At night 1st Division units wanted to be in their NDPs, "up tight," with the advantage to the defender. This practice made sense, but it reduced an infantry commander's flexibility in exploiting a situation as it developed. In the afternoon there was always the nagging feeling that the unit might be caught out after dark. Consequently the division had established some relatively inflexible rules that restricted creative thinking or action on the part of infantry commanders. This certainly was not the goal, but it was an unintended result.

Thus on October 16, Delta Company, commanded by first Lieutenant Clark Welch, and Bravo Company, commanded by Captain Jim Kasik, had gone on a two-company search mission to the southeast of the battalion's new NDP. A small command element from the battalion headquarters, headed up by Major Jack Sloan, the new battalion S3, had accompanied the force, traveling with Bravo Company, which was second in the column of march. Terry Allen's SOP, and therefore the battalion's SOP, was that if more than one company went on a mission, a battalion command element would go with them. Since one company always had to stay in the NDP for security, the normal force operating outside the NDP during the day (for search and destroy, recon in force, or whatever) was a two-company force. Sometimes this two-company force would include the recon platoon, which was a much smaller, but highly trained and motivated unit, and good to have around.

Terry and I had discussed this SOP, and many others, repeatedly. The SOP made sense to me. The NDP security company job could be termed rest, although continuous patrolling was required. The battalion commander (Terry Allen) and the S3 (Jack Sloan) were really the only people considered capable of commanding the battalion in the field. A force of two or more companies required a command element on the ground accompanying the force. Consequently the SOP required that if a contact developed, the command officer who was left behind in the NDP (battalion commander or S3) would immediately get airborne in an H-13 (light observation helicopter) to assist those on the ground with fire support and communications.

This system worked quite well. During extended operations, like this one, it meant the battalion commander was not always in the bush. Normally Terry wanted to be with the two-company force in the bush, but on the 16th he had stayed back in the NDP. This was a good move to get some rest. I can only imagine, however, that Terry's heart was in his throat when his two-company force got into a significant contact in the afternoon while he was back in the NDP.

Helicopter availability was also a problem. Brigade commanders always had a command and control (C&C) aircraft on a daily basis. Supposedly, the army's table of organization also provided for LOHs for each battalion, but under brigade control. On many days, however, battalions did not get a dedicated LOH. A battalion might get one for a few hours, or on call, but they weren't available as much as they were needed. We lived with this, and I don't think we whined about it. Helicopter maintenance was difficult, and there never seemed to be enough LOHs to go around. I don't know if the battalion had an LOH on October 16 or not, and probably no one else knows for sure, since that particular support could not be counted on, although it should have been.

Both First Lieutenant Clark Welch and Captain Jim Kasik, the company commanders involved in this action, have good recall of the details of this contact. Welch remembers that the enemy action and maneuver was confident, aggressive, and determined. Welch can describe how the enemy force was armed, how they moved during fire and movement, how they were dressed. At the time, Welch was the most experienced company commander in the Black Lions. He also states that the enemy force encountered on the 16th was formidable.

B Company, trailing Welch's D Company, could not see as much and was less involved in the contact. Captain Jim Kasik recalls that they saw a good number of the enemy through the trees trying to move along B Company's flank, but he could not see the effect of his unit's fire. Accompanying D Company at the time was a squad of South Vietnamese soldiers from a PRU (Province Reconnaissance Unit). These were highly trained South Vietnamese soldiers, and a U.S. captain and advisor was accompanying the squad: Captain Bernard Francis Jones from Coalton, West Virginia. First Lieutenant Welch remembers how he was standing next to Jones speaking with him when Jones was hit in the throat by small-arms fire and died instantly. Welch recalls helping to carry Jones to the rear. Captain Kasik remembers that later on that day he watched the Vietnamese squad members carry Jones's body in a poncho lashed to a sapling back through his company toward the NDP. Reports of the October 16 contact indicate that seventeen Viet Cong were killed. The U.S. casualties were Captain Jones killed and five or six members of D Company wounded. With the help of artillery fire and air strikes, contact was broken and Bravo and Delta companies returned to the NDP.

At division headquarters, the Dauntless contact of October 16 had generated some excitement. With this contact, Dauntless appeared to have struck a VC nerve and raised the possibility that there might be a bigger payoff coming. At the brigade level, the same feelings obtained. A picture taken by Specialist Fifth Class Verland A. Gilbertson, a combat photographer from the division's signal battalion, attests to the interest. This photo shows Lieutenant Clark Welch describing the October 16 action to an intent group of senior officers. Brigadier General Coleman (79er), Major Don Holleder (1st Brigade S3), Lieutenant Colonel Terry Allen, and Colonel Buck Newman (1st Brigade commander) all appear to be listening closely to Welch. Two other officers in the picture are not identifiable, but I believe one is Major Jack Sloan, S3, for 2-28 Infantry. This photo is doubly fascinating because Specialist Gilbertson, the photographer, was mortally wounded in the action at Ông Thanh the next day. Gilbertson probably took this photo at 1800, just before dusk.

Neither Colonel Newman nor Lieutenant Welch remembers much about what was said during that meeting. The others are all dead. One thing is for sure, Welch did not say anything in front of General Coleman or Colonel Newman about the plans for the next day's action. Welch was not a showman; nor was he comfortable hobnobbing with senior officers. On that day, he told his October 16 story and went back to his company area in the NDP to await instructions. Since Colonel Newman, the brigade commander, cannot recall what guidance he gave to Terry Allen on the night of October 16, a knowledgeable person can only speculate.

A point should be made here. The 2-28 Infantry Black Lions had never operated with Colonel Newman prior to the airmobile assault on October 8. Terry Allen knew Don Holleder, the brigade S3, better than he knew Colonel Newman. Colonel Newman had taken over command of the brigade from Colonel Bill Caldwell only about a month earlier. Eight days in a combat operation is, however, a long time. Terry Allen and Buck Newman were compatible, and there is no reason to believe that lack of familiarity between Allen and Newman was any factor in the October 17 battle. By this time, Terry Allen had a reputation in the division as a solid battalion commander, and he had given Newman no reason to think otherwise in the eight days that Allen had operated under Newman's command. My guess is that Newman and Allen quickly agreed on the plan for October 17, and Brigadier General Coleman, if he was there, concurred. The discussion of what to do the next day probably ended with Allen saying something like this:

"Well, we know the VC are in there, and tomorrow we should

be able to smoke them out. We'll order up a couple of air strikes tonight for tomorrow. We'll go in there tomorrow with Delta and Alpha. Welch was in there yesterday, so we'll lead with Delta. Bravo will secure the NDP. I'll [Allen] go with a small command group and Sloan [S3] will stay in the NDP. We'll also have artillery zeroed in with marching fire. If they are in there tomorrow, it should be a good fight. That's what we're here for."

The result was probably a fast consensus on Allen's proposed course of action being reached among the leaders of the division, the brigade, and the battalion. No big deal. SOP. Business as usual. What the hell, they'd been at it for eight days now.

With this general plan for the following day settled, General Coleman, Colonel Newman, and Major Holleder left, just before dark, to head back to their forward CP on Highway 13 at Chon Thanh. Keep in mind that Colonel Newman still had two other battalions and various units to watch over.

Terry Allen would then have called a commander's meeting at the battalion level. Those in attendance would be Major Sloan (the S3); the three company commanders, George (Alpha), Kasik (Bravo), Welch (Delta), the artillery liaison officer, the S3 air (to handle air strikes), the recon platoon leader (Second Lieutenant Bill Erwin), the battalion operations sergeant, the S2 (Captain Jim Blackwell), and Sergeant Major Francis Dowling. (That's a total of ten people, plus Allen; there may have been more.) With Allen outlining his plan, the meeting went something like this:*

"Well, guys, it looks like we're finally going to get some action. It went well today, and if we play our cards right tomorrow we can get a big kill. It should be a great day for the Black Lions. I want a couple of air strikes tomorrow—one to the southeast and one to the southwest. I want to discourage them from trying to slip out to the south. We'll lead off with Delta, followed by Alpha. I'll have a small

*Conversation reconstructed with the help of Clark Welch.

126

command group with me: S2 [Captain Jim Blackwell], Sergeant Major [Francis E.] Dowling, Specialist [Pasquale] Tizzio and at least one other RTO, and Sergeant Plier [assistant operations sergeant]. We'll travel with Alpha. Arty, I want marching fire out in front of us. S3 [Sloan], you stay back here at the TOC. If we make contact, get up in an LOH ASAP and help us out on fires and commo. We'll depart the NDP at 0800. Any questions?"

Lieutenant Welch: "Sir, that is big trouble in there."

Allen: "What do you mean, Al?" [Terry called Welch "Al," although most called him Clark, his middle name.]

Welch: "Sir, those guys are loaded for bear. They are well organized and know what they are doing. Frankly, I don't think we've got any business going in there."

Allen: "What the hell are you talking about, Al? That's what we're here for, to kill VC. You had a hard day today. Maybe Alpha should lead."

Welch was dumbfounded, and hurt. The battalion commander was accusing him of being yellow. The meeting then continued:

Allen: "Okay, switch assignments. Alpha leads out, 0800, that's all."

The meeting broke up. Welch approached Allen.

Welch: "Sir, if anybody has to go in there it should be me first. I was in there today."

Allen: "Too late, Al. Jim George will lead, you follow. I'll be with your company. That's all."

Welch was truly hurt. It seemed to him that the battalion commander thought he was gun-shy. Nevertheless Welch headed for A Company's area and found Captain Jim George. Using the map, he showed George where he had gone earlier in the day and told him to expect big action at this location. (He pointed the area out on the map.) Both company commanders then went to their units to issue their orders. Both knew it was going to be a rough day.

What follows is a copy of the battalion log for October 17 that was being kept by the battalion operations sergeant, back in the NDP, throughout the battle of Ông Thanh. On the night of October 18, after the battle, I went to the battalion area trying to get information. I found the log and copied it, and I have carried it with me for thirty-four years. Read the log, and then my commentary, speculations, and information garnered from some survivors of the action that day.

DAUNTLESS LOG: 0001 17 OCT. 67 – 2400 17 OCT. 67
[Earlier entries for that day have been omitted.]

11. 0802—"A" Departing NDP (B) [The "A" refers to A Company; the "(B)" means this information was also reported to the 1st Brigade, 1st Infantry Division.]

12. 0845—"A" Location – 684583 (B)

13. 0855—2-28 Infantry 1st Air Strike /XT 675585 Starting (B)

14. 0910—2d Air Strike Commencing/VIC XT 698567 (B)

15. 0920—Delayed Entry CO D Departed/NP 0815 (B)
    ["CO D" refers to D Company]

16. 0956-0958—CO A point located trail running SE X NW fresh footprints XT 686576, 1 VC observed. Will be taken under fire. (B)

17. 1000—Recon PLT Departing NDP (B) ["Recon PLT" refers to the Reconnaissance Platoon]

18. 1015—CO A contact right front VIC XT 686576 (B) E-W Trail – Many enemy footprints last night and early morning

19. 1020—CO D Receiving sniper fire from trees (B) [D Company is taking fire.]

20. 1030—A CO 6 and RTO hit w/head wound 6 R Other casualties reported # UNK at this time [This entry records that Captain Jim George, the A Company commander, and his RTO have been wounded.]

21. 1035—Dauntless 2 hit – 1 kilo w/Daunt 6

22. 1040—Senior Lima (Platoon) leader A CO directed to take command

23. 1040—A CO Pulling back – contact continues (B)

24. 1100—1st Air strike commencing

25. 1120—2d Air strike commencing

26. 1120—A & D CO's report contact broken

27. 1135—29 reports sniper fire on gunships VIC XT 680580 (B) [29 is recon platoon leader Bill Erwin]

28. 1135—D – A CO reports new contact (B)

29. 1145—B CO – sniper fire being received NDP (B)

30. 1145—29 Being held location 681588

31. 1150—B CO – Prepare assume blocking POS TOS

32. 1150—Delta 6, Dauntless 6, 6R Hit

33. 1153—29 moving to NDP

34. 1215—A & D still receiving fire

35. 1220—BN CMDR wounded, SGM KIA, BN S3 ordered to assume command by BDE CMDR [Colonel Allen is wounded; the battalion sergeant major is killed; and the brigade commander (Colonel Newman) directs that Major Sloan, the S3, take command.]

36. 1222—Dustoffs requested –3 (B)

37. 1255–1257—1st Dustoff (B)

38. 1256–1257—2d Dustoff (B)

39. 1300—3d Dustoff (B)

40. 1310—4th Dustoff 1st lift of 5 – Charlie on ground

41. 1350—Fire ceased

42. 1400—CO C closed perimeter

43. 1430—7th Dustoff – Total 42 WIA, 1 KIA (BDE)

44. 1515—RCN PLT located 30-40 wounded or dead soldiers from CO A, & CMD GP BN CMDR, BN SGM KIA (B)

45. 1515—CO A – 33 MIA, 20 air evacced – prior to operation CO A had 96 PFD ["PFD" means "present for duty"]

Examination of this log shows that the preplanned air strikes (at 0855 and 0910) were on time and put into the designated areas to the southeast and southwest of the suspected enemy locations. The information provided in the log indicates that the column made up of companies A and D was moving extremely slowly and cautiously. Item 16 states that fresh footprints were observed at location XT 686576 at 0956. Those coordinates plot out at about one thousand meters due south of the NDP, which means A Company had traveled one thousand meters in two hours. A Company then reported contact to its right front at 1015. Five minutes later D Company reported sniper fire from the trees. At 1030, fifteen minutes after the first report of contact, the log contains an entry of a report that Captain Jim George and his radio operator had been hit (this report appears to have come from the company's first sergeant, who is identified in the log as "6R") and that there were other casualties.

Then at 1035 the NDP received a report that Dauntless 2, Captain Jim Blackwell, had been hit and that another man in the command group had been killed. That meant that within the first fifteen minutes after making contact with the VC, both rifle companies and the battalion command group had sustained casualties. Reading further in the log, item 22 indicates that at 1040 Terry Allen presumably directed the senior platoon leader of A Company to take command of that unit. What we learn later, and not from the log, is the way that Captain Jim George, the A Company commander, was wounded in the first burst of enemy fire. George had been hit by a claymore detonated at virtually point-blank range.

Information about the action on October 17 that became available after the battle and which was not recorded in the log also established that the volume of fire in the front of the column was devastating. In all likelihood, Terry Allen had no clear idea what had happened to A Company. While Allen was in communication with Captain George's company, the log reports that his command group was also receiving fire. According to later information, Allen and his command group sought cover behind a large anthill. A log entry states that, around this time, Allen's S2 had been hit by enemy fire and that another person in the command element, presumably Sergeant First Class Eugene J. Plier, had been killed.

Later analysis of the battle revealed that A Company had been stopped dead in its tracks, hunkered down without a commander, and that a large part of the company of fewer than one hundred men had already been hit by enemy fire. Then men from A Company begin to run to the rear, where D Company had established a perimeter. There were no attempts at using fire and maneuver (i.e., maneuvering platoons or squads) and no use of fire and movement (individuals covering each other). By this time, the VC were intermingled with the retreating troops from A Company, and soldiers in D Company were shooting at both the VC and the retreating men from A Company.

The log reports that at 1040 A Company was pulling back under the pressure of continued enemy contact, but this was not an organized move. A Company had ceased to exist as a military unit and had become no more than a line of stragglers heading back for the NDP or joining D Company in its perimeter. The artillery fire, which had not been effective because the enemy was too close at the time of first contact, was lifted and air strikes were put in (1100 and 1120). The air strikes added to the confusion. They may have had an impact on enemy reserves, but they certainly had no impact on the VC who were engaging the remnants of A Company, D Company, and the battalion command group, which by then was clustered in a tiny perimeter, perhaps fifty meters in diameter, around the anthill. At 1150 an entry in the log reports that Terry Allen (Dauntless 6), LT Welch (Delta 6), and the battalion sergeant major have all been wounded. In the hour preceding that report, nothing of significance, other than the fact that B Company, which was providing security at the

NDP, had received some sniper fire, is recorded in the log.

This absence of significant entries in the log for the hour prior to the report that Allen, Welch, and the sergeant major had been wounded means that Terry Allen was talking on the radio to Colonel Buck Newman and Brigadier General Bill Colemen, both of whom were overhead in choppers. Unfortunately, senior officers Newman and Coleman were unable to do anything to help. Air and artillery fire had not been effective because the combatants were too close, while the command group and D Company had been pinned down and had made little or no attempt to move. At the same time, snipers were firing on the NDP. Consequently B Company and the recon platoon may have had their hands full defending the NDP. Under these circumstances, no reinforcements were immediately available and, if they were, there would have been difficulty in employing them effectively.

Later information and reports that are not a part of the log confirm that from 1150 to 1220 (thirty minutes), the VC further weakened the command group's small perimeter in the jungle around the anthill. During this time, Lieutenant Welch saw the battalion sergeant major killed, and Terry Allen also received what would prove to be a mortal wound. In the meantime Second Lieutenant Harold Durham, the D Company artillery forward observer, was calling artillery fire onto the company's perimeter. Welch, who was already weak from loss of blood, noticed that in making this call for help, Durham was operating his radio "press to talk" switch with a bloody stub where his hand had been.

Lieutenant Welch later gave an account of just how critical the plight of those left in the small D Company perimeter around the anthill was. As the perimeter grew smaller and smaller, Welch's ability to lead was hampered by his wounds. During the battle he was wounded five times and lost a great deal of blood. By then he was sitting inside the perimeter with his back against a tree. Some ten meters across from him he saw First Sergeant Clarence "Bud" Barrow, sitting in a similar fashion with an M-60 machine gun across his lap. Barrow had been wounded in both legs. Welch would lose consciousness for a few moments, and then regain it. As he was recovering consciousness at one point, Welch noticed Sergeant Barrow aiming the M-60 machine gun directly at him. The machine gun then began to fire, and Welch again lost consciousness. He remembers nothing after that until he woke up in the evacuation hospital at Long Binh. "Why did First Sergeant Barrow shoot me?" he wondered.

Welch later met Sergeant Barrow in a Tokyo hospital. He asked why Barrow had fired the M-60 machine gun at him. Barrow replied that a VC had grabbed Welch's equipment suspenders from behind in an effort to pull Welch to his feet. The equipment suspenders rode up Welch's body and the belt was around Welch's neck. Barrow had used the machine gun to shoot the VC who was holding Welch's suspenders.

On the night after the battle, Lieutenant David Stroup, a D Company platoon leader, reported a conversation he had had near the anthill with the battalion commander, Allen, who was covered with blood. The conversation went like this:

Allen: "Who is in charge of D Company?"

Stroup: "I am." [Lieutenant Stroup was apparently unaware that Lieutenant Welch, although wounded, was also within the perimeter.]

Allen: "What is your call sign?"

Stroup: "Delta 36."

Allen: "What are you going to do?"

Stroup: "I'm going to get my people [eight to ten soldiers] out of here."

Allen: "Okay, do the best you can."

Stroup said he then began moving north with his men. He had traveled about one hundred meters when he received a radio call from Allen.

Allen: "Delta 36, this is Dauntless 6. What is your status?"

Stroup: "This is Delta 36, pulling back approximately one hundred meters, still receiving sniper fire."

Allen: "This is Dauntless 6, roger, still receiving sniper fire?"

Stroup: "Affirmative, still receiving sniper fire."

Allen: "Roger, understand you are still receiving sniper fire. Be sure to keep your flank security out."

Stroup: "Wilco, sir."

Based on the log and other reports, this conversation between Lieutenant Stroup and Terry Allen must have taken place between approximately 1200 and 1230. It is obvious from what Terry Allen said that he was trying to regain control over his battalion. Essentially, Allen lost control of the battalion as soon as A Company's situation was unknown and Allen had no way of influencing the situation. My interpretation of the Allen/Stroup conversation is that although Allen really knew the battalion was in deep trouble, he wanted Lieutenant Stroup to know that he, Allen, was in control, passing orders and instructions. In my opinion, this method of handling the situation would be typical of Terry Allen. He may not have known what to do, but he did not want anyone thinking that he did not know what to do.

Returning to the record in the log: when the brigade commander, Colonel Newman, realized that Terry Allen was in serious trouble, at 1220 he ordered the battalion S3, Major Jack Sloan, who was back in the NDP, to take command of the battalion. In issuing this order, Colonel Newman was really referring to B Company and recon. Those two units were back at the NDP, where there was a real threat that the NDP could be attacked. Then, at approximately 1230, Colonel Newman landed at the NDP and took command of the entire operation. Newman's S3, Major Don Holleder, who was also aboard his C&C chopper, was killed shortly thereafter while attempting to rescue some wounded.

The rest of the story, as reported in the log, involved policing of the battlefield, which lasted all afternoon and into the darkness. All wounded were evacuated, and the dead and their equipment were stacked near what was now being called "the hole," a section of jungle that had been cut out to allow one Huey to get in and out. Artillery fire was plotted around "the hole," and Colonel Newman and General Coleman agreed that evacuation of the dead and their equipment would be completed the next day. Newman then returned to the NDP to get the 2-28 Infantry reorganized. By that time, C Company, which had been securing a firebase on Highway 13, had joined B Company at the NDP. The NDP had also been reinforced with two companies of the 1-16 Infantry (Devour) to assist in the afternoon evacuation and security operations. On the 18th, B and C companies of the 2-28 Infantry together with their recon platoon retrieved their dead and equipment, and the decimated battalion was extracted to Lai Khe to regroup. An early casualty report indicated fifty-eight U.S. soldiers killed, two missing, and fifty-nine others wounded. Enemy dead was set at 102, though no one knew for sure.

This is my version of the battle. I listened to parts of it on the radio in the 1st Infantry Division TOC in Lai Khe. While listening, I was at first elated that my battalion had done its job in finding the enemy. Then as the reports poured in and I listened to General Coleman and Colonel Newman desperately talking to Terry Allen and others on the ground, my elation turned to terror, then to despair, and finally, remorse. I should have been there, I thought. I could have made a difference. How could this have happened?

There are at least three other written versions of this battle. The first was published in the 1st Infantry Division's *DANGER Forward, The Magazine of the Big Red One, Vietnam* (June 1968). Captain Richard W. Flanagan, the division information officer and the magazine's editor at the time of the battle, wrote this account. Although well written, it is, by design, a glorification of the actions of the division. That is what the magazine was designed to do, and its articles were carefully edited to show the Big Red One and the U.S. Army in the best light possible.

Another account of the Battle of Ông Thanh is not identified as such, but nevertheless provides a very accurate version of the battle. It is in the book *Ringed in Steel: Armored Cavalry, Vietnam 1967–68* (1986) by Michael Mahler. The author's account of the battle is better, but it also dwells on what happened as best he can piece the story together. Mahler provides little analysis of why such a defeat occurred.

Lieutenant Colonel George MacGarrigle, U.S. Army (Ret.), who was employed by the U.S. Army Center of Military History in Washington, D.C., wrote yet a third account of this battle in his book *Combat Operations: Taking the Offensive, October 1966 to October 1967* (1998). Immediately following the Battle of Ông Thanh on October 18–20, 1967, and continuing for perhaps a month thereafter, Captain John Cash, a military historian working with a small team of assistants, made tape-recorded interviews with many of the Americans who had been present at the battle. Cash's notes and tapes were delivered to the army's chief of military history for possible publication. The chief of military history determined, however, that the information would be too controversial, had it marked Classified, and thereby made sure that the fruits of John Cash's meticulous interviews in October 1967 would not soon see the light. Lieutenant Colonel MacGarrigle subsequently got access to these tapes and used them in writing his recent book.

My version of why this defeat occurred contains no underlying secrets or revelations. The 2nd Battalion, 28th Infantry Black Lions (Dauntless), commanded by Lieutenant Colonel Terry Allen, was probably as ready to do battle that day as any battalion in the 1st Division. But the men were tired, having been continuously in the field for eight arduous days, and the rifle companies were woefully understrength, with A and D companies fielding about ninety to one hundred men each. Thus the battalion was in the field that day with fewer than two hundred men, making it really more of a beefed-up rifle company.

Why this occurred requires an explanation that is too long and detailed to go into here. Maintaining high foxhole strength is a difficult task for the U.S. Army in peace and war. It is a command responsibility that is easy to overlook, at all levels of command, and it certainly had an impact on the battle of October 17, 1967. Diminished foxhole strength was not, however, the primary cause of the tragedy that day.

The primary reason for the defeat was that Lieutenant Colonel Terry Allen failed to visualize what might happen to his battalion and was unable to influence the battle in his favor once it began. As Lieutenant Welch had predicted the evening before, at Ông Thanh the battalion became decisively engaged with a force at least as strong as the 2-28 Infantry and at a place where the 2-28 Infantry was at a disadvantage (i.e., not on their own ground). The decisive engagement unfolded so rapidly that Terry Allen was not able to bring firepower to bear on the enemy force. Further, he was not able to maneuver his force to affect the outcome of the battle. Hindsight is easy. Terry Allen was not a careless or incompetent commander. But Terry Allen was responsible for the battalion's predicament that day.

Others have proposed some dark and tawdry reasons why the battalion was defeated, such as adherence to a 1st Division SOP that demanded air strikes over artillery. This is simply untrue. There were problems with air strikes and artillery continuously in the 1st Division, and on that day, but they were not a primary cause for defeat. When the enemy closes with an infantry force, neither air support nor artillery support can do the job for which it is intended.

I have heard some arguments that Terry Allen was an incompetent officer and was only in command because his father had commanded the division in World War II. Although the reputation of Major General Terry Allen may have gained some recognition for his son, my analysis is that Lieutenant Colonel Terry Allen was as competent, knowledgeable, and able as any lieutenant colonel I knew in the division at the time, except perhaps for Lieutenant Colonel Dick Cavazos. Still others have said that Terry Allen had a "death wish" caused by a recent estrangement from his wife. That speculation is pure hogwash, and I will discuss it later in a separate analysis of Terry Allen.

Succinctly put, combat operations can never be "business as usual." This was the downfall of the 2-28 Infantry Black Lions on October 17, 1967. The battalion could conceivably have altered the outcome, but only if it had heeded Lieutenant Welch's warnings. Much has also been made of the question as to whether or not the 2-28 Infantry was ambushed. On the night of October 17, after the tragic battle, Major General Hay gathered the division staff in the conference room to talk about what had occurred that day. He spoke of the bravery of the men and all the efforts that had been made to turn the tide that day. He stated three times during his short discussion of the battle that it had been a "meeting engagement." I immediately knew in my own mind that General Hay was trying to make the best of a bad situation. This had not been a meeting engagement but, in my view, General Hay did not want to admit that a Big Red One battalion had been ambushed. Frankly, I don't think it was an ambush either. Here are some definitions of operational terms drawn from the army's *Operational Terms and Symbols* (FM 101-5-1 October 1985, Department of the Army):

1. Ambush—A *surprise* [italics added] attack by fire from concealed positions on a moving or temporarily halted enemy.

1A. Surprise—To strike the enemy at a time and/or place and *in a manner for which he is unprepared.*

2. Meeting Engagement—A combat action that occurs when a moving force, incompletely deployed for battle, engages an enemy *at an unexpected time and place.* The enemy force may be either stationary or in motion.

3. Deliberate Attack—An attack planned and carefully coordinated with all concerned elements based on thorough reconnaissance, evaluation of all available intelligence and relative combat strength, *analysis of various courses of action,* and other factors affecting the situation. It generally is conducted against a well-organized defense when a hasty attack is not possible or has been conducted and failed.

4. Hasty Attack—An offensive operation for which a unit *has not made extensive preparations.* It is conducted with resources immediately available in order to maintain momentum or to take advantage of the enemy situation.

5. Movement To Contact—An offensive operation designed to gain initial ground contact with the enemy or to regain lost contact.

I believe that the 2-28 Infantry was expecting to be hit by the VC on October 17, 1967. They fully expected a combat action, and it was really a matter of who opened fire first, who had the greatest volume of fire, and how well that fire was employed. The *hasty attack* and/or *movement to contact* really describe better what the 2-28 Infantry did that day. The fact was that at that time and place, the enemy force was more ready, more aggressive, and capitalized on its strengths to win a significant victory.

"**Truth is a stranger,
and a thousand times
more thrilling than fiction.**"

True Magazine

Chapter 15
The Battle of Ông Thanh:
From Other Perspectives

It is now the year 2002. There is a tight-knit little group of persons who ask themselves: "How could such a debacle have occurred on October 17, 1967?" It is etched into our souls! We meet annually in late October or early November at West Point. We call it the November Nightmare—not referring to the battle, but to the carousing, the football game, and the boisterousness of a weekend spent by a bunch of men with too much booze. Every night, seemingly without fail, we re-fight the battle, each from his own perspective. Those of us who weren't directly involved in the battle ask questions, but there are few answers.

Joe Costello and Tom Hinger each received a Silver Star and Purple Heart as a result of the battle. On that day, Hinger was a combat medic who saved or soothed many lives, and Costello was the M-79 grenadier who saved a man's life by putting paper from a cigarette pack over his sucking chest wound. Later, Joe would somehow get on a radio with the battalion command frequency and talk to both General Coleman and Colonel Newman, directing artillery fires and giving sitreps to these high-ranking officers in helicopters above. In the midst of all the fighting at Ông Thanh, Joe Costello was essentially the battalion commander. Terry Allen was dead, the battalion sergeant major was dead, and both company commanders were critically wounded. By default, Private Joe Costello was the acting battalion commander. Today, Joe is superintendent of one of New York's largest state prisons in Utica.

At a Big Red One officers dinner in April 1994, I sat next to General Bill Rosson, who had been Terry Allen Jr.'s commander in Germany and had participated in his 1961 wedding. General Rosson, now retired, is a highly respected airborne/special forces infantry general. I sent him a copy of the *Vietnam* magazine article I had written about the battle. He was complimentary of the article in his thank-you letter, but he also said:

> I wish you had provided a little more on the battle itself, including the circumstances attending Terry Allen's death. As it is, I have the image of a worm-like column, two companies in length, making its way slowly ("one thousand meters in two hours") through the light jungle of the Long Nguyen Secret Zone. No frontal or flank security. Suddenly, the head of the column is hit, and the enemy "maneuvered down both flanks of the U.S. column, inflicting massive casualties." Surely there was more to it than that.

Those words haunt me to this day because I have found it so difficult to explain the battle in more precise terms.

*

On October 17, 1967, the 2nd Battalion, 28th Infantry Black Lions was an exhausted group of soldiers. They had entered the jungle from their base camp at Lai Khe on October 8. For nine apprehension-filled days they had beaten the bush. Enemy contact had been expected at their landing zone on the 8th. Each day that followed added to their apprehension and mental and physical exhaustion. During the day everyone was working at a fever pitch, either moving through the jungle on patrol or continuously improving fighting positions. The heat and humidity sapped their strength. Most men didn't eat full meals, which were normally C rations. These are fairly palatable and high in calories, but soldiers tire of them as a steady diet. Men who were working as hard as these troopers needed three square meals a day, but they did not get them. Tired, undernourished soldiers are not ready for savage, close combat. On the other side, the VC soldiers probably suffered from the same symptoms, but the 271st Regiment—in fact, all regiments (271st, 272nd, and 273rd) of the 9th VC Division—were made up of battle-hardened veterans. Most of them had acclimated themselves to the rigors of jungle life. They still got hot and tired and hungry, but they were much tougher physically and mentally when dealing with such adverse conditions.

Perhaps neither side had an edge in handling the effects of mental exhaustion, but physical exhaustion adds to the weight of mental exhaustion. For the men of the 2nd Battalion, 28th Infantry, search and destroy operations, security patrols, ambush patrols, and listening posts were times of abnormal apprehension. The men knew that they always had to be at the ready. Have you ever watched a robin move across a lawn? It stops, looks, and listens—continuously. The same is true for soldiers conducting operations in the jungle. Their nerve endings are on a constant state of alert. Their muscles are poised to react instantaneously.

In 1962 I went through the Jungle Warfare School at Fort Sherman in the Panama Canal Zone. During the month-long training period, I developed what I thought was a prickly heat rash. It felt like a thousand needles were puncturing my skin at the same time. The pain wasn't constant, but it was most pronounced at a time of emotion. Grabbing a branch of black palm, a painful, thorny tree that abounded in the Panama jungle, caused this reaction in my nervous system that I equated to prickly heat.

Five years later, after several months in Vietnam, I began to have the same sensation. It could be brought on by something as simple as hearing the *thump thump thump* of our resupply chopper off in the distance bringing us much needed ammo, water, and

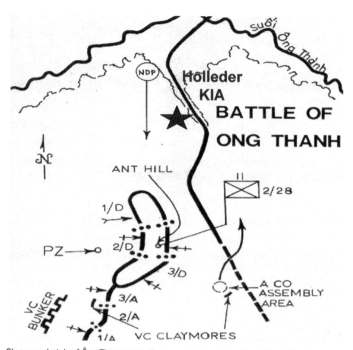

Close-up sketch of Ông Thang area shows route taken from the night defensive position to the battle site, general locations of the enemy, general route of the withdrawal, the ant hill, and approximate location (star) of Major Holleder when he was killed. (James Shelton/William Ostlund/*DANGER Forward Magazine*)

rations. I would hear the sound of that Huey and would feel as though I was being jabbed by needles. It was painful, and I thought it must be related to heat. In fact it was related to high emotion. The relief of knowing that we would be re-supplied that night caused this sensation. I am convinced that my nervous system had been brought to some heightened degree of tension so that emotions, such as fear and joy, affected my physical being in this way. If it happened to me, it must have happened to others. Fear, apprehension, and physical tension, all of which were seemingly continuous while on jungle operations, took a toll on my mind and body.

For leaders like me, the burdens of responsibility added to the stress. Our leaders knew that the men depended on them for making the right decisions and seeing to their well-being. Each minor decision that a leader made, such as pointing "go left" or "go right," could have huge consequences. For me, the sound of that re-supply chopper meant that our system, which I was partly responsible for, would arm, feed, and bring comfort to our soldiers. Hearing the chopper's *thump thump thump* thus became an emotional experience.

For these and other reasons, nine days in the jungle from October 8 to 17 would have taken their toll on everyone, the men and their commanders.

The number of American soldiers who took part in the Battle of Ông Thanh on October 17, 1967, was appallingly small. At the time, an infantry battalion in Vietnam had an authorized strength of approximately seven hundred men. It consisted of a headquarters company (administration and recon platoon, cooks, drivers, maintenance, supply and transportation, medics and the battalion commander and staff). There were also four rifle companies (A, B, C, and D) and a combat support company (4.2-inch mortars and anti-tank weapons). Each rifle company had an authorized strength of one hundred and forty men, while the combat support company numbered about fifty men and the headquarters company perhaps one hundred.

The force that began the search-and-destroy operation of October 17, called a "battalion minus," consisted of a total of approximately one hundred and fifty men. A Company had sixty-five men and D Company had seventy-three men, totaling one hundred and thirty-eight soldiers. The battalion command group consisted of Lieutenant Colonel Terry Allen Jr., Command Sergeant Major Francis Dowling, Captain Jim Blackwell (the S2), Sergeant First Class Eugene Plier, who was the battalion assistant operations sergeant, two RTOs, and perhaps two or three more men for security. B Company was left behind to secure the battalion's night defensive position and resupply area. C Company was off securing an artillery firebase on Highway 13 in Chon Thanh. That firebase provided supporting artillery fires to the 2-28 as well as other units within range of its guns.

Having such a small number of men, little over a rifle company, fighting a battle at Ông Thanh that day, was quite commonplace. How could a seven hundred-man battalion end up as a reinforced company? How could two rifle companies that had an authorized strength of about one hundred and forty men each become a force of one hundred and fifty men total, roughly 50 percent of the expected strength? Although "foxhole strength" was a term given to ensure that the number of soldiers assigned to fighting units was closely watched, it does not appear to have been of major concern for this battle until after the fact.

Foxhole strength was a matter of concern in units of the 1st Division in Vietnam, but the fact that rifle companies rarely fielded more than one hundred men was routine, and it was not a Vietnam War phenomenon. In World War II, for example, most ten-man rifle squads averaged about five or six men. In Korea the same problem existed. A rifle company is not a desirable place to be in war, and people can think of many reasons why they have to be somewhere else. Although there seemed to be an inordinate number of men who were not in the field at Ông Thanh, the actual number of soldiers who made up the two-company force that day was at the time unremarkable. A book could, and probably should, be written about this problem.

Looking back, we do know that approximately ten men from D Company had been evacuated for wounds since the battalion had entered the field on October 8. In addition, eleven men from A Company had been left behind at the NDP as a result of their having conducted an all-night ambush patrol on the night of October 16–17. Consequently on October 17, two understrength rifle companies, consisting of sixty-five and seventy-three men, respectively, must have made this particular U.S. Army infantry battalion a much more appealing target to the 271st VC Regiment.

And so, as the battalion log of October 17, 1967, dutifully reported, at 0802 A Company was "departing NDP." D Company, which included the battalion command group, moved out right behind A Company. At 0845, forty-three minutes later, A Company reported a new position five hundred meters south of the NDP. This information reflects a cautious advance, only five hundred meters in forty-three minutes. The slow progress of this patrol was due to continuous cloverleafing. The entire rifle company would wait while two three-man patrols would move out to the front, beyond the sight of the column, both to the right and the left, and circle out and back in their respective directions before they returned to the column in the manner shown below:

After the cloverleafing patrols returned, the column would move forward through the area that the patrols had covered. Then new men would move forward, and new patrols would again advance ahead of the column. Seen from above, the forward progress of the column would have looked like an inchworm, inching its way along. Concurrently, artillery marching fire provided coverage to the front of the column. The A Company artillery forward observer was with the company commander. He would call for one marking round, and the round would land approximately five hundred yards forward of the lead elements. As the column moved forward, the marching fire was moved ahead. The marching fire was also a registration point from which heavier fire could be brought to bear with a rapid shift of fires by the forward observer. In most instances, marching fire in the jungle was not so much observed as it was heard. The forward observer would have to estimate how far the round had landed from friendly troops based on the volume of noise produced by the incoming round. Thus controlling the artillery marching fire was also an exercise in map reading on the part of the maneuver element, the forward observer and the company commander, and precision with zero defects on the part of the artillery fire direction center and gunners who set azimuth, elevation, and level bubbles on the gunsights.

Background Situation and Planning

Joe Costello, the nineteen-year-old M-79 grenadier from A Company, recalls how that day went:*

October 16 was an easy day and dinner chow was hot and decent. Throughout the evening, there was a lot of talk about the next day. Word among us was that the day's contact was brief and surprised Charlie. A Company was going to go out the next day to engage the enemy again.

Allan Reilly, who was an older guy (about twenty-five) with good in-country experience, said we were going to get into some "bad shit in the morning." He volunteered to walk point and was charged up. He and Mike "Pee Wee" Gallagher had just gotten new fatigue uniform pants that day on re-supply. They were as happy with their new fatigues as most people are with a new $500 suit. Most of us had guarded respect for Reilly's jungle savvy and knowledge of how to maneuver and get comfort and recreation items (socks, booze, etc.). He had

---

*Unless otherwise indicated, the first-person accounts of the Battle of Ông Thanh that appear in this chapter were obtained by the author through interviews and personal correspondence with the contributors and are used with their permission.

been involved in Operation Billings and was always willing to walk point.

The word was that the area where contact was made was going to be pummeled all night with artillery fire. We were worried and, in an odd way, anxious about what was going to happen the next day.

The morning of the 17th started like any other: heating C rations with a chunk of C-4. A quick "shave and shit" and then collect my gear to make sure everything is straight and ready. I carried an M-79 and plenty of ammo. I topped off my canteen and made sure I had enough cigarettes.

Soldiers were moving around within the field perimeter with a quickened pace as the morning progressed. Everyone seemed to know there was going to be a big fight ahead.

When we finally moved out, it was in the typical column formation. It was damp and hot and seemed like we would go fifty yards and everything would stop for five to ten minutes before we moved again. The stop-and-go progression was nothing new and it usually had something to do with the cloverleaf patrols or unusual sightings. It was obvious the officers were being very careful.

The sixty-five men of A Company were like the point of a dagger stabbing into a hornets' nest. The hand holding that dagger was the battalion command group and D Company, which moved behind the point. On the preceding day, D Company had been the point of the dagger leading B Company into the jungle, surprising the enemy, inflicting many enemy casualties, and losing one of their own men, Captain Jones, who along with his special team had been traveling with the company.

Colonel Buck Newman, the brigade commander, describes what he remembers about the initial movement of the 2-28 Infantry on October 17:

> Without trying to shirk my own responsibility or failures on 17 October 1967, let me just say that the 2-28 mission was only one of several concurrent operations going on in the division and 1st Brigade areas. The areas of operation were extensive, so much so that most operations such as that by 2-28 were essentially independent reconnaissances in force with such artillery and air support as might be available rather than the nice textbook-type operations taught in service schools where you have coordination with other units on your flanks or at least a recon screen of some type.
>
> Also there was no element of surprise in the 2-28 operations. They went into their fight on foot in a deliberate probing and searching action having departed from their assembly area in the vicinity of their NDP. There was no sudden heliborne air assault so beloved by those who write about Vietnam but have never experienced it. This was a standard infantry operation with patrols and cloverleafing under the canopy of the jungle. An air assault on the objective would not have been practical even if division and brigade had been able to spare the lift, which neither had. At this time period in Vietnam, helicopters were still a very precious luxury, and there were many competing requirements for lift. Division had only one single slick company (ten helicopters) available and all other aviation came from 1st Aviation Brigade.
>
> I dwell on this point at some length because I believe it is essential to understand that the 2-28th was basically an understrength U.S. infantry battalion operating independently under the jungle canopy in an area where the enemy had much better knowledge of the terrain and the advantage of surprise, being able to position himself in the anticipation of the 2-28

advance. In my opinion based on my limited conversation with Terry Allen before he was killed, the enemy was perhaps equal to or superior in strength on the battlefield to the 2-28th.

Medic Specialist Tom Hinger recalls his initial actions that morning:

Activity in our platoon was normal prior to leaving the NDP on October 17. I did my normal check of the men's feet, and treated ailments. As for myself, I did the normal things: check my aid bag, clean my weapon, and get ready for the day. Since the odds of making contact were high, I swapped my pistol for an M-16 with one of the men in the weapons platoon since they would be remaining in the NDP. I was scared as always before a patrol, but in no way did I have any premonition of what the day would bring.

The departure from the NDP was uneventful. If we left early or late, I have no idea, for it always seemed we were subject to that phrase of "Hurry Up & Wait." Alpha was the lead company, and we were in platoon formation: 1st platoon in the lead, 2nd platoon (our platoon) next, then 3rd platoon. When we entered the jungle, we were in double column, and I was in the right column with Joe Costello behind me. We moved slowly, and stopped frequently and sent out cloverleafs. If we moved slower than normal, it was not apparent to me. The heat in the jungle was stifling as always, and the fear and excitement of the patrol added to the emotional drain.

Captain Jim Kasik, the B Company Commander, remained in the NDP to secure the battalion's perimeter while A and D Companies moved out on October 17. He recalls those days and moments leading up to the action:

15 October 67: Things were getting more tense. We had seen a lot of VC signs and there were numerous small contacts, claymorings, etc. that I have omitted. Although tense, in general the troops felt we could handle whatever we ran into (my opinion) since the battalion had been doing well. On this day Bravo and Recon S & D's [search and destroy operations] south from the NDP. I'm fairly certain recon was in the lead (that was their normal place).

We discovered a kind of trail that was really spooky. It was in solid jungle and consisted of broken saplings to your left and right as you walked down it. Believe it was used by VC to move at night. If you were not directly between the broken small trees you would totally miss it. We followed this trail for several hundred yards the way porcupines make love (carefully) and came to a larger, more permanent, trail. Recon cloverleafed the area and found a VC rucksack or pack sitting against a tree. We set up a hasty ambush and pretty soon two or three VC appeared walking north. Recon opened up and hit at least one but the others dragged him off and out of sight. I'm fairly certain Lt. Erwin has the VC's sandals, as the guy was literally shot out of them and they were quite bloody. I've still got the canteen he dropped. Our patrol route called for us to break east at this point, which is what we did rather than proceeding further south—perhaps avoiding the fate of Delta and Alpha two days later. There was some talk of us continuing south; but since we were only a "single company force," battalion opted against it. The area obviously had seen a lot of use by the VC, but so had all the other areas we'd been in. Delta and Alpha were in the NDP working in positions and doing local patrolling. Believe a Delta patrol took some VC under fire crossing an open area to our northwest.

16 October 67: Search and Destroy. Delta lead, Bravo trail.

Route further to the east. This was done to avoid going south on a 180-degree track since there were limited ways out of the NDP. In some ways what happened this day was almost a preview of the following day. We had a Province Reconnaissance Unit (PRU), Vietnamese irregulars, led by a U.S. Army captain, Bernard Jones. He seemed a solid soldier. I remember talking to him, and he telling me what a fine group he had. They all looked out for one another. He talked of his hopes to earn an award for valor, which he held in high esteem, but didn't see much chance of it since he had what most considered a rag-tag outfit. Anyway, he and his group were on the point with Delta and picking up all kinds of signs. We were calling in marking/spotting artillery and mortar rounds. I'm certain our 81s were fully up during this period. There was a series of fairly violent, but brief, contacts. The captain and PRU soldiers moved forward to scout things out. Al Welch told me later in the day that as the captain started forward he turned to Al and said, "Well it looks like the sons-a-bitches are try'n to kill us again." They did. He took a round through the head shortly thereafter, as all hell broke loose.

Bravo tightened up on Delta's trail platoon and we kept our connecting file so as not to lose contact. We were laying low on the ground, only getting up to move as Delta's rear positions changed, and holding fire listening to the snaps of bullets overhead. We were in a fairly oval perimeter linked to Delta. One of my platoon leaders, a fine and courageous black Lt., radioed that he saw/sensed movement to our right or southern flank. We got the word out to hold fire until we actually saw something. All of a sudden a group of twelve to fifteen VC materialized moving toward us. I'm talking twenty to twenty-five yards max. Fleeting glimpses through the trees. We opened fire and shot them up pretty good but remained in position as Delta was still engaged to our front but only lightly. I remember one VC throwing a grenade that hit a tree and bounced back toward them.

They stopped firing and disappeared in the jungle. We stopped firing on them as there were no real targets, and I believe to this day that they were trying to feel their way around it, so it may have been better to let them commit and key on them when they presented a moving image through the foliage.

Shortly after this, we got the word to begin moving back to the NDP as air and artillery (I also fired the company 81s) pounded the area. We reversed direction. My trail platoon became battalion point and Delta following us. I remember seeing the PRUs carrying their captain's body, wrapped in a poncho and slung under a pole. They were crossing the stream that ran down "the draw" and joined the Ông Thanh. Their group left the NDP that evening and I remember them telling anyone that wanted to listen that there were "beaucoup" VC out there. I think it was Lieutenant Bobby Fortenberry who said to me, "Damn, sir, those guys are scared shitless and glad to be leaving. They say there's a shit-load of VC all over the place." That evening orders were issued to go back into the area of contact and proceed further south. Colonel Allen was adamant about getting into the area south of the NDP, only much deeper than before. Tension was very high in the NDP that night and I, to be quite honest, was glad to have drawn the straw to secure the NDP.

It may very well be that the totally "bad vibes" I had about the next day's operation block any memories of the orders meeting that night—I don't think so—but it is possible. I do know that it was Colonel Allen's intent to actively press into whatever was found the next day. We all knew they were there—somewhere. "The beast was out there, and the beast was hungry."

The Battle Begins

And so the dagger that probed into "the belly of the beast," the sixty-five-man A Company, moved forward. At 0956 the point reported sighting a well-traveled trail running northwest to southeast with fresh sandal prints and freshly cut trees close by. Lieutenant Colonel George L. MacGarrigle, the eminent army historian and a West Point classmate of Terry Allen, recounts the action in his book, *Taking the Offensive:*

> At that time most of Allen's men were in moderate jungle that did not form a complete canopy. The vegetation did not obstruct movement by foot, but it obscured ground visibility beyond fifteen to twenty meters. At a greater distance to the flanks and to the south, where the lead unit of Company A was moving, the jungle was more dense, with some trees as high as forty meters.
>
> Almost immediately, the men of the 1st Platoon, scouting west of the trail, sighted a Viet Cong soldier. Moments later a group of enemy troops appeared on the trail just ahead. The commander of Company A, Capt. James D. George, told the patrol to form a hasty ambush, but by the time his men were in position the enemy had disappeared and all was quiet.
>
> As they lay silent on the jungle floor, the 1st Platoon leader heard movement in the trees, the clicking of rifle bolts, and the rattle of metal. George told him to reinforce the ambush patrol at once. Moving out, the rest of the men of the platoon immediately ran into sniper fire. They pressed on until a

machine-gun burst from a well-camouflaged bunker killed one man and wounded two others. Then heavy fire poured into both flanks and the platoon was pinned down.

The next platoon in the column, the 2nd, tried to reinforce but was brought up short by the same hidden machine-gun nest. As the bullets flew, the radio went dead and the company commander could no longer communicate with either platoon.

Captain George had few options. His trail unit, the 3rd Platoon, had only eleven men, and since he needed to maintain a link with Company D, George decided to move his own command group forward to join his beleaguered platoons. Maneuvering to a position some fifteen meters in front of the enemy bunker, he tossed in a flurry of grenades and temporarily silenced the troublesome machine gun.

But the enemy was still in the fight. Perhaps an alert Viet Cong soldier spotted the antennas on the radios carried by members of George's command group and realized the importance of what he had found. Whatever the case, one soldier dashed forward with a claymore-type mine and set off the explosive before the Americans could cut him down. The blast killed a radio operator and wounded Captain George and most of the rest of the command group.

As Company A battled on, Company D began drawing sniper fire from trees west of its position. The shooters wounded two men before return fire silenced them. Colonel Allen directed his command group to remain in place beside a prominent anthill and told the Company D commander, 1st Lt. Albert C. Welch, to form a two-platoon perimeter around the command group. Welch's leading platoon, the 3rd, was to stay in contact with Company A's rear. Since he needed to call in artillery and air strikes, Allen radioed George to break contact and withdraw into Company D's perimeter, the same kind of maneuver the battalion had conducted successfully the day before.

Captain George, blind and deaf from the explosion of the claymore, gave the order to pull back. But all three of his platoons were under heavy fire, and all three platoon leaders were wounded. With his officers out of action, George radioed Allen that he was placing his senior noncommissioned officer, M. Sgt. José B. Valdez, in command of the company.

Company A's plight was serious. The fight had unfolded so quickly, and it was so difficult to see through the underbrush, that few survivors would remember seeing the enemy. Despite heavy return fire by the Americans, enemy fire continued undiminished. And with most of the company's officers wounded early in the action, communication within the unit broke down almost immediately.

The blade of the dagger, which had been Company A, 2-28 Infantry, had been broken off by the massive firepower that had erupted from the west, and Company A had ceased to exist as a fighting force. The men in D Company, the hand holding that dagger, were now fully engaged with enemy soldiers positioned to the southeast, south, west, and in the trees overhead. Two platoons protected the battalion command group and established a collection point for the wounded. One platoon moved forward toward the trail units of A Company, which by then were badly hurt, and provided covering fire during the evacuation of the wounded as well as weapons and ammunition.

D Company's command group positioned and encouraged each platoon, then it moved forward into A Company so that it could locate the enemy, evacuate wounded, and get the artillery forward observer team far enough ahead of the company that it could control counter fires. Enemy fire hit key men early. The battalion's sergeant major, S2, and a radio operator were all killed. D Company's company commander, first sergeant, forward observer, radio operators, senior medics, two platoon leaders, and all three platoon sergeants quickly received wounds or were killed. Enemy fire hit all of D Company commander's radios and made them inoperable. Thus as the company's leaders moved around the perimeter, communications within the company were by direct voice. The only way that Lieutenant Welch of D Company could communicate with Colonel Allen was to crawl to the battalion commander's position and speak directly with him, which Welch did often. Although ordered to withdraw into Delta Company's protective perimeter, which resembled a hand that had been holding the dagger but was now curled into a fist, most of the ambulatory men who remained in Company A withdrew from the withering enemy fire, moving with First Sergeant Valdez and the incapacitated Captain George. This withdrawal complicated D Company's defensive efforts because many of the wounded from A Company moved to the west of D Company's position, thereby not only missing a possible refuge with D Company, but also screening and limiting the fires that D Company had been directing toward the enemy to the west.

Tom Hinger describes his situation in A Company:

We were stopped and had out cloverleafs. I was facing the right flank, and both Joe Costello and I saw movement about forty feet up in one of the trees just beyond where our cloverleafs should be. It looked like someone was trying to reposition himself to remain out of sight to the men below him. Within the next few seconds, the sound of metallic clicks could be heard, and then the first firing broke out. I remember Joe firing his M79 into the tree where we had seen the movement.

Seconds later I heard someone up toward the point call for

a medic, and that would be the last I would see of Joe and my platoon until late in the afternoon. The volume of fire was so heavy that you could almost taste the cordite, and the sounds of claymores and a heavy machine gun rose above the noise of the rifles.

I made my way to the front of the 1st platoon and treated the wounded as I found them. I have no idea of the time frame, but while I was treating a man shot in the knee, I heard someone give the order to pull back. Two men (Olin Hargrove and Paul Fitzgerald) stayed with me and fired while I completed what I could for the man who'd been hit in the knee. We soon found out that we were alone and our position was in immediate danger of being overrun, so we began to fight our way back. With only three of us, it was not possible to carry the wounded man, so I supported him so he could hobble on his good leg as we fought our way back.

By pure dumb luck we stumbled into the temporary perimeter of about twenty-five or so men. The group included first platoon men and the company command group. Neither Hargrove nor Fitzgerald were wounded at that time, and as I recall they were sent to the left flank of the position. I never saw either of them again. Again, I have no idea of the time frame that had transpired. Several of the men were wounded, so I was trying to treat as many as I could. Sometime during this period I swapped weapons with the wounded Alpha FO, and took his .45 and ammo. I have no idea how long we remained in this area, or of any tactical decisions being made during this time. Captain George was one of the wounded, and I think his hearing was damaged. First Sgt. Valdez was not wounded and was maintaining control of our situation as best as he could. The sounds of the battle were deafening, and most of the men in our group were wounded.

Joe Costello describes what he remembers:

Our second platoon followed the first. I was on the right side of the column. During one of our stops, there was word of an enemy sighting ahead of us. Shortly after, there were a few shots fired. Myself and everyone near me were in the prone position facing out trying to see through the dense jungle. There was some firing and those of us near anthills scrambled behind them. Doc Hinger and I were studying the right flank when Doc pointed out some treetop movement 50–60 yards out. I dropped a 79 round in the treetop, and the movement stopped. Shortly after, heavy firing started. Most of it was enemy fire on our column. As we fired back, people started yelling, "Hold your fire! Some of our guys are out there." It quickly become clear that we were taking heavy casualties and fire superiority was essential to protect the unit.

There was a sudden lull in firing and guys were yelling for medics, God, and Mom, everywhere. Doc and I were split up at this point. I remember trying to help a guy who was shot in the front, below the belt. He was on his back arching upward in pain and shock. His intestines were hanging out. I remember having a flashback to training where they warned not to push them back in and to use the wounded soldier's own bandage to cover it. I felt helpless putting a bandage on this terrible wound and telling him he is okay when I knew he would die. As I kneeled over him (don't remember his name), there was an explosion behind me and I felt a sensation in my back.

Now came a second heavy volume of fire. It was so intense you couldn't make out individual rounds and blasts. It was one big racket of explosions and small-arms fire. After firing my remaining ammo, I laid [sic] as flat as I could on the ground, prayed briefly, and tried to collect myself. As I lay with my head to the side, I saw rounds hitting the ground, walking right past my head. I believe they were heavy machine gun rounds based on their relatively slow, deliberate pace. I was scared like never before.

At this time, orders were given to move back to the NDP. We started going back. Sporadic small arms fire continued and then dropped off. After going 100–200 yards back, someone mentioned guys up front needed help to get out. Another guy (unknown) and myself reversed and went back out, passing many retreating, wounded, and stunned soldiers on the way. On the way back we passed an anthill where Col. Allen, his Sgt. Major, and their radioman were. The Sgt. Major saw we were going back and recognized I only had a .45 in my possession, and he gave me his M-16 and bandolier of ammo clips. They all were killed, apparently, shortly after our encounter. Further out, the firing intensified for a third time. I found several dead Americans and myself among a group of about 8 men, all wounded. At one point, I noticed ants all over my arms biting the hell out of me, yet I couldn't feel it. My back was soaking wet with what I thought was sweat, and it turned out to be from blood. I had caught a fragment from the earlier explosion. My body was numb with adrenaline.

Captain Jim Kasik, then with B Company in the NDP, recalls what happened:

About mid-morning we (in the NDP) began to hear firing from the south. I remember Jim George and Colonel Allen over the radio, Alpha 6 [George] was receiving fire from his front and was deploying people to "develop the situation." I still have strange feelings about this because I thought at the time that "it sounds like we're not going to pull back this time but rather take it to them."

There was a lot of maneuvering, a lot of small-arms fire heard over the net before Jim George was hit; in fact, he was describing it: "I can see them placing claymores, there's a lot of them, etc., etc." When he was finally hit, he was hit hard, and there's not much memory left there.

Somewhat later—30 minutes—the sound of firing really got intense and Alpha 6 was reporting taking fire from VC on the ground and in the trees as well as Chicom [Chinese communist] claymores being detonated against them at close range. A short time later, there was a report that the S2 had been wounded in the back or shoulder and was being attended to. Colonel Allen radioed later that he was okay, his wound apparently not critical. The command group seemed to be functioning normally. Jim George was very shaken and reported a lot of wounded, including himself, and that he was not in contact with all his elements. To my recollection Colonel Allen was still in control when Alpha began pulling back. They obviously were not able to make an orderly withdrawal. Shortly thereafter, Delta 6, Lt. Welch, reported fire from the trees and his flanks.

Clark Welch, commander of Delta Company, was highly agitated. He found himself in a situation that he had predicted the night before and that he had encountered the day before. It was clear to him at this time, perhaps 10:30 in the morning and thirty minutes into the battle, that the VC were accomplishing today what they had tried to do the previous day: hug the U.S. force so closely that the effectiveness of air strikes and artillery would be nullified. Supporting fire—air and artillery—was like striking the enemy with a sledgehammer. The hornets that Alpha Company had stirred up while acting as the point of a dagger were now swarming out of the hive with enormous fury, massing all around the closed fist of Delta's perimeter, and rendering those sledgehammer blows as lethal to the friendlies as they were to the foe. By now the battalion was decisively engaged.

Allen, who miraculously was still not yet wounded, was on the radio desperately describing the terrible situation and requesting support from any available helicopters and the air force. His battalion command group maintained its position by the anthill while popping colored smoke grenades, treating the wounded, and attempting to repair their radios, and with the dwindling number of survivors in the two-company force continuing to shoot when the enemy appeared. The initial enemy fire had hurt A Company so badly that it could no longer deliver effective fire or maneuver. D Company's lead platoon had by then moved forward into A Company while the company's two trail platoons had stretched out their lines to both cover and assist A Company and protect the battalion command group. All three D Company platoons were firing, but they could no longer maneuver. Very early on, Lieutenant Welch, the D Company commander, had taken a hit in his chest, but his wound was quickly treated by the company's senior medic. With the forward observer team, Welch moved forward far enough to set up an artillery fire plan. Both 105mm and 155mm artillery, but no mortars, quickly responded. He then returned to the company perimeter, moving among the soldiers, firing his own weapons, and talking often with Allen.

Welch could move through the jungle effortlessly. His slim, wiry, six-foot-two-inch frame, legs longer than his torso, let him move like a cheetah. His mind worked like a trap, analytical, fast, and propelled his actions. Before he became the first commander of Delta Company, Welch had led the battalion reconnaissance platoon and later had commanded A Company. When D Company had been established, he and First Sergeant Clarence "Bud" Barrow had been the first two men assigned to the new company. Together they had organized, trained, and then successfully fought their new rifle company. Both men were very close with all their soldiers. Welch and Barrow knew each man's strengths, problems, families, friends, and girlfriends back home.

Now they were all in the fight of their lives, and Welch felt completely and personally responsible for each one of his soldiers. He moved quickly from man to man, encouraging them, getting them into position, directing fires with his own fire. He dived on his belly beside Colonel Terry Allen, who was crouched behind a large anthill in the center of the Delta Company perimeter. Allen told him he did not know what Alpha Company's situation was. He told Welch to go forward and assess the situation of A Company. Welch was off in a bound. He moved quickly around the anthill and ran straight south towards his 3rd platoon, which had been maintaining contact with Alpha's rear. As he reached the forward edge of his own troops, he was astounded by what he saw. Many wounded and dead were already on the ground. His men were firing at figures moving through the sparse jungle to his front. Unfortunately, the figures were both VC and the remnants of A Company who were trying to pull back into the Delta perimeter. The VC were using fire and maneuver, and the Alpha survivors were firing and running away from the area of initial contact.

Welch could see that some of his men's fire was hitting the Alpha survivors. He also noted fire coming from the southeast. This meant that the VC had penetrated through the A Company position and were now working down Delta Company's left (east) flank as well as the right (west) flank, where the bulk of the enemy fire was coming from. The official Combat After Action Interview Report describes the Delta Company perimeter:

The 2nd platoon was split with half of its personnel on either side of the battalion command group (anthill) and tied in with the lead platoon (3rd) to the south and the rear platoon (1st) to the north, which completed the perimeter by covering the rear. The initial enemy fire was directed into Alpha, not Delta, but very quickly the enemy fired into Delta and moved north along both flanks. The close jungle made observation very difficult, and few individual enemy targets could be seen by Delta's soldiers. The flank (cloverleaf) security had been called in and the Company Commander [Welch] passed the word throughout the company to hold their fire until targets could be seen.

Few targets appeared except muzzle flashes, and these were taken under fire. As the firing increased, a M-60 machine gun could be distinguished firing into the company [Delta] from the south or southeast, which created some confusion as shouts of "CEASE FIRE" were given. Company A was in this general direction and was to withdraw through Company D. It was feared that the two companies were firing on each other; however, the M-60 did not cease its fire, and some valuable moments were lost before it was realized it was enemy operated.

The friendly and enemy fire was very quickly and violently tearing away any cover and concealment. The enemy fire included rifles, heavy and light machine guns, claymores, hand grenades, and rocket-propelled grenades. Our soldiers were engaging the enemy at ranges of five to thirty meters with rifles, M79 grenade launchers, light machine guns, and by placing claymores on the forward sides of large trees, then firing them while crouched against the trees' backsides. Everyone in D Company was concerned about A Company: trying to fire into the enemy positions that had punished Alpha so badly, trying to drag Alpha's wounded back to care for them, and making sure they were not firing into Alpha's soldiers moving outside the Delta perimeter. Throughout this time enemy fire was increasing, and although no one can relate the time, this could have been the point at which the enemy gained fire superiority. Although a few Company A personnel, mostly wounded, had come into Company D, Company A was still expected. The 3rd platoon was still prepared to let them pass through and did not know that what remained of Company A was some one hundred meters or more to the east.

Welch, now wounded, continued to move among his men and encourage them. Suddenly, a lone enemy soldier ran into the D Company perimeter. He appeared to be crazed-looking and without a weapon. The company's one surviving platoon leader tackled the confused enemy, then after securing him, told Welch that he had always wanted to take a prisoner. Those who heard the platoon leader's remark thought it was funny for a moment, but then they quickly returned to the deadly serious business at hand.

Enemy fire hit First Sergeant Barrow in the legs, keeping him down but not out. Then a machine gunner right next to Barrow was killed. Barrow took the M-60 and continued to fight. Then Welch took another hit, which tore out his left bicep. Again a soldier's quick action and a tight bandage repaired the damage, but Welch could no longer bend his arm.

After a short time, this close, intense battle had resulted in shortages of ammunition, water, bandages, and morphine. The two-company force had gone into battle with as much ammunition and water as it could carry, but even with the addition of the ammunition and water from A Company's position and the redistribution of what D Company had, there was not enough of either. After the issued bandages were used up, the men used their extra socks and then tore up their shirts to make more bandages. The morphine and the medics were quickly exhausted, but the mental and physical shock of the fight kept many of the wounded immune to their terrible pain.

By this time Welch was no longer able to hold a rifle with his straightened arm, so he gave the weapon to a soldier whose M-16 had a bullet hole through the barrel. As Welch moved around D Company's perimeter, he saw an enemy RPD team firing into the wounded and the battalion command group. Welch killed the RPD gunner with his .45, but he realized that many Americans had already been hit.

About this time, an enemy RPG slithered across the ground right into the battalion command group, but it failed to detonate. The sergeant major laughed at this dud, but just a few moments later he was cut down by a RPG that exploded right between him and Welch.

D Company had gone into the jungle that day with ten radios: two in each platoon and four with the company commander. Very quickly, however, the radios and the operators were taken out. Two of the good radios were provided to the D Company forward observer team. Members of the company then dragged the remaining radios or radio parts into the battalion command group in an effort to provide Allen with a good radio. Colonel Allen continued to maintain his position and his composure. Welch and others could hear him reporting the situation and demanding air force and helicopter support, but they didn't know who he was talking to. The air force support eventually arrived, but it came in too far south. They never saw or heard any helicopters.

Allen then told Welch to pull back with A Company, but there were not enough able soldiers available to carry out the dead or wounded in both companies. So Welch didn't pull out. D Company's machine gunners were effective but loud, and they were also special enemy targets. All were hit. Whenever a gunner went down, a brave rifleman would crawl to the now-silent gun and get it back into action. The enemy kept up the fire from three sides (east, south, and west), shooting at anyone who moved. All the leaves, vines, bushes, and low branches that had helped conceal both sides were by now blown away, exposing some enemy fighting positions to the south and some enemy snipers in the trees overhead. Everyone in D Company had been killed or wounded. Those who were able continued to protect themselves as best they could. Consequently soldiers were often holding bandages on themselves or their buddy as they fired. One soldier ran from one side of the perimeter to the other and from there crouched behind a tree before killing two enemy who were trying to get into D Company.

Lieutenant Colonel MacGarrigle's account from his book, *Taking the Offensive*, picks up the action:

> Within Company D's perimeter, the situation was also deteriorating. Allen himself had been wounded, and enemy snipers in trees and machine gunners firing low grazing fire six to twelve inches off the ground were pounding the trapped Company D from three sides. Any American who tried to move instantly became a target. Many of the company's leaders were now casualties, including the company commander, Lieutenant Welch.
>
> Shortly before noon Allen ordered the wounded Welch to pull the unit back to the battalion base and Company B to come forward to cover the withdrawal. Refusing assistance from those men about to leave, the battalion commander elected to remain with those wounded who were immobile
>
> The withdrawal proved costly. As the troops began to move back, enemy fire cut down several of them, and the movement north quickly turned into a disorganized scramble. A platoon sergeant moving to the rear was the last to see Allen alive. With

the help of the sergeant, Allen had begun removing a radio from the back of a dead operator to call in more artillery fire. Moments later a short burst of machine-gun fire grazed Allen's helmet, knocking him down. Allen told the sergeant to forget the artillery and get his people "the hell out of there." Shortly after leaving, the sergeant looked back and saw either an RPG round or a claymore mine explode near Allen, followed quickly by a burst of machine-gun fire, which killed him.

While members of D Company were trying to withdraw, a wounded Lieutenant Harold Durham, Welch's forward observer, shouted to Welch that he had ordered artillery fire very close on both the south and west sides of their position, as planned earlier. The requested mortar fire never came, but Durham's 105mm and 155mm fire was very close and very effective. The artillery team paid dearly for this life-saving fire support, as Durham remained forward where Welch had placed the team. Durham smiled at Welch, and then he turned back to his team and continued his calls for fire. Welch remembers seeing the brave artillery lieutenant pressing the "press-to-talk" switch of his radio handset with the stub of his wrist because his hand had been blown off. (Durham was awarded the Medal of Honor posthumously for his actions that day.)

At that point in the battle, Welch was sitting against a tree. He could see artillery rounds actually coming through the tops of the trees, and explosions all around. He was sticky with blood, and it seemed that all he wanted to do was go to sleep. Blood loss had sapped his strength. Once more Welch crawled part of the way around the perimeter, but he found few fit surviving soldiers. At the artillery forward observer's position, Welch saw that Lieutenant Durham had been hit again and killed, but his sergeant was keeping up the fire. Welch moved back toward the battalion command group, where, as best he could tell, only Colonel Allen was still alive. Allen was still in position and still on the radio, talking in a voice that was determined, calm, and resolute. As Welch approached him, Allen dropped the radio handset, and Welch thought he could see where a bullet had hit the colonel's helmet near the rank insignia. Colonel Terry Allen died; still in position and still on the radio.

Welch moved closer to Allen, but he was now sure the battalion commander was dead. Then Welch saw the first sergeant and crawled toward him, but the company commander covered only a few meters before he lost consciousness. Some time later, in a haze of blood and pain, he could feel hard jerks on his combat harness. He opened his eyes and saw First Sergeant Barrow, his first sergeant, sitting across from him, some twenty feet away. Barrow was also propped up against a tree, facing Welch. Welch could see the dark stains of blood on Barrow's jungle fatigues. Barrow cradled an M-60 machine gun in his lap, and Welch could see Barrow turning the gun in his direction. "My God," thought Welch, "he's getting ready to shoot me." As the M-60 began to fire at Welch, he lapsed into unconsciousness. He would not regain consciousness until he found himself in a hospital bed in the evacuation hospital at Long Binh. He had been wounded five times.

Welch next encountered Barrow in a hospital in Tokyo. Welch thought Barrow had been killed. After they exchanged greetings, Welch asked Barrow why he had shot at him. Barrow replied, "There was a VC standing behind you trying to pull you up by your suspenders. The suspenders pulled up around your neck as you stayed on the ground, and I chopped the VC in half with the M-60."

According to the Combat After Action Report,

Company D's commander (Welch) and First Sergeant (Barrow) were by this time wounded and the Artillery FO (Durham) and 1st Platoon Leader were dead. The ranks of the

1st and 2nd Platoons, although suffering many casualties, were still holding when the order to withdraw was passed. The 3rd platoon had fewer casualties to this point, however, withdrawing through the command group area was most difficult and casualties mounted. No one could stand and survive. The withdrawal was a slow and exhausting process as the survivors and less severely wounded crawled a few inches, fired, and crawled a few inches further, helping whoever [sic] they could. There were not enough able-bodied personnel left to assist all the wounded out and several remained, to include the First Sergeant, who killed two VC that ventured into the perimeter the wounded had managed to scratch out.

Joe Costello, the A Company grenadier, who was back near D Company's perimeter recalls what happened next.

We formed a makeshift perimeter in preparation for the enemy, should they try to overrun us. Private Edward Grider gave me the battalion frequency numbers and I used a discarded field radio to try to make radio contact for help. I was answered immediately by a general in a chopper who dropped us some medical supplies, had us mark our position with green smoke, and gave me some great tips on assisting the wounded; i.e. cigarette pack cellophane on Grider's sucking chest wounds. Sporadic fire from the underbrush killed a few more of us, and then there was silence.

The general assured us help was on the way. He was a Godsend. It was then, when it looked like we might live, that I remember becoming emotional. So many good American men had died. I remember becoming upset when I realized they wanted to evacuate Colonel Allen's body while there were still some live, wounded American soldiers on the ground.

Lieutenant Colonel MacGarrigle reported on this unique circumstance.

> [A] wounded grenadier from Company A, Pfc. Joseph J. Costello, managed to locate a radio near Allen's last position and about 1330 sent a message over the battalion command net: "This is Costello, please help, we need help." Overhead, General Coleman heard his call and told him to mark his position with a smoke grenade.
>
> Seeing the smoke rise from the trees, Coleman told Costello that help would soon arrive. Instructing those stations on the battalion command net to switch to an alternate frequency so he and Colonel Newman could remain in continuous contact with Costello, Coleman planned to vector Newman's relief to Costello's position. Meanwhile, he encouraged Costello to set up a perimeter defense with the surviving troops and gave him advice for treating the wounded. When the enemy fire around Costello's position finally ended at 1430, a helicopter dropped bags of smoke grenades and medical supplies.

Joe Costello's resourceful and fortuitous action in using a discarded radio to try to make contact may have saved many lives. For some time before Private Costello made his call for help, both Colonel Newman and General Coleman were unable to speak to anyone on the ground at the battle site, and they were fearful that there might be no survivors. Costello's radio call enabled them to pinpoint the unit's location and direct the evacuation efforts. I distinctly recall the excitement in General Coleman's voice as he spoke on the radio to Private Costello. Coleman's voice was compassionate and instructive. We could not hear Costello's voice since he was on the ground and out of range, but General Coleman in the helicopter was coming through loud and clear. With the help of Joe

Costello, General Coleman now had a positive link with the ground. Lieutenant Colonel MacGarrigle continues his account of the battle:

> Meanwhile, Colonel Newman obtained helicopters to evacuate the casualties and to bring Allen's Company C from CAISSON V. Newman planned to lead Company C and the battalion's reconnaissance platoon to Company D's former position while Company B kept a corridor open to the base. Expecting to find many wounded, he instructed the battalion surgeon and medical aid men, augmented from division by another physician and other aid men, to accompany him. Unsure as to where the wounded were, he intended to advance without artillery support for fear of hitting them.

Lieutenant Bill Erwin, the recon platoon leader, took part in the evacuation. According to him,

> Colonel Newman and Major Holleder had landed in the NDP for an update. I had returned to the NDP by that time and was in the TOC when they arrived. I had put my platoon in defensive positions on the perimeter and was told to report to the TOC to get an update when they arrived. Colonel Newman decided that he wanted to go to the south edge of the perimeter and he needed a radio. I think it was Major Sloan who told me to carry a radio for Colonel Newman and go with [him] and Major Holleder. Anyway, I was suddenly a 2nd Lieutenant RTO, but I knew all the call signs, etc., and so maybe it made sense. We were on the edge of the perimeter and Major Holleder was really pumped. He kept saying, "We have got to get in there and help them," and, "They are in trouble and need help." Colonel Newman kept telling him to basically take it easy until he could

assess the situation. We were there for some time and then a few troops from A and D Companies started coming back to the NDP. Some had no weapons and [had] lost steel pots, etc.

One of them was the A Company 1st Sergeant José Valdez. He looked me in the eye and said, "It's a massacre, sir." We all realized that the battalion was in a lot worse shape than we imagined, and then Colonel Newman decided that he would send Recon in to find out what was going on. I told him that he was going to have to get someone else to carry his radio because I was the Recon platoon leader. I think he was surprised, but I did not have any rank on the collar. There was no reason for him to know that I was a lieutenant. Anyway, he decided to carry his own radio, and Holleder had convinced him that he should go in also. Colonel Newman told Holleder to wait for Recon, but he didn't. I do not think he went a hundred yards before he took a full burst. One of my troops helped put his body in the OH 13 that landed and brought him back to the NDP. A side bar to all of this: The OH 13 was flown by a Warrant Officer Howard Bennett. He and I sat beside each other a few months later as we flew to Hawaii to meet our wives. Unfortunately, he was killed during Tet.

Recon went in. We found Lieutenant Colonel Allen, Sergeant Major Dowling, and the rest of the command group next to and around the anthill. Captain Blackwell's body was a few feet away on a jungle litter. He had been wounded earlier in the chest. Allen reported on the radio that he, the SGM, the S2 and one of the RTOs had been hit. Blackwell had taken another bullet in the forehead. There is no doubt that he was helpless on the litter when he was shot. I saw at least one other soldier who suffered a similar fate. He stood out because he had those red ants crawling all over his body. He had been stripped almost naked in order for our people to treat his wounds, but he was killed like Blackwell.

I remember very clearly seeing one NVA soldier dead behind a Chicom light machine gun (the drum-fed MG). I counted nine dead U.S. immediately in front of the gun. He may have taken out more, but he certainly got nine. Our guys were facing the gun and were clearly trying to take it out. That one NVA killed a lot of our guys before he was killed.

Aftermath

Captain Jim Kasik, with B Company in the NDP, recounts their efforts to come to the aid of men in A and D Companies:

After stripping out [personnel from] the listening post and the combat outpost, B Company consisted of 45–55 men with 5 or 6 PRC 25s. We moved south on the west side. About one hundred yards out of the NDP, I met Jim George, who was being helped back. He was walking but not in good shape. I stopped and asked him what I could do for him. He said, "Help get my people out of there." He had been hit with claymore pellets below the eye. My troops knew this was a bad deal and were arming themselves to the teeth with weapons they got from the small bands of soldiers making their way north to the NDP.

Three quarters of the way down the draw, we came upon a black soldier who must have weighed 110 pounds carrying a 180-pound white soldier with a head wound. The black soldier had been hit in the ankle. We told him it would be easier going in open area to the west, but he replied that there may be VC over there. I told him we had a small security element on that side. He picked up his burden and headed north. There was no lack of bravery or sacrifice on that day.

As I got to the southern end of the draw, I was told to hold there, set up a perimeter and provide cover for what troops were still coming back. An H-13 had landed and was sitting at idle. When I got to it, my 3rd platoon sergeant and a couple of soldiers were putting a body into the passenger side. I had no idea who it was. He was dead and covered with mud. I said, "Who the hell is this?" The platoon sergeant responded that the major [Holleder] had landed there as they were arriving and told them to go running into the jungle with him. "We told him there were VC out there—lots of them," said the sergeant. "But he just said, 'Come on.' He got about thirty yards, and they nailed him," he said.

I think I found out it was Don Holleder when Colonel Newman arrived and asked if he'd been in the area. In any case it was the Brigade S3 who had made a very brave attempt to help. After Colonel Newman arrived, I spread my platoons even thinner and began popping smoke like crazy to mark our positions. The firing had all but ceased by now with only an occasional round coming out of the jungle to our south. I was very concerned that the VC might come up and threaten the NDP as my force was not of sufficient size to stop whatever had chewed up Alpha and Delta. At around 1430 Captain Tom Reese with his C Company arrived. We moved south into the contact area.

I remember putting a machine gun crew in position; several dead from the battalion lay nearby. We found the S2's body on a stretcher, his wounds neatly dressed, except for the hole between his eyes. 15–20 yards south was the anthill behind which were Colonel Allen, Sergeant Major Dowling, and the radio operators, all dead. As I said earlier SGM Dowling had thrown his body over Colonel Allen's as though to shield it. From the way they were lying, it appeared they had been facing to the east. The majority of the dead and wounded were further south and slightly west; others were widely scattered.

In the meantime, Colonel Newman was trying to reestablish control and evacuate survivors. According to him,

Terry Allen was already dead when I reached the 2-28 forward assembly area and took control of the battalion. There were several trails leading from the forward assembly area to the battle site. My plan was very simple: push down to the site of the battle with the relief force; rally the 2-28 troops still in the area; reorganize; establish a secure perimeter as near the battle area as possible; set about regaining control, recovering all wounded and dead, policing the battlefield; and preparing for further operations. All orders were oral and fragmentary. There was no time or place for any formal planning, assessment of the situation, detailed estimates, or anything of the sort. Everything was extemporized on the spot with whatever resources were at hand until about mid-afternoon—by which time, we had regained control in the battle area, located a small clearing in the canopy, and enlarged it to begin evacuating the wounded.

Initially we could only get H-13s into the small clearing. The pilots were truly magnificent. To reduce some weight, the armored seats were jettisoned and every effort made to improve lift. At first this was almost a vertical hover in and out. There was some risk all afternoon from sporadic enemy ground fire at the evacuation ships; fortunately the jungle canopy offered protection.

Also as soon as we regained control and established a perimeter encompassing all the battlefield area, I asked for all the artillery and air support I could get. The ADC [assistant division commander] Brigadier General Coleman had taken over as 1st Brigade Commander after I assumed command of the 2-28th. He did a super job of providing air and artillery support and encouragement and suggestions from his airborne CP. I told him I wanted to box in the relief position to ensure that the enemy could not maneuver to counterattack while we were evacuating the wounded, collecting the dead, and policing the battlefield. We brought the artillery concentrations in as close to our positions as possible, and he placed air strikes out to the flanks to inhibit any enemy reinforcements or setting up of mortars to hamper us in the evacuation clearing.

As darkness approached I recognized that I had the surviving elements of the 2-28 and the relief units spread out much more than was wise. I knew that Terry had selected his NDP position well and had left his exec to plan a defensive position. Therefore I decided to withdraw from the battlefield site and helicopter evacuation clearing to the NDP. In anticipation I placed security elements on either flank in the route from the helicopter clearing to the NDP. We stayed at the evacuation clearing until I was satisfied that all the wounded and dead had been recovered and the battlefield policed to the extent possible.

By this time night had arrived, and I had to make a decision, which I found very difficult. We had given priority to evacuation of wounded, and there were still a considerable number of dead when it became necessary to cease helicopter operations because of the hazardous nature of the clearing and the lack of light. I realized that transporting the dead by litter back to the NDP was not feasible considering the number to be evacuated, the exhaustion of the troops, and the problems this might cause if necessary to fight en route to the NDP. Therefore, I decided to group the dead in a concentrated area at the edge of the helicopter evacuation clearing and to leave them there for recovery the next day.

I conveyed this decision to Brigadier General Coleman who agreed with me, even though it violated Big Red One policy of never leaving a dead comrade on the battlefield. I asked him to arrange artillery concentrations to protect the dead and also to protect our rear as we began our retrograde movement to the NDP. This maneuver went off with no difficulty. We had the benefit of some moonlight through the canopy as we broke into the clearing leading to the NDP. On reaching the NDP I reviewed the organization of the perimeter, visited several key positions to be sure everyone was alert, and that control had been restored satisfactorily, and that the 2-28 was again a functioning organization. I considered this last point to be all-important. I pointed out to the 2-28 staff and commanders that the battle was over, that they were still capable of fighting, and that I expected everyone to pull together and get on from there. As you know and as the record will show, they did so with honor. The 2-28th may have lost a battle, but they were not destroyed on the battlefield.

I spent most of the night talking to division, reviewing the situation and planning for the next day's operations. I insisted that the 2-28th under its own XO and staff go into the battlefield area the next day and recover its own dead and finish the job of policing the battlefield. They did so in a methodical and professional manner. After this was accomplished, I recommended and division approved that the 2-28th be pulled out of action, rested, refitted, casualties replaced, and placed back into operations under a new commander as soon as possible.

Fire Support: Doctrine and Practice

In his 1978 book, *Summons of the Trumpet,* Lieutenant General David Richard Palmer describes in some detail the results of tactical changes in the use of fire and maneuver in Vietnam that had application, or perhaps misapplication, in the Battle of Ông Thanh. In his chapter, "The Phalanx of Fire," General Palmer explains how firepower had replaced maneuver in the army's tactical thinking as the way to dominate the enemy. This approach to infantry tactics influenced the actions of the 2-28 Infantry at Ông Thanh. The 1st Infantry Division's policy on the role that firepower played in infantry tactics is contained in *Fundamentals of Infantry*, particularly pages 33–35, which is reproduced in Appendix 2. At one point in this manual in the section dealing with "Actions upon Contact," commanders at all echelons are told:

> Once the enemy position is established, all commanders must strain their resources to bring available fires to bear on the enemy. Each commander from company on up must be capable of employing air and artillery, practiced in utilizing the channels of communications for each, and quick to initiate action to bring each into play.

Lieutenant Colonel Terry Allen Jr. was well aware of these policies. He had been a battalion S3 for several months in Vietnam prior to becoming a battalion commander. Unknown to most, he was also a school-trained air/ground operations officer. He had graduated from the air/ground school at Hurlburt Field in Florida and was very familiar with the use of tactical air support. On a number of occasions while I was the Battalion S3, he insisted on wargaming the use of artillery fire and tactical air strikes simultaneously. During these sessions he was adamantly opposed to ever "check-firing" artillery; that is stopping artillery fires while putting in air strikes. His SOP, which he hammered into my head, was NEVER to check-fire artillery for the less accurate air strikes. He said, "Put air strikes whenever you can but do not interfere with the artillery gun/target line and do not check-fire artillery."

In his official history of the army's combat operations in Vietnam in 1966–67, Lieutenant Colonel George MacGarrigle, reports the following:

The use—or possibly misuse—of air strikes influenced how the battle would play out. Earlier that morning F-100s and B-57 Canberras had flown preplanned air strikes against known and suspected enemy base camps within the 1st Brigade's sector, but none were in direct support of Allen's advance. The last was completed at 1012, only minutes before Company A ran into the enemy and Colonel Newman, flying overhead at 1020, called for close air support for Allen's battalion. Even so, apparently no planes were immediately available to answer Newman's request. Thirty minutes would pass before A-37 Dragonflies on strip alert at Bien Hoa Air Base, nearly sixty kilometers from the fight, could arrive. Another ten minutes would elapse before a forward air controller could brief the pilots on the target. By then, about 1100, only sporadic fire threatened Allen's men.

Believing that the Viet Cong were withdrawing south, Newman directed the air strikes to two hundred meters south of the southernmost point where he had seen smoke, which Company A had used to mark its position. Before the first of what would eventually total sixteen strikes went in, Newman agreed to halt the supporting artillery fire coming from CAISSON III-S and CAISSON V; during the partial check-fire only the two artillery batteries at LORRAINE III continued to fire, striking an area west of Company A's initial contact. According to Colonel Allen's operations officer, Maj. John F. Sloan, the check-fire was against Allen's wishes, but he deferred to the judgment of the brigade commander.

The target that Colonel Newman had indicated was in

dense jungle and the forward air controller who was to vector in the fighter-bombers had no direct communication with the troops on the ground. For these reasons, the air controller had the attacking aircraft make several passes over the designated target to ensure that the pilots knew exactly where to deliver their bombs. After obtaining final clearance, the first of two aircraft attacked at 1110. The second began its run ten minutes later, at which time Allen informed Newman that all enemy fire had ceased.

The duration of the check-fire was difficult to reconstruct. Conflicting reports ranged from fifteen to forty-five minutes. Whatever its length, the enemy, far from withdrawing, used the respite to redeploy into a horseshoe with troops west, south, and east of Company D.

....Colonel Newman later recalled that as soon as the new enemy attack began at 1135, Allen contacted him by radio, saying, "Sir, I can use my artillery now." Newman halted all further air strikes and ordered the artillery to resume firing. Newman later noted that the switch took about two minutes, but explained "it was never made known to me that he, Allen, was experiencing difficulty with artillery fire support."

Captain Fred Gantzler, commanding a 105mm artillery battery of six howitzer tubes, recalls the role his unit played in the battle:

My battery, B Battery, 6th Howitzer Battalion, 15th Field Artillery (CAISSON III N), was either attached or OpCon to the 2nd Battalion, 33rd F[ield]A[rtillery]. We did that kind of thing often in the 1st Infantry Division. I don't recall the name of the firebase we were in, but we were secured by the 2-2nd Infantry. I know that because the 2-2nd was the only mechanized infantry battalion in the 1st Division, and I remember

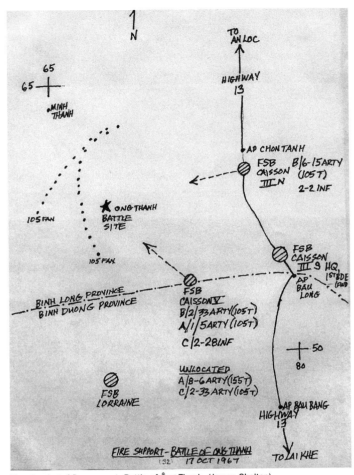

Line drawing of fire support, Battle of Ông Thanh. (James Shelton)

them using their organic VTR ["Vehicle, Tracked, Recovery," a maintenance vehicle] to help move A-22 bags [of ammo] to the howitzer positions.

We were providing marching fires for the 2-28th Infantry that day, as we had for some number of days. When they were hit, we were the only direct support (105mm) battery in range of them. A 155mm also became engaged in the fight, but we were the only unit that could provide close-in fires. I believe that a battery of the 2-33 FA was in the process that morning of being moved to some firebase that would allow them to also support the 2-28th Infantry. I think that they began supporting by early afternoon.

At some point early in the fight, we were called by the 2-33rd Battalion Fire Direction Center and were put on a DivArty-directed check-fire. I recall getting on the radio and asking the nature of the check-fire. I was told that there were some Air Force close air support sorties coming in, and they would not make their runs until the artillery had been turned off. I called the FOs that we were responding to, and told them of the check-fire.

About 2-3 minutes (maybe not that long) after the check-fire, I was called by one of the FOs. He stated that the VC were right on top of our infantry, and he asked for us to resume firing. I called the 2-33rd FDC and asked if I could begin firing again, but was told that the Air Force had not yet completed its runs. I relayed that to the FO. The commander of the infantry company then got on our fire net and demanded that we resume firing, stating that his unit was being overrun and that the Air Force [ordnance] was falling behind the enemy and was basically ineffective. I notified 2-33rd FDC and informed them that I was resuming firing and that they should inform the Air Force. I recall giving them firing data (gun-target azimuth, max ordinate) just in case the AF wanted to continue its runs while I was firing. (I recall that the FAC was on the net and copied my data.) I was again told that the check-fire was not lifted, and that I should wait until the AF had completed dropping its ordnance. I don't recall even responding to that message—I only recall resuming firing and praying that the AF planes would be okay. We were firing over the heads of our own infantry, and the AF was making its runs in a fashion that never got them close to the GT line, unless they banked into it. The data that I gave to the FAC was meant to prevent that.

There was one transmission from someone senior who was airborne above the fighting—a statement that artillery rounds had started landing and that they needed to be stopped until the AF had departed. Either the FO or the company commander that I had spoken to minutes before replied that his men were being killed and that only the artillery was preventing a total massacre. We continued to fire. I believe that the AF missions were quickly modified to provide primarily blocking fire rather than close-in support.

As the fighting quickly made it obvious that this was no small skirmish, I requested resupply of ammo. It began arriving, and the commander of the 2-2nd Infantry on the firebase detailed to his VTR to move the A-22 bags as close as possible to my howitzers. His soldiers also helped us break out the ammo and fuse it. In all, we fired over 6,000 rounds that day.

Captain Gantzler's recollection of what his artillery unit did on October 17 is an example of how command judgment and moral courage was required of all commanders in combat. Personally overriding the check-fire order could have been grounds for court-martial. He chose the high ground. It was a courageous act by a brave artilleryman.

All in all, these accounts of what happened at Ông Thanh that day indicate that fire support never played a decisive role in the battle. Only if Lieutenant Colonel Terry Allen had foreseen how decisive engagement would disadvantage his smaller and wearied force and pulled it back out of the killing zone into which his unit had proceeded, could fire support then have conferred a significant advantage. As it was, tactical air strikes did nothing to solve Allen's immediate dilemma. Even if helicopter gunships had been available that day, they, like tactical air strikes, could only have operated on the periphery of the action. Similarly, the 105mm artillery fire, the savior of the infantry at Ông Thanh, could not get inside the forty- or fifty-meter range at which the two opposing forces found themselves. By all accounts, on October 17, 1967, the Black Lions were out-positioned, out-gunned, out-manned, and out-maneuvered.

The Death of Major Don Holleder

Major Don Holleder was Colonel Newman's operations officer. Playing end at West Point in 1954, he had been an All-American football player. In the 1955 season, Colonel Earl ("Red") Blaik, the Army football coach, had made Holleder the Army quarterback. Although Holleder had not made All-American in 1955 as a quarterback, he was renowned for captaining the Army team in 1955 and defeating Navy in the last game of the 1955 season. I knew who he was because in 1955 I was a linebacker calling defensive signals for the University of Delaware in a preseason scrimmage against Army held in Michie Stadium at West Point. In that scrimmage, I had tackled Don Holleder a number of times. He was not a passer, and he carried the ball himself many times, simply rolling out to his left or right and keeping the ball. He was big and strong, and he dared you to tackle him. It was a punishing task. He gave no quarter. After being tackled, he would bound up off the ground, knocking people aside like a bull with an air of indomitability. He was a ferocious competitor. As I had been the battalion operations officer and he was the brigade operations officer in Vietnam, I observed that he was much the same kind of man. He was confrontational, demanding, forceful, and brave. The accounts of his actions on October 17 are easy to visualize.

The Combat After Action Report provides the following account:

> The brigade S3 (Holleder) had also arrived on the scene and on his own volition organized a small party of three or four beside himself. There was a sergeant, a medic, a PFC with a machete and possibly one other. None of these men knew the major but followed his simple instruction, which was, "Come with me, we are going to help get the wounded out. I want one man to have a machete." The major led, going in almost a dead run through tall grass and knee-deep water. He had out-distanced the rest of the group by 50 meters in the 350 to 400 meters he plunged. The draw narrowed with a tree at the end of the draw. Shots sounding like those of an AK-47 rang out from the tree, mortally wounding the major. He was dead by the time the medic applied the first bandage. The sergeant sprayed the tree; something fell, hidden by bushes. No more shots came from that location.

During the battle, Colonel Newman had airlifted Major Bob Gillard, the battalion executive officer, into the NDP from Lai Khe and told him to assist in casualty evacuation. Gillard remembers working in the NDP and recalls the following:

> Survivors had just told me they thought the VC were still in the area. It was about this time that Don Holleder said he was going to the battle site to see if he could get out any survivors. I advised against it until we could get up a force, but he insisted, and Colonel Newman did not object. He took off out of the NDP with a radio operator and ran across the clearing. This was the last I saw of him.

Medic Tom Hinger was the last man to see Holleder alive. He recounts the action:

> We began to try to evacuate the wounded back out of the jungle as best as we could while maintaining security. During one of these trips back with walking wounded, I ran into a major at the mouth of what we called the Draw. That is where we were turning over the wounded to other men from Recon or Bravo. The major shouted that there were still wounded in there, and we had to get them out. He took the point and was making his way down the Draw when an automatic weapon opened up and cut him down. I made my way to him while Recon provided covering fire, but when I got to him and started to treat him, he died in my arms. That major was Donald Holleder. A few men from Recon helped me to carry his body back to the rear.
>
> Again I have no sense of time, and events tend to become muddled. During this time I think I returned to bring out more wounded, and this may or may not have been when I was hit myself. I have no memory at all of being wounded, or the exact sequence of events during this time. I do remember going back into the battle area later with Lieutenant Tom Grady and other men. I vividly remember that I was completely dehydrated, and all my canteens were empty. I had used most of my water on the wounded, and Lieutenant Grady gave me one of his canteens. I was so thirsty that I drank the entire canteen of water. During our movement to the front, we did have sporadic contact, and I remember firing the .45 pistol. This event is best described by Lieutenant Grady since my memory of it is somewhat cloudy. Bodies, both ours and the enemy's, were everywhere. Many of the enemy dead were dangling from the trees still held by the ropes they had used to tie themselves. We treated and evacuated the wounded as we found them.

Sometime during all this, I remember the sounds of the chain saws being used to clear a hole wide enough for a chopper to get in and lift out the wounded men. There was sporadic fire during this time, but the battle had basically ended. When the last of the seriously wounded men had been lifted out, we policed up all of our dead that we could find along with their weapons. There were not enough of us to get the bodies out, and it was approaching nightfall. We returned to the NDP with the rest of the walking wounded. It was getting dark when we reentered the perimeter, which was held by Charlie Company and elements of the 1-16th Infantry.

First Lieutenant Tom Grady was both the executive officer and 1st platoon leader of Company A. He recalls his part in the battle:

On the morning of October 17, Captain Jim George had sent me back to Lai Khe. I should have been with the 1st platoon. The day started as normal. I arranged for the resupply at 1200 hours and then headed up to battalion to report to Major Gillard, to let him know that I was back in Lai Khe. As I drove south on Highway 13, Major Gillard approached me in his jeep. He was very excited. He told me to get back to A Company, get my gear and get ready to go to the forward area. I remember him saying, "A/6 has been wounded. Go out and take over A Company." I returned to A Company and picked up my gear. I was to go out on the resupply flight.

On my way to the resupply pad, I saw "dustoff" ships coming in to D Company (Med). I knew it was bad. I stopped at D Company. One of the first off was Jim George. He had been hit with a claymore. I tried to pump him up and left for the resupply pad. By the time I got there, I needed someone to pump me up. I loved the army and wanted to be a company commander, but not under these circumstances. As I stated, I left Lai Khe with only my web gear. I remember it like it was yesterday. One M-16, 10 magazines of ammo (18 [rounds] to a magazine; a full magazine of 20 put too much pressure on the spring and could result in a double feed), a compass, two canteens of water, first aid pouch, two smoke grenades, three frag grenades, flash light, C rations, and a K-Bar knife. I also had a .45-cal pistol with three clips.

The resupply Huey I flew out on was filled with small arms ammo and machine gun ammo. We landed at the NDP. It was total confusion. No one knew what was going on. I'm not sure if First Sergeant Valdez was in or not. I quickly arranged for a relief party to be assembled. I had mostly medics and anyone who could walk and carry a weapon. We prepared to leave the NDP within minutes.

As I headed out toward the wood line, Sergeant First Class Van Peski stopped me and the column to clear the wood line. Van Peski was my first platoon sergeant and…one of the finest soldiers I have ever met. We cleared the wood line and got into what was the main battle area. It was at this time I linked up with Specialist Hinger. I have no idea where he came from. He probably came out with the relief party. I told him to take me to the forward most point of the battalion when contact was made earlier in the day. Hinger reminded me that at that time he had no water, since he had used all of his on the wounded. I gave him my canteen. He drank the whole quart as we stood there.

We found the front of the column. Dead and wounded were everywhere. We started to carry back the wounded. More people came to help us. First Sergeant Valdez organized a central location for the wounded and coordinated "dustoffs." When we thought we had them all, we went out and looked for more. Once we were sure we had reached the outer limits of the battle area, we started to bring in the dead. During this time there was sporadic small-arms fire from outside the perimeter. I told First Sergeant Valdez that if they came after us again, it would be over in a hurry!

Once we were sure we had all the wounded, we headed back to the NDP. Doc Hinger was still with me. I still don't know how he made it through the day. First the battle and then having me take him out again. By the time we moved from the battle scene, it was dark. Real dark! I think that was the most frightened I was all day. Moving in the jungle at night. There was still sporadic small-arms fire. We were all carrying wounded. All I could think of was getting caught in the jungle at night carrying wounded. We wouldn't have lasted long. We made it back to the NDP.

On the morning of October 18, A Company only needed 5 ships to return to Lai Khe. There was an SOP in A Company that the CO was first in on an insertion and last out on an extraction. The rear detachment NCO, Sergeant Bevins, was always there to meet us when we returned from an operation. He was there on 18 October also. He had heard the news, but he didn't want to believe it. When Tom Grady, the new A/6, got off the fifth and last Huey, Sergeant Bevins, crying like a baby asked, "Is that all that's left?" The answer was simple: "That's all." I brought back 27 people out of an entire rifle company. It was the lowest point in my life.

Postscript

In the early fall of 1969 I was working in Infantry Branch, Officers Personnel Directorate, Office of Personnel Operations, Department of the Army in Temporary Building A (TEMPO "A"), Fort McNair,

Washington, D.C. Colonel Buck Newman was the branch chief. After attending the Armed Forces Staff College, Class #44, from September 1968 until February 1969, I was moved to the Washington, D.C. area and assigned as an assignments officer in Infantry Branch. It was a good job, and I was happy that Buck Newman saw fit to bring me to Infantry Branch. It was a pleasant surprise since I had not sought the job, but I admired and respected Colonel Newman, and I knew that working in Infantry Branch was as good an assignment as an infantry officer could get in Washington.

Since the fall of 1967, the Vietnam War had only intensified and making assignments at Infantry Branch was a hectic operation. My job was assigning infantry captains overseas. Another major was assigning infantry captains stateside. The two of us were busy making assignments for some twenty-five thousand captains who were bouncing back and forth to Vietnam, returning to the States for twelve to fourteen months, and then heading back to Vietnam. It could be a subject for another book.

One day I looked up from my desk and saw a wiry, dark-haired infantry captain standing in the hallway looking around. He was dressed in a khaki uniform and was wearing a Combat Infantry Badge, a Purple Heart with four clusters, a Vietnam Service Medal, and Master Parachutist Wings. I jumped up from my desk and literally ran to him. It was Clark Welch—Dauntless Delta Six. I hadn't seen him since I had left the battalion on October 5, 1967, in Vietnam. I thought he had been killed in the Battle of Ông Thanh.

I pulled him into my office cubicle, and we sat there for awhile just grinning at each other. I was overjoyed to be looking at this great soldier whom I had known only two or three months but greatly respected. He told me that at some point during the battle he had lost consciousness from loss of blood and had awakened in the hospital in Long Binh. He told me that while he was lying in the hospital bed, General Westmoreland had visited him and pinned a Distinguished Service Cross on him. I asked him where it was. He told me he had no orders in his records that he had been awarded the DSC, the second highest decoration for valor—second only to the Medal of Honor. I was aware that he had won two Silver Stars while he was the 2-28's battalion recon platoon leader, and I asked him why he wasn't wearing them. He told me that he never received any orders on those, so he could not wear them.

I said, "Let me get your file." I went back into the stacks of official military records that we kept at Infantry Branch and quickly found Welch's file. I brought it back to my desk and began to look through it. I was astounded. There was no DSC, no Silver Stars, and no record of his ever being in the Black Lions or the 1st Infantry Division. In his chronological record (Form 66), there was an entry assigning him to Vietnam, another to a hospital in Japan, and then to the 5th Special Forces Group in Vietnam. His official record was void of any assignment to the 1st Infantry Division. I knew he had served as the recon platoon leader, then for a short time as A Company commander, finally commanding D Company during its initial organization at Lai Khe through the Battle of Ông Thanh. There was no record of it. How could this have happened?

Welch then brought me up to date. Medical personnel were able to stabilize his wounds at field hospitals in South Vietnam. From there he was evacuated to a general hospital in Japan where he underwent major surgery. Following his subsequent recovery, Welch returned to South Vietnam where he worked with Project Omega, 5th Special Forces Group. After finishing his Vietnam tour, he had received orders to report as an instructor at Florida Ranger Camp at Eglin Air Force Base, Florida, and he was on his way there.

I told Clark that I would try to reconstruct his file and get him those decorations. He headed for Florida. General Westmoreland was then in Washington serving as U.S. Army chief of staff. I called his office and spoke to one of his aides, telling him the story of Clark Welch. He apparently asked General Westmoreland about Welch's DSC, but General Westmoreland could not recall the specifics. Handing out awards was so commonplace for the general, it was not unusual that he couldn't remember. I went to work writing up the Silver Star recommendations for Welch that I knew he had been awarded. They were awarded to him a year or so later. Trying to get the DSC was too difficult.

We also tried to reconstruct his history as a member of the battalion. There were no efficiency reports for the three great jobs that he had done. Nonetheless, he pursued a distinguished army career and achieved the high honor of being selected for battalion command in the early 1980s. Welch commanded an infantry battalion in the 4th Infantry Division, Fort Carson, Colorado, and later in the 1980s the 4th and 7th Ranger Training Battalions at Fort Benning, Georgia, and Dugway Proving Ground, Utah. Soon after, he retired from the active army but remained close to the service in consulting jobs associated with military operations. In the 1990s he was advising in Bosnia and Kuwait. A great warrior and son of the United States of America—A. Clark Welch.

Clark Welch had survived the Battle of Ông Thanh, but he was one of the lucky ones. The Combat After Action Report listed fifty-six U.S. KHA (Killed Hostile Action), seventy-five WHA (Wounded Hostile Action), and two MHA (Missing Hostile Action). The death of Major Don Holleder, the 1st Brigade S3, raised the total of KHAs to fifty seven; the two MHAs, both of Company A, Private First Class Paul L. Fitzgerald, and Private Olin Hargrove Jr., were never found and were declared dead by U.S. authorities years later.

REQUIESCANT IN PACE

"We few, we happy few,
we band of brothers;
For he today that
sheds his blood with me
Shall be my brother."

Shakespeare, Henry V

Chapter 16
Personalities

This chapter is an attempt to capture a flavor for the major personalities of the Battle of Ông Thanh, as I knew them. JS

Hay

Major General John H. Hay, commanding general, 1st Infantry Division (call sign: Danger 77) was an impressive man, primarily because of his physical appearance. He certainly "looked" like a general. Hay was tall, well groomed, and graceful in his movements. I first met him when he was the commanding general, Berlin Brigade, as a brigadier, and I was a captain, assistant operations officer, G3, Berlin Brigade. During that time I briefed General Hay on many occasions, and I was flattered that he called me by my first name. I think he realized then that I was relatively knowledgeable for an officer of my grade and experience, and that I worked hard at my job. He always treated me well, except to lecture me occasionally on my being overweight. He was trying to advise me about something for my own good.

The most outstanding characteristic I noticed about General Hay, other than his outstanding appearance, was his stubbornness. He was willing to talk and discuss almost anything, but his mind was not easily changed. I don't remember ever being impressed by the substance or rationale of the arguments he made during briefings or discussions, and he had a stubborn streak, which is doubly difficult to deal with when it resides in the senior officer. On occasion he may have been in a bad mood, but by and large he was friendly, always a gentleman, and serious about his responsibilities.

In Vietnam, General Hay was very much the same. At that time, I considered him almost as a mentor, because I believe General Hay was responsible for giving me the opportunity to be a battalion S3. There were many other majors in the division who coveted a battalion S3 job, which in combat is the best job for an infantry major. I went to the Black Lions because General Hay sent me there. Unfortunately, I also believe he had something to do with my being pulled out of the battalion at the end of September 1967, when Lieutenant Colonel Pendleton, the division G3, was looking for an operations officer.

General Hay lived in the shadow of the DePuy/Hollingsworth team and its cult of forceful personality and dynamism. I think he realized exactly what he was facing, and I think he realized that the "old timers" in the division who had served under DePuy resented his presence. Although Colonel Pendleton was also a "DePuy man," General Hay and Colonel Pendleton had known each other in Berlin, when Pendleton had brought his battalion from the 24th Infantry Division into Berlin as a reinforcing battalion. Colonel Pendleton was a harsh taskmaster and a first-rate battalion commander. In Berlin his battalion had performed well. In Vietnam Colonel Pendleton helped bridge the gap between the DePuy era and General Hay's taking over the Big Red One.

In fact, General Hay never tried to change anything in the division that General DePuy had started. General Hay only wanted to codify the DePuy systems. Thus he expanded the manual, *Fundamentals of Infantry,* and incorporated most of General DePuy's practices into his own rules. General Hay also lacked the flexibility of General DePuy. He made the rules, and then he concentrated on making sure they were followed. General Hay was obdurate and prevailing, while

General DePuy was polemic and dialectic. What seemed to matter most with General Hay was how well his subordinate commanders followed the rules. General DePuy seemed to search more for those who could prevail by intellect and personal ingenuity. General Hay felt the pressures of his position as commanding general of the 1st Infantry Division in an extreme way. He felt fortunate to be commanding this division, the oldest in the army. Because Hay and General William C. Westmoreland had both had prior service in the 101st Airborne Division, General Hay was somewhat of a Westmoreland protégé. Westmoreland was then the commander of all U.S. forces in South Vietnam; thus Hay wanted to do well. Perhaps most importantly to General Hay, he wanted to carry on the proud tradition of the Big Red One and to make sure that while he was in command (on his watch), there would be no blots of shame or infamy on the division's escutcheon.

For some almost mystical reason, this feeling seemed to prevail to a greater extent in the Big Red One than in any other unit I have ever served in. There was a feeling in the Big Red One, at least at the professional soldier level, that the division was something special that you wanted to preserve. This parochialism was, however, a double-edged sword. Esprit de corps is admirable and should be cherished, but in modern warfare, particularly at the levels of battalion and above, it can be an invitation to disaster. I believe it had an impact on Terry Allen's thinking; that somehow the unit had to prevail. He could not visualize defeat as a possibility and failed to address it in his planning.

I also saw General Hay as a very cautious commander, perhaps overly so. He did not like to take calculated risks, although operations in Vietnam were full of them. As commanders go, I believe he was the most cautious commander I have ever known. He always wanted the upper hand before a fight started. Consequently what happened to the 2-28 Infantry at Ông Thanh was an absolute aberration from General Hay's point of view. I'm sure to his dying day he wondered how, with all his attention to detail, his rules, and his checking on subordinate commanders' plans, such a disaster could have befallen one of his units.

Major General Hay was a fine man. He could only be what he was and give his best, which he did. Protective of his division and greatly concerned for the welfare of every one of the soldiers in his division, General Hay was not a harsh and unfeeling man. He strived to be the most responsible and caring commander that he could be. Whatever his minor faults may have been as a division commander, he certainly was not the villain of the Battle of Ông Thanh.

Coleman

Brigadier General Bill Coleman (call sign: Danger 79) was a graduate of Clemson University in South Carolina. He spoke with a pronounced South Carolina accent, but he spoke quickly, and his mind worked quickly. Because General Hay was at a meeting in Saigon at the time the battle took place, General Coleman represented the 1st Infantry Division at the Battle of Ông Thanh. The fact that General Hay was not present at the time of the battle did not matter much. After all, the head football coach's main responsibility is to get the team prepared for the game.

Trying to sort things out on the battlefield is another matter. On October 17, 1967, at least in the early critical stages of the battle, General Coleman was calling the shots at division. He was in on the meetings on the evening of October 16 in the Dauntless NDP (a photograph confirms that), but neither he nor Colonel Newman, the 1st Brigade commander, were aware of First Lieutenant Welch's apprehensions concerning the capability of the enemy.

Bill Coleman was a good assistant division commander. He

was field wise; he asked good questions and could get to the root of a tactical problem quickly. He was not slow on his feet. Very early in the battle that day, I could hear the concern in 79er's voice on the radio. This concern was not fear, but a gut seriousness that foretold of the grievousness of the situation. During the battle, General Coleman helped with the artillery and air strikes, he voiced encouragement to the commanders on the ground, and he assisted Colonel Newman in the futile command and control activities from the air. While they were flying over the battle area, refueling the helicopters was a problem. Consequently Colonel Newman and General Coleman tried to ensure that one of them was orbiting the contact area at all times. If Coleman could be faulted for anything that happened at the Battle of Ông Thanh, it could only have been in sensing the possibilities of what could occur. On October 11, however, under similar circumstances in the jungle only three to four kilometers from the site of the Battle of Ông Thanh, Lieutenant Colonel Dick Cavazos and his Dogface battalion had done well. Why shouldn't Dauntless be able to do the same?

Brigadier General Bill Coleman was a good soldier and a good leader. He understood the problems of the men and their leaders. He was there on October 17 to do everything he could to make the best of what became a tragic situation. Some of his efforts were not in vain that day; for example, he greatly assisted in the evacuation of the wounded. Although he was a general, with supposed magical powers, and although he was there, General Coleman's impact on the outcome of the battle was not decisive because it could not be.

Newman

Colonel George E. Newman was the commander of the 1st Brigade, 1st Infantry Division (call sign: Devil 6) during the Battle of Ông

Thanh. He was a 1943 graduate of West Point, and an infantry combat veteran of World War II and Korea. I first met Colonel Newman in Korea in 1959, where he was the deputy battle group commander of the 1st Battle Group, 7th Cavalry, 1st Cavalry Division and I was a lieutenant.

Our battle group commander at the time (a colonel) was a survivor of the Bataan Death March. On occasion he would have a mental seizure and revert to his drastic experiences. Colonel Newman was very protective and loyal to the battle group commander, and he took it upon himself to ensure that the battle group commander was always taken care of. All officers in the battle group admired and respected Colonel Newman for his loyalty, a quality that he continued to demonstrate throughout his years of service and which remains today as one of his most significant traits.

George (Buck) Newman did not simply recite the motto of West Point: Duty, Honor, Country. He lived that motto with every fiber of his being. He was a man of high intellect, although he was not outwardly so. Mostly, he knew and respected people. I never saw Buck Newman treat any man with less than the full respect and dignity to which every human being is entitled, regardless of his station in life.

Colonel Newman was not what he appeared. Although he came across as somewhat overweight, puffy, and pompous, beneath it all he was a man of great moral strength and courage. He was compassionate, strong-willed in the best sense, physically courageous with great stamina, and a truly professional soldier. He was comfortable as an infantryman, but he was also capable of understanding army politics. He was not devious, however, but a man of truth. He might bend the rules when they needed to be bent, but he was a man of honor, selfless even when surrounded by the selfish. This is how he commanded, and why he had the absolute respect of the soldiers he commanded.

Those who knew Colonel Newman respected and loved him; yet many people did not really know him. Colonel Newman had commanded the 1st Infantry Division Support Command while waiting for command of a tactical brigade. He took command of the 1st Brigade around October 1, 1967, and had been in command less than a month when the Battle of Ông Thanh took place. Although he accepts responsibility for allowing the 2-28 Infantry to proceed on its relatively incautious maneuver on October 17, 1967, no man could have done more to try to get the battalion out of the mess it was in. Colonel Newman's professionalism, personal courage, and physical stamina will be remembered by all of us who witnessed his actions that day. Buck Newman cannot be maligned for his efforts on behalf of the Black Lions at Ông Thanh.

Allen

Lieutenant Colonel Terry Allen Jr. was the commander of the 2nd Battalion, 28th Infantry Black Lions (call sign: Dauntless 6) at the Battle of Ông Thanh. His father's father had graduated from West Point. His own father, Major General Terry de la Mesa Allen, had attended but not graduated from West Point. General Allen's son, Terry Jr., had graduated from West Point in 1952, but by the skin of his teeth. Terry did not do well academically at West Point, and at the time his father's heroic reputation in the U.S. Army undoubtedly helped him.

Like many young men with a famous father, Terry lived in his father's shadow, as did John Eisenhower and George S. Patton, whose fathers both had gained renown in World War II. Terry showed little of this pressure on the surface. He knew that he had his father's reputation as a soldier to uphold, but he certainly was not a martinet.

Most people would have described Terry Allen as a "nice guy." He had no airs of superiority or braggadocio. He had a quiet manner, and he was usually a good listener. He enjoyed quiet conversation, though several of his West Point classmates have described him as a "loner." Allen enjoyed being with people, but he was not an extrovert. He normally had a soft, quiet smile on his face. He enjoyed a good time but not necessarily as the center of attention. Some might say that Terry Allen lacked aggressiveness, but as his battalion S3, I never thought that of him. Although he never made a lot of noise or commotion, and rarely raised his voice, he had a commanding presence when among his subordinates and was conscious of the fact that he was the commander and had certain responsibilities in that regard.

As I explained earlier, I first met Terry Allen out in a jungle NDP, where he was the battalion S3 and I was to replace him. He impressed me with his helpfulness and forthrightness, as well as the way he treated soldiers around him with dignity and respect. He struck me as a genuine and concerned human being with very little posturing and puffery, faults that can sometimes be associated with many army officers who feel they must impress all around them with the idea that they are somebody special because they have been told they are "officers and gentlemen." Terry was just not cut from that bolt of cloth. He enjoyed talking about a wide variety of subjects, and both of us expressed our personal opinions that although we had spent a good amount of time in the military, we both felt we could have done well in another profession. Terry told me one day that he might consider leaving the army after the war, maybe after serving his time; he wanted to try something else completely different than soldiering. He certainly did not have his eyes on being a general.

Some have said that perhaps Terry Allen was not competent to be commanding an infantry battalion in combat and that he wasn't well prepared and had only been given the battalion through favoritism. On the contrary, my observation was that he was highly qualified both in technical and tactical competence and in leadership ability. During the three months that I knew him, I never saw him do an irrational, stupid, or unthinking action, nor did I have reason to question his judgment. He knew his stuff, much more than his predecessor, and he genuinely cared about his men. Neither of us really agreed with the "ass-chewing" mode of the Big Red One, but he was better than I was at taking it without passing it along.

Others have stated that they thought Terry Allen might have had a "death wish," caused by an estrangement from his wife. During our time together after he came back to the battalion, Terry confided to me that while he had been at division headquarters he had taken some leave to visit his wife. He told me his wife was having an affair with another man, in spite of the fact that they had three small girls at home. Terry did not express hatred toward his wife. He told me she had been much younger than he at the time of their marriage, and she hadn't totally understood what the life of an army wife really entailed. He told me he loved his wife, but it appeared that their marriage was over. He was concerned about the custody of their children.

Having said all this, I believe he certainly was not distraught. In my opinion, this situation had no effect on his mental state or on his feelings and responsibility for the battalion. He felt badly about the situation, but he certainly was not preoccupied by it nor did it interfere with his ability to command. He was mature and levelheaded about it. Any speculation to the contrary, perhaps originating in gossip-ridden army social circles, should be put to rest. It simply was not so.

When I left the battalion, I asked Terry to write to my wife and tell her he had not fired me. I did it in a half-joking way. Nevertheless, he followed through on my request. His letter is reproduced here:

Lai Khe, Vietnam October 6, 1967
Dear Mrs. Shelton,

Your husband, Jim, who had been my battalion S3 in the "Black

Lions" is now the G3 Operations Officer at Division. He left, not through any desire on my part, but, because he can best serve the Division and the Army in that position at this time.

Even though we had only been together for two months, I've been as close to Jim professionally and personally as anyone I've known. I consider him to be the finest Battalion S3 in the Army. His tremendous sense of humor and outgoing manner does wonders during the toughest situation, as I'm sure you're aware.

Hope our paths will cross in the future. From Jim's description of you, he is a very lucky man.

Sincerely,
Terry Allen

I did not know that Terry had written this letter until after I had returned from Vietnam and my wife showed it to me. Does this letter look like the work of a self-centered libertine?

Terry Allen was a first-class person and soldier. Unfortunately, on October 16, 1967, when First Lieutenant Clark Welch voiced his concerns over the advisability of the battalion proceeding into that VC haven, Terry was not in a listening mode. It was probably a combination of being tired and looking forward to the opportunity of finally getting into some decisive action. In retrospect, Allen never once even considered the possibility that the VC might get the upper hand. He knew that the battalion had to proceed with caution, and it did. He knew that air strikes should be placed to the enemy's rear to discourage their escape, and he went ahead with the mission. He knew that artillery marching fire was important, and by all accounts, it was used that day. But he never thought of what would happen if his lead company commander was knocked out immediately and that he would essentially lose control over that entire company. He didn't visualize that air and artillery fire would be useless to him (except to block enemy reinforcement) as the enemy closed on his unit. He didn't visualize that the Big Red One—the great division his father had commanded and his source of strength and confidence— was incapable of helping, in spite of the concern expressed by both Colonel Newman and General Coleman, who would be orbiting uselessly overhead. He didn't visualize that the enemy force was, pound for pound, better trained, better conditioned, better armed for jungle battle, and at least the size of his own. The reports of his conversation with Lieutenant Stroup, very near the end of the fighting, show either his inability to believe or to grasp the total seriousness of the situation, or that he had not given up hope for his battalion. He was still waiting for someone to do something, right to the end.

Terry Allen was a good man. He would have given anything to have avoided placing his battalion in this predicament, but it was too late. Combat is a very unforgiving environment, and there was no chance for the Black Lions that day. The chance had been missed the night before, when Terry had been concentrating on what might be gained, rather than what might be lost.

George

Captain Jim George (call sign: Dauntless Alpha 6) was the lead company commander (A Company) in the movement of the 2-28 Infantry into the site of the Battle of Ông Thanh. He had commanded A Company since late July 1967, fewer than three months, but a relatively long time for a rifle company commander. Jim George was a native of Spartanburg, South Carolina, and had graduated from Wofford College in Spartanburg. He had majored in theology, hoping to eventually become a minister. Because he went through the Reserve Officers Training Corps (ROTC) program at Wofford, he was obliged to serve time in the army. He went in as an infantry officer, graduated from parachute school and the ranger training course at Fort Benning, and decided that he liked the army. Herman Melville's description of Billy Budd, the young sailor, in Melville's story of the same name, is a very close description of Jim George. George had blonde, curly hair, chiseled features, a cleft chin, and blue-gray eyes with long eyelashes. Not only was he handsome, he had a warm and bright smile, which was his trademark, and a cheery disposition to go with it. He was really a happy-go-lucky guy, although he was very serious about his job and his responsibilities. His religious training helped him greatly in dealing with people, which is the main job of a commander.

Because of Jim George's personality and his attitude toward his job, his men respected and trusted him. He wasn't afraid to get down in the dirt with the men, and he lived in the mud with them while he encouraged them. He had a temper, but it did not show very much unless it was on behalf of his men. Jim George was a first-rate rifle company commander. Unfortunately, on October 17, 1967, the first man knocked down by the blast of an enemy claymore was Jim George. He really played no part in the battle. He was blinded and deafened by the claymore and would most likely have been killed with his men had not First Sergeant Valdez taken him by the arm and guided him back to safety. George's company led the battalion into its predicament, and the enemy force immediately gained fire superiority over A Company. This is attributable in part to training— even relatively seasoned U.S. soldiers would not fire their weapons unless commanded to do so—but it is also due to the fact that the VC knew more about A Company's location than A Company knew about the VC's location. The blanket of fire delivered by the VC force on that day had the same impact that volley fire had in the Napoleonic era: a shock effect that was difficult to recover from. Although the battalion had advanced less than one thousand meters from its NDP in two hours, the two-company force had exercised caution as it proceeded. Unfortunately, the well-trained VC regulars "got the drop on them," and a leaderless and immobile A Company was chopped to ribbons in the first ten minutes of battle.

Welch

First Lieutenant Alfred Clark Welch (call sign: Dauntless Delta 6) was the most elusive and enigmatic of all the personalities involved in the Battle of Ông Thanh. Clark Welch had joined the U.S. Army at age seventeen, right out of high school. He rose through the enlisted grades rapidly because of his native intelligence, high motivation, and Yankee New Hampshire doggedness. He was a Sergeant First Class (E-7) by age twenty-four, with most of his experience gained as a member of the newly formed U.S. Army Special Forces (Green Berets). Although he was highly trained in the techniques of warfare, Welch had, however, little or no experience in dealing with line soldiers. Most of his experience had been with the volunteers, who composed the special forces in its early days.

In 1966, Welch applied for and received a direct commission in the army for two years under a special direct commissioning program. In the 2-28 Infantry, Welch had served as the battalion's reconnaissance platoon leader, and he had more combat experience than any other officer in the battalion, including Terry Allen. When Delta Company was added to the battalion as a fourth rifle company, the captain who had originally been selected to command the new unit failed to follow orders given by Major Bob Gillard during the company's initial training in Lai Khe. Consequently First Lieutenant Clark Welch found himself assigned as commander of D Company. Terry Allen, Bob Gillard, and I considered Welch the best company commander in the battalion. In our judgment, Welch was the most field-wise of the battalion's company commanders, and he understood better than anyone how the enemy operated. He also had few other interests besides the army and his men.

At the time he and I were in the battalion, I believed Welch felt inferior to the rest of the battalion's officers because of his lack of a college education and social graces. He was somewhat of a loner, who only spoke when he was addressed, or when he had a point he thought should be made. Since none of us (Allen, Gillard, or Shelton) ever told him we thought he was the best, he may have felt that we did not have a high regard for him. Actually, Welch was highly respected by all. He really did not lack self-confidence; he just felt he was not of the same cut as the "college-educated" guys. Very quickly, the men of D Company knew that Welch had it all together, and they were proud of him as their commander.

Welch had a short-fused temper, and he did not tolerate fools. If he thought something was wrong, he spoke his piece. He was not diplomatic or particularly persuasive, but he was forceful. He also expected to be treated forcefully. That kind of approach doesn't work well in a discussion because it leaves little room for negotiation. The boss says one thing, and he disagrees. Then the boss says this is the way it's going to be, and that's the end of the discussion. On October 16, 1967, Clark Welch was dead right in his assessment of the enemy's capabilities and the danger of going into that jungle under the prevailing circumstances. Unfortunately, he was really the only one who recognized this, and no one listened to his reasons. The five wounds he received during the fighting attest to his steadfastness in a battle that unfolded in a way he foresaw and tried to prevent. He still resents the implication made by Terry Allen that he was "gun shy," rather than wise. He also resents, very personally, the loss of lives that day because he feels those losses could have been avoided. His bitterness has softened, but the experience has not been forgotten. Clark Welch is a man of competence, responsibility, integrity, and courage. Few could match his strength of character and self-possession. He gave his very best. On that day and in that place, it was not enough.

Cavazos

Lieutenant Colonel Dick Cavazos was battalion commander of the 1st Battalion, 18th Infantry (call sign: Dogface) through most of 1967. During the Korean War, he received a Distinguished Service Cross, second only to the Medal of Honor, for gallantry in combat as an infantry leader. He received his second Distinguished Service Cross as a battalion commander in combat in Vietnam. His Dogface battalion was the most highly acclaimed infantry battalion in the 1st Infantry Division in Vietnam. He retired from the army in 1985 as a four-star general, commanding all U.S. army forces in the continental United States. He was one of the greatest tactical combat leaders in the history of the United States Army.

The 1st Battalion, 18th Infantry (Dogface), with Dick Cavazos in command, figured prominently in the events leading up to the Battle of Ông Thanh. The Dogface battalion had established an NDP, which was identified on the map as Dai Yeu, on October 6, 1967, along the Binh Duong/Binh Long Provincial boundary south of the Long Nguyen Secret Zone. A 105/155mm firebase at Chonh Tanh on Highway 13 provided artillery support. The Dogface NDP was situated on the crossing point of a network of trails, a main enemy line of communications. Determined VC attacks took place on the Dogface NDP at Dai Yeu on October 6. Cavazos also made some offensive probes into the jungle north of his NDP, which was about three kilometers south of the area where the Battle of Ông Thanh took place some ten days later.

On one of these probes, Cavazos used a scout dog to give advance warning of the presence of enemy troops in the area. The dog kept signaling that enemy troops were nearby even though none was apparent. After many warnings from the dog, Cavazos called a halt and directed his troops to conduct reconnaissance by fire in the suspect area. The reconnaissance by fire was immediately answered by a huge volume of enemy fire—a veritable blanket of fire—laid down on the area where the 1-18 Infantry was expecting to proceed. In this way, Cavazos's intuition, with the help of the dog, had allowed his battalion to escape the fate that later befell the 2-28 Infantry on October 17.

There has been speculation that if Dick Cavazos had been commanding the 2-28 Infantry on October 17, the battalion would not have suffered the fate it did. That may be true. Comparing Dick Cavazos to any of the battalion commanders in the 1st Infantry Division at that time would, however, be very difficult. Cavazos was a very special and different person. He was not the average infantry officer. For that matter, he was not really a recognizable product of the army's officer commissioning and schools system. He had attributes that went far beyond the normal infantry lieutenant colonel. Cavazos had possessed realistic self-confidence; he was supremely confident of his own abilities and those of his unit to control events. He was not the type to trust others to assist him or his unit in carrying out its responsibilities. He was extremely aware of his command responsibility and therefore knew he had to control things and not leave the outcome to chance or to others. In most circumstances Cavazos was a team player, but not when exercising his command responsibilities. If he wasn't sure he had a very good handle on the control of the operation, he would not get involved; that is, he would influence those in control either to do something another way or to give him control. He had the power to do that within himself.

Dick Cavazos is a man of the earth; it shows in his intellect, his will, and his intuition. When he talks tactics, he gives personification to the military organization. As I watched him for a few moments, I could almost see him using his senses: looking, hearing, smelling, tasting, touching. His intuition was superb, and he commanded by intuition. He was not an inveterate planner, perhaps because he knew that too much study of the supposed circumstances might cloud his mind to the real situation when it occurred.

Cavazos was a wolverine; the epitome of the ferocious fighter, who was ready in every direction. He was also a bull—one who never lost a bullfight. According to tradition, when a bull survives a certain number of bullfights (he is not supposed to survive his first), his ability should be recognized, and he should live the rest of his years providing stud service and resting in the barn or pasture. That is Dick Cavazos.

Cavazos believes that if he had not used his intuition and his five senses on October 6 at Dai Yeu, he would have found himself in the same combat situation that Terry Allen did on October 17. He also states that among the many attributes he was blessed with, he was also extremely lucky. Many feel they have been lucky to know him.

Prior to the death of Terry Allen, a major waiting to be promoted to lieutenant colonel and to take command of an infantry battalion in the Big Red One was sent to the 1st Battalion, 18th Infantry to study under Dick Cavazos. He was doing that when Terry Allen was killed. Subsequently this major replaced Terry Allen as battalion commander, 2-28 Infantry Black Lions. The major's name was Lou Menetrey, and he too received a Distinguished Service Cross for bravery in a battle some three months after assuming command. Menetrey subsequently became a four-star general and commanded all U.S. and Allied forces in Korea. Dick Cavazos was certainly a man to emulate. In addition, his brother, Lauro, became the secretary of education in the Reagan administration and subsequently the Bush administration. The Cavazoses are a family of achievers in the highest sense.

Reputation was another personal quality that Dick Cavazos had going for him. He was the standard for the division. All other commanders were measured and benchmarked against him. Dick Cavazos was not perfect, and he would be the first to admit that. At the time he was held up as the benchmark battalion commander in the 1st Infantry Division, he certainly was not about to present himself to the division commander and others as a leader who was less than they had described him. He liked being the benchmark. Unfortunately for many who admired Dick Cavazos, he was not the benchmark because he had studied the *Fundamentals of Infantry* booklet published by General Hay as the division bible. (Cavazos largely wrote the second version of that book immediately after leaving command of his battalion and on special assignment to the division G3 office. Working with him there was like being trapped in a small room with Genghis Khan after he had stepped down. Staff duty, especially sitting at a desk writing, was not Cavazos's cup of tea.)

Cavazos's personal leadership qualities were what set him apart from others, and others would have been foolish trying to duplicate them. He had a personal magnetism and an air of confidence in an earthy, infantry-like way that always placed him in the limelight, even when he didn't want it. He made the most of that quality. Senior commanders would listen to him and let him do things that others might not dream of doing. Cavazos had that special something that other battalion commanders didn't have.

In my opinion, if someone were to say that Cavazos could have succeeded that day at Ông Thanh where Terry Allen had failed (and Terry would have been the first to admit that he had failed), my response would be that Dick Cavazos would be as dead as Terry is today, given the same set of circumstances. Cavazos might, however, have been able to alter the circumstances prior to moving out that day to ensure that he was in better control. I doubt that he would have allowed the pressures of "getting a big kill" to cloud his mind to the reality of the situation and the real jeopardy that a moving force might encounter in the jungle.

By the time Terry Allen really understood his situation at Ông Thanh, his unit was decisively engaged. He probably hoped then that someone could bail him out. Cavazos was a master at not getting into those kinds of predicaments, largely because he didn't do it, if he didn't like the "smell" of it, and he had the power and presence to alter the circumstances.

Cavazos never followed instructions unless he essentially wrote them, and accomplishing that is no mean trick. There was a lot of badgering of commanders in the Big Red One. Cavazos was never badgered. He never lost a battle on the battlefield because he never lost a battle anywhere, even when those above him thought they had prevailed. If someone were to try to emulate Dick Cavazos as a commander, the best approach would be to study the essence of command responsibility.

Command responsibility means: "You got it. It's yours." No one can be allowed to take it away from you temporarily and then give it back. You are the master of your own destiny. It is your ship to sail. No one can keep you from your course. Command responsibility means a leader must do what he or she has to do to accomplish the unit's mission. This does not mean ruthlessly crushing those around the leader in the process, but it also means not allowing fools and hangers-on at any level to affect the leader's ability to do what he or she must do. Lastly, command responsibility means that the things that a leader does and that all that those who serve under the leader do—good or bad—are the leader's responsibility. That was Dick Cavazos as a commander. Men of his cut are few and far between—anywhere. He was the kind of man that men would follow and men would die for. I believe that is still true today.

"Were there other Americans such as this one?
Or was he one of a kind?"
—Louis Lamour, *The Last of the Breed*

"So you'll live, you'll live,
Young Fellow My Lad,
In the gleam of the evening star,
In the wood-note wild
and the laugh of the child,
In all sweet things that are.
And you'll never die,
my wonderful boy,
While life is noble and true;
For all our beauty and hope and joy,
We will owe to our lads like you."

Robert Service, "Young Fellow My Lad,"
Rhymes of a Red Cross Man, *on the dead following World War I*

Chapter 17
The Men

The conditions of war have never been easy. War has frequently been a result of human failure to find a solution to a disagreement through less destructive means. Some wars may have been more gentlemanly than others, but it would be difficult for me to envision a war fought under worse conditions than those that I saw in Vietnam. True, helicopters brought in supplies at a phenomenal rate and evacuated the wounded very effectively. I'm sure that German soldiers on the Russian front suffered greatly after the Russians turned the tide in World War II. But the life of the 11 Bush—the grunt, the infantry rifleman—who lived twenty-four hours a day, seven days a week in the mud and dust of Vietnam was abominable. Later in the war, after the Tet Offensive in 1968 and the assassinations of Martin Luther King Jr. and Robert Kennedy, the morale of the soldiers dropped, and the ability of unit pride and esprit to carry the day was over. But in 1967, in spite of the terrible conditions, the heat, the rain, the mud, the dust, insect bites, the apprehension, the cuts that didn't heal, body sores, diarrhea, leeches, ticks, and the amount of effort it seemed to take to try and stay clean and keep your weapon and equipment clean, the men cared for each other. I never expect to see again in my life young men of eighteen, nineteen, or twenty years of age who understand the true meaning of the word "love" as I saw it in Vietnam, in the men who cared about each other and would sacrifice for their buddies. Men who grew up overnight, who understood what was really important, and who valued other human beings and held them to their hearts. And when one of them had "made it," and was leaving, the genuine and heartfelt good-byes between buddies that would tear my heart out.

These men understood the value of human life, and they knew that there was a higher purpose in life than self-aggrandizement and covering your backside. This is not to say that there were not con-men, goldbrickers, and underachievers in that army. One of the reasons for low foxhole strength (number of soldiers in the field) was the number of soldiers who had been excused from field duty because of sickness and assorted maladies of body and mind, all of which had to be treated even though they might be trifling, fabricated, or even imaginary. That system was, and always has been, difficult to police, putting the burden on the organization rather than on the individual. Additionally, the tables of organization never seemed to provide for enough clerks and other positions of dubious value that were, nevertheless, unofficially justified. All these positions were filled at the expense of foxhole strength.

But the men who filled the foxholes were an extraordinary lot. In that time, in 1967, they cared and were proud to be the Black Lions in the Big Red One. They did their share of bitching, but they didn't need to be driven. In general, none had received sufficient, and sufficiently demanding, training. As a matter of fact, it would be difficult to envision training that would prepare men for day-to-day life in an infantry battalion in Vietnam (more about that in the Epilogue). Most of the men gave one hundred percent and more. They tried to do what their leaders wanted them to do. Their ingenuity and industry were astounding, and they were a mixture of bona fide volunteers (identified by RA in front of their serial numbers) and draftees (identified by US in front of their serial numbers). I really couldn't tell them apart. And they were an ethnically diverse group from all over the country: whites, blacks, and Hispanics; from the Northeast, Southeast, Midwest, Northwest, and the Far West; from cities and farms.

In 1967, because they still believed their country cared about them, they were great. Stanley Karnow's book, *Vietnam: A History*, describes the breakdowns that occurred in our army later in the war. In a democracy the army is a reflection of the people and their concerns and values. In Vietnam in the Big Red One in 1967, the men served their nation well. American men will serve their nation well in war again, as long as the reasons can be justified, their objectives are clear, and the sacrifices seem worth the gain to the majority of the American people. For me, Specialist Fourth Class Ray Neal Gribble, the man to whom this book is dedicated, epitomizes the American soldier in war in Vietnam. After the Battle of Ông Thanh when I went to the battalion on the night of October 18, I knew that he would be one of the casualties. As I found out, he was on or near the point that last day, leading his men, trying to keep them alive. He was a draftee. He didn't ask to be there, at least not until he saw how much others—his squad—needed him.

In the early 1970s, when the U.S. involvement in the war was drawing to a close, a great many soldiers left the U.S. Army and took with them bad feelings about their service. Many in the general populace identified them as losers, and there was very little about their time in the military that gave them pride. By then the My Lai massacre was known to the public, and many other reports of wrongdoing in the army had surfaced. As well, it had come to light that some decorated war heroes who had supposedly made great sacrifices for their country were self-seeking embezzlers and worse. The leadership of the army was shaken to the core.

At the time, I was a lieutenant colonel serving in the 82nd Airborne Division. The division's senior officers were asked to go to the army separation centers and give talks to the men who were leaving the service. This was no easy task. The men were generally surly, to the point of being disrespectful and insubordinate. They didn't want to hear any army bullshit, and peer pressure was heavy on them to rebel. On the several occasions that I had to perform this difficult, but necessary and important task, Ray Gribble pulled me through. I told these men the story of Ray Gribble. I also told them that since I never got the chance to thank Ray for the service he had rendered to this country, I asked them to accept my thanks for their service and for Ray Gribble's. Once they understood what I was trying to say, they were much more receptive and understanding. And, for me, this was not a gimmick. It was true, and I meant it, and I think those disgruntled men knew that. Somehow Ray Gribble's story and my expression of thanks for his and for their service made the memory of their time in the army more palatable. Perhaps by identifying with Ray Gribble, these men were better able to understand what they had done in serving their country. At least it did for me.

In Memoriam

Adkins, Donald W. PFC 11H10 US
Allen, Terry LTC 1542
Anderson, Larry M. PFC 11B10 RA
Barker, Gary L. SGT 11B40 RA
Blackwell, James L. CPT 1542
Bolen, Jackie Jr. SP4 11B10 RA
Booker, Joseph B. PFC 36K20 RA
Breeden, Clifford L. PFC 11H10 US
Camero, Santos PFC 11B10 RA
Carrasco, Ralph SP4 11B20 US
Chaney, Elwood D. SP4 11B20 US
Cook, Melvin B. SP4 11B20 US
Crites, Richard L. PFC 11B20 RA
Crutcher, Joe A. PFC 11B10 RA
Dodson, Wesley E. PFC 11B10 US

Dowling, Francis E. SGM 11G50 RA
Durham, Harold B. 2/LT 01193
Dye, Edward P. PFC 11B10 US
East, Leon N. SP4 11B20 US
Ellis, Maurice S. SP4 11B20 RA
Familiare, Anthony SP4 11B10 US
Farrell, Michael J. SP4 11B20 US
Fuqua, Robert L. Jr. PFC 11B10 RA
Gallagher, Michael SP4 11B20 US
Garcia, Arturo SP4 11B10 US
Garcia, Melesso PFC 11B10 RA
Gilbert, Stanley D. SP4 11B20 US
Gilbertson, Verland SP5 84B20 RA
Gribble, Ray N. SP4 11B20 US
°Holleder, Donald W. MAJ 52162 [1st Bde. S3, not 2-28]
Jagielo, Allen D. PFC 91B20 US
Johnson, Willie C. J. SFC 11B40 RA
Jones, Richard W. PFC 11B10 RA
Krische, John D. PFC 11B10 US
Lancaster, Jerry D. SP4 11B20 US
Lincoln, Gary G. PFC 11B10 US
Lovato, Joe Jr. SP4 91B20 RA
Luberda, Andrew P. 2/LT 01542
Megiveron, Emil G. PFC 11B10 RA
Miller, Michael M. SP4 11B20 RA
Moultrie, Joe D. PFC 11B10 RA
Nagy, Robert J. PFC 11B10 US
Ostroff, Steven L. SP4 11B20 US
Platosz, Walter PFC 11B10 US
Plier, Eugene J. SFC 11B40 RA
Porter, Archie A. SP5 91B20 RA
Randall, Garland J. SP4 11B20 US

Reece, Ronney D. PFC 11B10 RA
Reilly, Allen V. PFC 11B20 RA
Sarsfield, Harry C. SP4 11B20 US
Schroder, Jack W. PFC 11B10 RA
Shubert, Jackie E. PFC 11B10 US
Sikorski, Daniel SP4 11B20 RA
Smith, Luther A. SSG 11B40 RA
Thomas, Theodore D. PFC 11B10 US
Tizzio, Pasquale SP4 11B20 US
Wilson, Kenneth SP4

Missing in Action
Fitzgerald, Paul L. PFC
Hargrove, Olin, Jr. PVT

Epilogue

Writing in his autobiographical account of his army service, *A Soldier's Story,* Omar Bradley states:

In time of war the only value that can be affixed to any unit is the tactical value of that unit in winning the war. Even the lives of those men assigned to it become nothing more than tools to be used in the accomplishment of that mission. War has neither the time nor heart to concern itself with the individual and the dignity of man. Men must be subordinated to the effort that comes with fighting a war, and as a consequence men must die that objectives might be taken. For a commander the agony of war is not in its dangers, deprivations, or fear of defeat but in the knowledge that with each new day men's lives must be spent to pay the costs of that day's objectives.

These words of Bradley have always puzzled me. They sound more like the words of George Patton, or Mars, the Roman god of war. In my early years as a soldier, I tried to understand words such as Bradley's. Omar Bradley was one of my favorite generals, for I thought he was down-to-earth, unassuming, and the champion of the infantry soldier. But as I read those words and thought of the bodies of the men I was asked to identify on October 18, 1967, I couldn't bring myself to accept them.

Even today, as I remember those dead men, I cannot accept the premise that their lives were worth whatever gain we may have accomplished. I know that Omar Bradley knew of the many men who died under his command, but he never had to identify a large group of his personal friends as war casualties. Bradley never fought in an infantry battalion, or even a division. I doubt he could have written those words if he had. On the other hand, at the time those words were written, Omar Bradley was justifying four years of a total, global war, where everything in American society, including freedom itself, was subordinated to the winning of the war.

I do not believe I am a pacifist, but the contemplation of the real consequences of war must be put into very tight perspective. The settling of issues by force of arms or intimidation has existed throughout human history. Consequently, in spite of disarmament efforts and the eternal hope for peace, any nation that greatly values its freedom has to be prepared to fight for it, or it might be subjected to some form of servitude to others.

In the realm of human conflict, Americans have learned that history teaches two guiding principles:

1. Develop a warrior class within the nation that is a part of the nation rather than mercenary in nature. Train this warrior class rigorously and equip it well, but ensure that its leaders always subordinate themselves to the Constitution, the rule of law, and elected civilian leadership.

2. Try to avoid armed conflict at all costs, but ensure that potential adversaries know that Americans are willing to use their power, if necessary, to defend their vital national interests.

One of the greatest threats to our national security today is the lack of understanding about why we need a combat-ready military, one that is highly trained and well-equipped. This force must have the best-trained leaders that we can provide, and it must be trained rigorously in the most strenuous and live-fire conditions possible. The training standards of the U.S. Army Rangers should be the army's standards, not the exception.

In analyzing the Battle of Ông Thanh, there are at least two major tactical lessons evident that could help military leaders in the future if study and concentration are applied in training. The first lesson is improvement in interpersonal relations or interactive skills between leaders and their subordinates. This improvement involves teaching our leaders how to listen to their subordinates. It does not necessarily mean consensus decision-making in combat, nor does it imply a democratic discussion process. As we now know, there was a breakdown in communications between Lieutenant Colonel Terry Allen and First Lieutenant Clark Welch on October 16, 1967. Had this breakdown not occurred, the outcome on October 17, 1967, might have been different. In the U.S. Army, a malaise that I refer to as the "prevail syndrome" afflicts many senior commanders. I know that it afflicted me when I was a senior officer, and I believe that most senior officers are afflicted with the "prevail syndrome" today. The "prevail syndrome" manifests itself in a tendency not to listen, not to carefully analyze the *substance* of the argument or point made by a subordinate. Instead the senior leader concentrates on a counterargument that will convince everyone that the commander's proposal is the best. The result is, of course, not a proposal at all, but an edict of what must be done.

What we must do in the army, in our leadership training, is concentrate to some degree on teaching listening skills. This involves creating an environment where the commander can benefit from the ideas/arguments of his subordinates without their presenting a threat to the commander's authority. This training should concentrate on both the role of the commander and the role that subordinates play in ensuring that the commander is able to process all ideas and viewpoints objectively prior to making a decision. This point is touched on in a book entitled *Leadership In Organizations* produced by the Department of Behavioral Sciences and Leadership at West Point, but it needs more development. Mike Malone also touches on the subject of listening in his book *Small Unit Leadership* (Presidio, 1995), but his ideas are not fully developed.

The second lesson from the Battle of Ông Thanh that cries out for systematic attention is the failure of the 2-28 Infantry to use fire and maneuver or fire and movement effectively. There are several explanations for this failure, but because these tactical methods are the bread and butter of infantry units in offensive action, as well as in any retrograde action, they should be the subject of continuing study and concern throughout the army's training program. Part of the problem at Ông Thanh lay in the SOPs of the Big Red One. These SOPs caused commanders to ignore or overlook fire and movement, or fire and maneuver, when engaged in a firefight with the enemy. In a chapter called "The Phalanx of Fire" in his book, *Summons of the Trumpet* (Presidio, 1995), Lieutenant General Dave Palmer covers very well the importance of these infantry tactics. By emphasizing the capabilities of indirect fire (mortars and artillery) and tactical air strikes in killing the enemy, the SOPs of the 1st Infantry Division usurped the old tried-and-true methods of infantry combat: gain fire superiority using techniques of rifle fire and gain the initiative either by fire and movement (by individuals) or by fire and maneuver (by units). The real problem with this approach is that these infantry tactics are very difficult to employ in actual combat because they require considerable training, up to the point where they become automatic, or what we call "battle drill."

The Battle of Ông Thanh also highlights the danger of overcontrol by superiors, which froze subordinates in action. Overcontrol is a real problem for concerned senior commanders who may be only a stone's throw away by helicopter, but who are unable to influence the action that is so near at hand. Terry Allen was almost paranoid about the commander being on the radio, giving directions. Therefore, he had difficulty moving on the ground to exercise personal control over the action and leading the ground action. I say "paranoid" because his major objective in doing this was to keep his superiors off his command net, where too often they were giving directions and taking up valuable time "trying to help."

The main job of the commander on the ground is maintaining control and directing the action of his subordinates. He is trained to do this. But in Vietnam, and in training exercises in the U.S. Army today, senior commanders supervise their subordinates so actively that they take away the subordinate commanders' prerogatives and, in many cases, freeze them into inaction. Overcontrol is an invitation to disaster. The only action that might have gotten the 2-28 Infantry out of their disastrous situation on October 17, 1967, once the two-company force had come under enemy fire, was old-fashioned fire and movement, and possibly fire and maneuver. This didn't happen mostly because restrictive SOPs, lack of training in proven infantry tactics, and the widespread syndrome of overcontrol in the division caused Terry Allen to be frozen to his radio instead of personally and physically directing the action of his men on the ground.

*

Epilogues usually contain information about what happened later to the people in the story. Lieutenant Colonel Clark Welch, U.S. Army (Retired), now has a bachelor's degree in engineering, two masters degrees, and is retired in Colorado. Colonel Jim George lives in South Carolina and does consulting work for military contractors. Colonel George M. Newman, U.S. Army (Retired) is retired in Alabama. Brigadier General Bill Coleman, U.S. Army (Retired) is deceased. Lieutenant General John H. Hay, U.S. Army (Retired) is deceased. General Richard Cavazos, U.S. Army (Retired) lives in

Texas. Second Lieutenant Harold B. "Pinky" Durham is buried in Tifton, Georgia. The soldier with the M-79 round embedded in his leg had the round removed by a U.S. Army surgeon without incident. Lieutenant Colonel Terry Allen is buried next to his father in El Paso, Texas. Specialist Fourth Class Ray Neal Gribble is buried in Muncie, Indiana.

Under a new battalion commander, Lieutenant Colonel Lou Menetrey, the 2nd Battalion, 28th Infantry participated in a victory over Viet Cong forces less than three weeks after the Battle of Ông Thanh. General Lou Menetrey is now retired after commanding all U.S. and Combined Forces in Korea.

Like many other phenomena in life, history has a tendency to be fickle. In 2002, some thirty-four years after the Battle of Ông Thanh, and the subsequent withdrawal of U.S. forces from Vietnam in 1973, which was followed by the "honorable peace" that saw the North Vietnamese army conquer South Vietnam in 1975 in violation of the Paris Peace Accords, most historians, as well as a large majority of the American people, may consider the U.S. involvement in Vietnam a disastrous and tragic waste, and a time of shame in U.S. history.

Consider, however, the fact that since the late 1940s, the Soviet Union was the greatest single threat to U.S. security. Yet for forty years, war between the Soviet Union and the United States was averted. Each time a Soviet threat surfaced during that time (Greece, Turkey, Korea, Berlin, Cuba, Vietnam, and Afghanistan), although it may have been in the form of a "war of national liberation," as the Vietnam war was characterized, the United States gave the Soviet Union the distinct message that each successive threat would not be a Soviet walkover. In fact, the Soviets were stunned by the U.S. reactions in both Korea and Vietnam. They shook their heads, wondering what interest a great power like the United States could have in those two godforsaken countries. They thought:

"These Americans are crazy. They have nothing to gain; and yet they fight and lose thousands of men over nothing. They are irrational." Perhaps history in the long-term—two hundred or three hundred years from now—will say that the Western democracies, led by the United States, survived in the world, and their philosophy of government of the people, by the people, for the people continues to survive in some measure because of the resolve and the resolute sacrifices made in the mid-twentieth century by men like those listed in the last chapter of this book. Then the words of Lord Byron, as quoted in this book's preface, will not ring hollow, but instead they will inspire other men and women of honor in the years to come.

Photographs

Lt. Col. Terry de la Mesa Allen Jr., commander of the 2nd Battalion, 28th Infantry Black Lions. A cordial, thoughtful, and competent officer who lived in the shadow of his illustrious father. (U.S. Army Photo)

The legendary Maj. Gen. Terry de la Mesa Allen (left, without helmet), charismatic and beloved commander of the 1st Infantry Division in North Africa and Sicily in World War II, father of Lt. Col. Terry de La Mesa Allen Jr. Shown with journalists Clark Lee (International News Service) and Don Whitehead (Associated Press) in Cerami, Sicily, August 4, 1943. (U.S. Army Photo)

Father and son. Terry de la Mesa Allen Sr. and Jr. in 1944. (U.S. Army Photo)

Maj. Gen. William E. DePuy, second commander of the 1st Infantry Division in Vietnam (call sign Danger 77). Dynamic, cerebral, fiery. (U.S. Army Photo)

Maj. Gen. John H. Hay, third commander of
the 1st Infantry division in Vietnam (call sign
Danger 77). Gentlemanly, concerned,
resolute, obdurate. (U.S. Army Photo)

Brig. Gen. Bernard W. Rogers, assistant
division commander under Maj. Gen. Hay (call
sign Danger 78). A Rhodes Scholar, he later
served as army chief of staff and supreme
Allied commander in Europe. Keen of mind,
intense, ambitious. (U.S. Army Photo)

Brig. Gen. William S. Coleman, assistant
division commander under Maj. Gen. Hay
(call sign Danger 79). Earthy, beloved,
knowledgeable, caring. Later commanded
Fort Jackson, South Carolina; retired as a
Maj. Gen. (U.S. Army Photo)

Lt. Col. Allen talking to his men. Soon after taking command, Lt. Col. Terry Allen made a point of visiting each company area to speak directly with the troops and answer questions. He was not his father, but he was surely his father's son. (U.S. Army Photo)

Capt. Ed Burke, feisty commander of C Co. and widely praised by Lt. Col. Terry Allen. He is now the heart and soul of the 28th Infantry and executive director of the Society of the 1st Infantry Division. (Ed Burke)

1st Lt. Mel Adams (right), commander of B Co., on the receiving end of a "donging" ceremony. Adams was a courageous officer who went on to command the division's Long Range Reconnaissance Patrol (LRRP) Co. Alabama's finest. (U.S. Army Photo)

1st Lt. Billy Murphy. After serving as a 1st Division platoon leader (and being awarded two Silver Stars for heroism), Murphy returned to Vietnam as helicopter pilot with the Big Red One. He went on to command the 1st Aviation Brigade as a colonel. A courageous, self-made soldier. (Billy Murphy)

Billy Murphy and an unidentified soldier examine a VC fatality. (Billy Murphy)

Capt. (Dr.) Jim Swink. The consensus All-American tailback at Texas Christian University in the mid-50s was the battalion surgeon for the Black Lions and was awarded a Silver Star for heroism and a Purple Heart for wounds. Courageous and unpretentious. (U.S. Army Photo)

Albert Clark Welch, a living hero of the Battle of Ông Thanh, with two of Lt.Col. Terry Allen's daughters, Consuelo on Welch's right, and Bebe on his left. Picture taken at Black Lions Centennial celebration in May 2001. (James Shelton)

L-R: The author, Maj. James Shelton, then battalion operations officer; Lt. Col. Terry Allen; Sgt. Maj. Francis Dowling. Photo taken at Uniontown (Long Binh). (James Shelton)

Battalion commander and staff, 2nd Battalion, 28th Infantry Black Lions, 1st Infantry Division, Republic of Vietnam, September 30, 1967. L-R, back: Maj. Jack Sloan, incoming S3; Maj. Jim Shelton, outgoing S3; 1st Lt. Tom Shuttle, 2-33 Artillery, FSO; Cpt. Jerry Edwards, S4; Cpt. Jim Blackwell, S2. L-R, front: Cpt. William Whitfield, S1; Maj. Bob Gillard, executive officer; Lt. Col. Terry Allen Jr., battalion commander; Cpt. (Dr.) Ed Crum, battalion surgeon; Lt. Levinson, communications officer. (U.S. Army Photo)

Commanders, 2nd Battalion, 28th Infantry Black Lions, 1st Infantry Division, September 30, 1967. L-R: Capt. Karl Kizer, HQ Co.; Cpt. Jim George, A Co.; Cpt. Jim Kasik, B Co.; Lt. Col. Terry Allen Jr., battalion commander; Cpt. Al Ziegler, C Co.; 1st Lt. Al (Clark) Welch, D. Co; 1st Lt. Brad Boehm, E Co. Kizer and Boehm were killed in action in 1968. (U.S. Army Photo)

Senior noncommissioned officers, 2nd Battalion, 28th Infantry Black Lions, 1st Infantry Division, September 30, 1967. L-R: 1st Sgt. HHC (N.A); 1st Sgt. Valdez, A Co.; 1st Sgt. Maddox, B Co.; Cmd. Sgt. Maj. Dowling; 1st Sgt. C Co. (N.A.); 1st Sgt. Barrow, D Co.; 1st Sgt E Co (N.A.). (U.S. Army Photo)

CH-47 Chinook. The workhouse of helicopters in Vietnam was an unsung hero that resupplied the grunts in the field, delivering ammo, rations, equipment (among countless other items), and placing artillery when and where needed. (U.S. Army Photo)

DEPARTMENT OF THE ARMY
HEADQUARTERS 1ST BRIGADE
9TH INFANTRY DIVISION
AFO San Francisco 96371

AVDE-BA-C

18 September 1967

SUBJECT: Letter of Appreciation

THRU: Commanding General
        1st Infantry Division
        AFO San Francisco 96345

TO: Commanding Officer
        2d Bn, 28th Infantry
        1st Infantry Division
        AFO San Francisco 96345

1. It is with considerable pleasure that I extend my appreciation to you and the officers and men of the 2d Bn, 28th Infantry for the outstanding manner in which you performed the Uniontown mission during the period 29 August to 19 September 1967.

2. During this period your command was highly successful in the accomplishment of a difficult and demanding mission. This result was due largely to the aggressiveness with which you approached the assigned tasks. Your patrol plan was by far the most comprehensive yet developed for the Uniontown area, and resulted in complete coverage of your area of operations. The use of extensive eagle flights combined with both mounted and dismounted ground reconnaissance patrols provided maximum use of the resources available to you. Your constant movement and the ability of your units to cover so large an area was largely responsible in keeping Viet Cong activities to a minimum. This contributed immeasurably toward the success of the recent election in Duc Tu and Cong Thanh districts.

3. Please express my full hearted thanks and deep appreciation to the officers and men of your command who performed so admirable during this period. Their courage, skill and dedication to duty are of the highest order.

A TRUE COPY

William L Whitfield
WILLIAM L WHITFIELD
CPT, Infantry

/s/ Donald A. Seibert
/t/ Donald A. Seibert
Colonel, Infantry
Commanding

Letter of commendation to the 1st Infantry Division from Col. Don Seibert, commander of the 1st Brigade, 9th Infantry Division, thanking the Big Red One for conducting a month-long security mission in the Bien Hoa/Long Binh area in August 1967. (James Shelton)

AVDB-CG (18 Sep 67)   1st Ind
SUBJECT: Letter of Appreciation

Headquarters, 1st Infantry Division, AFO 96345, 21 September 1967

TO: LTC Terry D. Allen, Headquarters & Headquarters Company, 2d Battalion
    2Cth Infantry, 1st Infantry Division, AFO 96345

    It is with great pleasure that I forward Colonel Seibert's highly
complimentary letter to you. I also want to extend my appreciation to
you and commend you for representing the division in such a fine manner.

                              /s/ J.H.Hay
                              /t/ J.H.Hay
                                  Major General, USA
                                  Commanding

A TRUE COPY

William L. Whitfield
WILLIAM L. WHITFIELD
CPT, Infantry

AVDB-WB-CC   2d Ind

HEADQUARTERS, 2D BATTALION, 28TH INFANTRY 26 September 1967

TO: All Officers and Enlisted Men of the 2d Battalion, 28th Infantry, who
    participated in the Uniontown Mission.

    1. I wish to add my personal thanks, to those of Colonel Seibert
and Major General Hay, for your fine performance during The Uniontown
Mission. It was only through the professionalism with which you performed
your duties that this battalion was able to so successfully accomplish
its assigned mission.

    2. The complimentary remarks of Colonel Seibert and Major General
Hay exemplify the Esprit de Corps and devotion to duty which have been a
tradition of the "Black Lions".

                              TERRY ALLEN JR.
                              LTC, Infantry
                              Commanding

The Black Lions were proud of Col. Seibert's letter commendation, which was passed down to all ranks. (James Shelton)

Lt. Col. Dick Cavazos (left), commander of the 18th Infantry's 1st Battalion ("Dogface"), confers with Lt. Gen. Fred Weyand, II Force field commander. Both would become four-star generals, Weyand as U.S. Army chief of staff, Cavazos as commander of all U.S. forces in the United States. Cavazos was a great tactical commander who received a Distinguished Service Cross (DSC, the nation's second highest award) for heroism in Korea as platoon leader, and a second DSC in Vietnam for heroism as a battalion commander. A true combat leader. (Dick Cavazos)

Planning the battle. 1st Lt. Clark Welch, commander of D Co., describes the action of October 16, 1967, to (from Welch's right), Brig. Gen. Coleman, Maj. Don Holleder, Lt. Col. Terry Allen, Col. George "Buck" Newman, and two others unidentified. Allen and Holleder were killed the next day; also killed was the photographer, Sp5c Verland Gilbertson, from the division's 121st Signal Battalion; the photo was found in his camera. (U.S. Army Photo/Verland Gilbertson)

Well before he became the Big Red One's 1st Brigade S3—and, subsequently, a fatality in the Battle of Ông Thanh—Don Holleder was an All-American at West Point. Featured on the cover of Sports Illustrated just prior to the 1955 Army/Navy game, he went on to lead his team to victory over the Midshipmen in the fall football classic. (Richard Meek/Sports Illustrated)

American soldiers. The mortal and inevitable consequences of military conflict. (James Shelton)

Sp4c. Ray Neal Gribble, A Co., 2-28 Inf.: "A hero among heroes." Gribble, a self-possessed leader of men, voluntarily returned to his rifle squad from the relative safety of battalion HQ because "they needed him." Killed in action, October 17, 1967. (James Shelton)

2nd Lt. Harold Bascom "Pinky" Durham Jr., 6th Battalion, 15th Artillery. Durham, the artillery forward observer of D Co., 2nd Battalion, 28th Infantry, was posthumously awarded the Medal of Honor for his heroic action in the Battle of Ông Thanh. "His golden smile of confidence lifted the spirits of others." (Durham Family Photo)

Harold Durham's final resting place, Oakridge Cemetery, Tifton, Georgia. (James Shelton)

The lifesavers (L-R): Combat medics Morris Blumenfeld, Tom Hinger, and Jim Norgon. Tom Hinger was awarded the Silver Star and Purple Heart for his actions on October 17, 1967. (James Shelton)

Pvt. Joe Costello on October 8, 1967, ready to move out. On October 17 Joe became the temporary battalion commander when all around him were killed or wounded. He was awarded the Silver Star and Purple Heart. (James Shelton)

Lt. Tom Grady ("Eltee") after the Battle of Ông Thanh. Executive officer and 1st Platoon leader, A Co. Tom assumed command of A Co. on October 17 after Capt. Jim George was evacuated. Philadelphia's finest. (James Shelton)

Appendices

Appendix 1

Second Lieutenant Harold B. Durham, Jr.
Medal of Honor Recipient, Class 1-67

Harold B. "Pinky" Durham, Jr., was born at Rocky Mount, North Carolina, 12 October 1942 to Harold B. and Grace Eidson Durham. He attended Ft. Lewis College, Durango, Colorado, before enlisting in the army in 1964 and attending basic training at Fort Jackson, South Carolina. He subsequently served in Vietnam as a rotary wing maintenance mechanic, stationed at Vung Tau. He also did volunteer work as an English teacher in a local Vietnamese village.

When the opportunity came to attend OCS, he willingly accepted. He graduated from OCS Class 1-67 on 17 December 1966 and was commissioned as a Second Lieutenant of Artillery. He volunteered to return to Vietnam.

Lieutenant Durham distinguished himself by conspicuous gallantry and intrepidity at the cost of his life above and beyond the call of duty while assigned to Battery C, 6th Battalion, 15th Artillery, 1st Infantry Division, in Vietnam.

Lieutenant Durham was serving as a forward observer with Company D, 2d Battalion, 28th Infantry, during a battalion reconnaissance-in-force mission. At approximately 1015 hours, contact was made with an enemy force concealed in well-camouflaged positions and fortified bunkers. He immediately moved into an exposed position to adjust the supporting artillery fire onto the insurgents.

The President of the United States of America, authorized by Act of Congress, March 3, 1863, has awarded in the name of The Congress the Medal of Honor posthumously to

SECOND LIEUTENANT HAROLD B. DURHAM, JR.
UNITED STATES ARMY

for conspicuous gallantry and intrepidity in action at the risk of his life above and beyond the call of duty:

Second Lieutenant Harold B. Durham, Jr., Artillery, distinguished himself by conspicuous gallantry and intrepidity at the cost of his life above and beyond the call of duty on 17 October 1967 while assigned to Battery C, 6th Battalion, 15th Artillery, 1st Infantry Division, in the Republic of Vietnam. On this date, Lieutenant Durham was serving as a forward observer with Company D, 2d Battalion, 28th Infantry, during a battalion reconnaissance in force mission. At approximately 1015 hours contact was made with an enemy force concealed in well-camouflaged positions and fortified bunkers. Lieutenant Durham immediately moved into an exposed position to adjust the supporting artillery fire onto the insurgents. During a brief lull in the battle he administered emergency first aid to the wounded in spite of heavy enemy sniper fire directed toward him. Moments later, as enemy units assaulted friendly positions, he learned that Company A, bearing the brunt of the attack, had lost its forward observer. While he was moving to replace the wounded observer, the enemy detonated a claymore mine, severely wounding him in the head and impairing his vision. In spite of the intense pain, he continued to direct the supporting artillery fire and to employ his individual weapon in support of the hard pressed infantrymen. As the enemy pressed their attack, Lieutenant Durham called for supporting fire to be placed almost directly on his position. Twice the insurgents were driven back, leaving many dead and wounded behind. Lieutenant Durham was then taken to a secondary defensive position. Even in his extremely weakened condition, he continued to call artillery fire onto the enemy. He refused to seek cover and instead positioned himself in a small clearing which afforded a better vantage point from which to adjust the fire. Suddenly, he was severely wounded a second time by enemy machine gun fire. As he lay on the ground near death, he saw two Viet Cong approaching, shooting the defenseless wounded men. With his last effort, Lieutenant Durham shouted a warning to a nearby soldier who immediately killed the insurgents. Lieutenant Durham died moments later, still grasping the radio handset. Lieutenant Durham's gallant actions in close combat with an enemy force are in keeping with the highest traditions of the military service and reflect great credit upon himself, his unit, and the United States Army.

During a brief lull in the battle, he administered emergency first aid to the wounded in spite of heavy enemy sniper fire directed toward him. Moments later, as enemy units assaulted friendly positions, he learned that Company A, bearing the brunt of the attack, had lost its forward observer. While he was moving to replace the wounded observer, the enemy detonated a claymore mine, severely wounding him in the head and impairing his vision. In spite of the intense pain, he continued to direct the supporting artillery fire and to employ his individual weapon in support of the hard-pressed infantrymen. As the enemy pressed their attack, Lieutenant Durham called for supporting fire to be placed almost directly on his position. Twice the insurgents were driven back, leaving many dead and wounded behind.

Lieutenant Durham was then taken to a secondary defensive position. Even in his extremely weakened condition, he continued to call artillery fire onto the enemy. He refused to seek cover and instead positioned himself in a small clearing that offered a better vantage point from which to adjust the fire. Suddenly, he was severely wounded a second time by enemy machinegun fire. As he lay on the ground near death, he saw two Viet Cong approaching, shooting the defenseless wounded men. With his last effort, Lieutenant Durham shouted a warning to a nearby soldier who quickly killed the insurgents. He died moments later, still grasping the radio handset. Second Lieutenant Durham's gallant actions in close combat with an enemy force are in keeping with the highest traditions of the military service and reflect great credit upon himself, his unit and the U.S. Army. For these heroic actions he was awarded the Medal of Honor.

Appendix 2

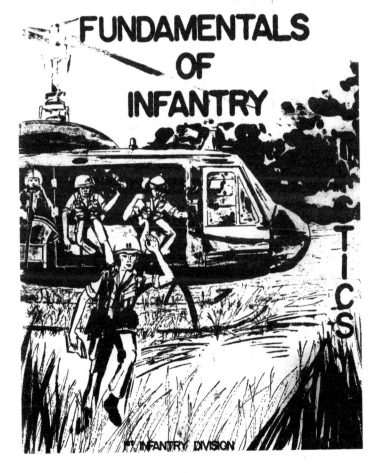

FUNDAMENTALS OF INFANTRY TACTICS

9TH INFANTRY DIVISION

DEPARTMENT OF THE ARMY
HEADQUARTERS 1ST INFANTRY DIVISION
APO San Francisco 96345

AVDB–CG

SUBJECT: Fundamentals of Infantry Tactics

TO: Brigade, Battalion, and Company Commanders

1. Swift and enduring lessons in tactics are taught by the Viet Cong, but combat experience is a hard and costly school. I am concerned that as our leaders rotate, our battle-won wisdom shrinks. However, I am convinced that if we help successor leaders to grasp a few tactical principles and basic techniques, victory--and comparatively inexpensive victory--will invariably crown our future undertakings. Therefore, I have asked a group of seasoned officers to draw up the enclosed compendium based on their combat experiences. I direct each of you to study it carefully, and to use it as your guideline for operations and training.

2. I will expect to find in your command, at the minimum, evidence of your attention to and emphasis upon:

    a. Exploiting artillery and air firepower for all missions.

    b. Maintaining security and dispersion under all circumstances.

    c. Moving to contact with particular care to find the enemy with scouts.

    d. Controlling advanced elements tightly, so that at any time precise position of units is known, and immediate use of air and artillery is possible.

    e. Searching the battlefield with system and thoroughness.

    f. Digging defensive positions which are well fortified to the front and overhead, with weapons sited painstakingly for maximum surprise and flanking fire upon an assaulting enemy.

3. The hallmarks of 1st Division leaders, our distinctive professional traits, have been (1) violent, massive firepower; (2) firm control of maneuver at all times; (3) security under all conditions; (4) cloverleaf patrolling; and (5) deep foxholes with full frontal berm overhead cover, and 45

AVDB—CG
SUBJECT: Fundamentals of Infantry Tactics

degree firing ports. That future leaders of the Big Red One are similarly
endowed is my most serious responsibility, and yours.

J. H. HAY
MG, USA
Commanding

4 Incl
   1. The Enemy
   2. Big Red One
      Battle Principles
   3. Defense
   4. Offense

2

THE ENEMY

1. <u>INTELLIGENCE IS FOR ALL COMMANDERS</u>: The tactical area of interest (TAOI) of the 1st Division encompasses BINH DUONG Province—the seedbed of armed communism in Vietnam—eastern War Zone C, western War Zone D, and the infiltration routes through BINH LONG and PHUOC LONG Provinces. Table I identifies the principal Viet Cong formations operating within the TAOI, both main force and local force. 1st Division leaders should take advantage of every available opportunity to learn about these units, and their strengths and weaknesses. In this war, intelligence cannot be relegated to staff specialists; it governs our tactics no less than our plans and operations.

2. <u>MAIN FORCE UNITS</u>: a. Since 1962 the Viet Cong have relied strategically on main force units of regiment and division size, composed of full time soldiers. The 9th Light Infantry Division, among the oldest and most successful of the VC main force organizations, operated during 1965 north of SAIGON down to the metropolitan suburbs. Since 1965 operations of the 1st Division have driven the 9th Division northward, away from the centers of population, into the jungles of War Zones C and D. A series of tactical defeats by the 1st Division have seriously depleted the regiments of the 9th Division, and its original South Vietnamese soldiers have been replaced by North Vietnamese to a significant degree, especially among the cadre and leaders.

    b. Main force units normally operate in elements no smaller than battalion, and are well equipped with a full range of modern infantry

3

weapons, including heavy machine guns, mortars, and recoilless rifles. Within the War Zones, 120mm mortars have been encountered, and artillery and artillery rockets also must be expected. Unit communication equipment—largely wire, with some radios—is adequate. Some weaknesses may lie in the morale, motivation, and state of training of the VC soldiers within main force units stemming from tensions between Northerners and Southerners, continued deprivation of the pleasures of civilization, lack of familiarity with the terrain, disease, and in some instances starvation. These occasionally detract from unit efficiency, but not dependably so.

3. LOCAL FORCE UNITS: The Viet Cong continue to wage intensive war with full time guerrillas (organized usually into district companies or provincial battalions), part-time guerrillas (usually district companies), and village militia (clandestine activists). Local force units are often, but not always, poorly equipped in most respects, but the local force guerrilla can be a better trained, more resolute foe than his main force counterpart. The style of the main force is regimental attack or ambush; that of the local force a two-man claymore attack or a road mining. The strength of the local force is the guerrilla's ability, through long familiarity with his own neighborhood, to merge with the populace or fade quickly into a base camp once he strikes.

4. BASE CAMPS: a. For both main force and local force units, base camps are essential for survival. Deeply rooted in Communist doctrine is the importance of a "secure base area" for guerrilla operations. The local force units tend to place their reliance on numerous small camps dispersed throughout their areas of operations. In BINH DUONG Province virtually every

4

patch of woods conceals at least one small circular entrenchment with associated bunkers and tunnels, and each local force unit has at least one ela-
borately fortified refuge; larger units have a tunnel complex in which their
hospital and headquarters are located. Some of these tunnels are more than
20 years old, and many are hundreds of meters in length. Local force base
camps are usually extensively booby.trapped, and often protected by punji
pits. Main force base camps are usually not so well guarded by mines; they
are, of course, larger, and frequently include training facilities, such as
rifle ranges and classrooms. Having constructed numerous, well fortified,
pre-stocked base camps throughout his area of operations, the enemy may
shift his forces as the situation dictates, either for offensive or for
defensive reasons.

      b. Any defended Viet Cong base camp presents a formidable problem
to attackers. One local force squad has been known to withstand assault by
two US infantry companies, and even a VC sniper or two, firing from within
a mined camp, can inflict numerous casualties on a maneuvering force.
Obliteration of local base camps and surrounding jungles using bulldozers
has unquestionably been effective. However, our attempts to demolish base
camps, using explosives, have been comparatively unsuccessful. Evidence
suggests that the enemy soon re-enters and restores partially damaged base
camps unless constant patrolling, or other US counter-action prevents him.

      5. <u>COMMUNICATION-LIAISON ROUTES</u>: The military organization of the
enemy is patterned after the cellular organization of the Communist party.
General dissemination of combat intelligence, and even information on Viet
Cong dispositions is rare; leaders are discouraged from inquiring into

5.

situations beyond their own unit and area of operation. Accordingly, fixed communication-liaison routes assume great importance to the Viet Cong units moving from one zone to another, since they must usually follow an established chain of base camps using a series of guides to pass from one area to the other. Supply parties and messengers follow the same routes; frequent "cut-outs" and transfer points are prescribed. US interdiction of such routes invariably causes confusion and dismay.

6. VC ATTACKS: Viet Cong offensive operations are usually launched from a base camp, and participating troops are well rehearsed in withdrawal routes, primary and alternate, from the point of attack to the same or another base camp. It is important to appreciate that all enemy military doctrine is couched in offensive terminology. Viet Cong "counter sweep" operations—the posture the Viet Cong assume to defend against large search and destroy operations—are described in their orders and other documents in terms of attacks by small groups upon the advancing enemy. In practice, this means the enemy units dispatch small elements to conduct harassing counter-attacks with mortars, rifle grenades, claymores, and other mines as the situation permits. This tactic is intended to maintain close contact with our forces, thus reducing vulnerability to our fires. Counter sweeps also visualize the gradual intensification of harassing actions up to and including all out attacks upon our forces once they appear fatigued or depleted, and their strengths and vulnerabilities have been accurately appraised. The terminology "attack" embraces any means of producing casualties among allied forces, including setting pressure mines in the road. Mortar attacks on US bases, both artillery field positions and our permanent

6

bases, is a preferred Viet Cong mode of offensive action. A meeting engagement outside fortifications with Viet Cong forces larger than platoon is rare, but there have been at least three instances in the past year of a Viet Cong force engaging, by what appeared to be an impromptu ambush, a US rifle company patrolling in the jungle. The Viet Cong prefer better odds and more carefully reconnoitered and planned operations. One favored form is the regimental ambush of a vehicular column on a road—a tactic to which the 9th Light Infantry Division resorted three times in the course of two months in the summer of 1966. Another preference is a regimental assault upon a US defensive position. Post-battle analysis suggests that the enemy plans his maneuver basically on terrain information, that is, knowing we were occupying a position in a given clearing, he maneuvered into position to attack the clearing. However, usually his attack was preceded by ground reconnaissance and probes designed to single out locations of our automatic weapons, and identify weak points in our defense. Invariably, his attacks were preceded by intense mortaring and numerous volleys from direct fire weapons. His assault, when it was launched, was delivered over a wide front, but he concentrated a large mass of his infantry in considerable depth upon one small sector of our position in an effort to penetrate at that point. A number of these large scale attacks were launched in the early morning hours, as though the attackers expected to capitalize upon the first daylight during the latter stages of their assault, when they had penetrated our position. The assault itself was intense and aggressively pressed, with heavy reliance being placed on hand grenades as well as the submachine gun. All these attacks were markedly unsuccessful; enemy initiated ground attacks were the greatest single source of enemy losses over the past year.

7

TABLE I   PRINCIPAL VIET CONG FORCES 1ST INFANTRY DIVISION TAOI

MAIN FORCES	AREA OF OPERATIONS	REMARKS
9th VC Division 271st VC Regiment 272d VC Regiment 273d VC Regiment	War Zones C&D	A highly mobile light infantry division which normally conducts regimental size operations. Oldest VC division in the III Corps Tactical Zone, this division has been the 1st Infantry Division's primary opponent.
7th NVA Division 52d NVA Regiment 141st NVA Regiment 165th NVA Regiment	PHUOC LONG and BINH LONG Province War Zone C	Elements of this division entered the Corps Tactical Zone in 1965. It is believed the division was formed during 1966. Ridden with disease, this unit is only just beginning to be a combat effective unit.
101st NVA Regiment	War Zone C&D	Independent mobile regiment formerly under the operational control of the 9th VC Division.
LOCAL FORCES		
PHU LOI Battalion	BINH DUONG Province	A well trained, high morale provincial battalion. The 1st Infantry Division has had frequent contacts with this battalion. It is the principal local force battalion in the division area.
C61 Company C62 Company C63 Company C64 Company C70 Company C81 Company	South BEN CAT District CHANH THANH District LAI THIEU District DAU TIENG District BINH LONG North BEN CAT District	Viet Cong district companies which vary in strength from 50 to 120 men. These companies are armed with mixed weapons. Their combat effectiveness varies from the highly proficient with high morale to those which are combat ineffective in other than platoon level operations. These companies operate within their districts and reinforce the hamlet and village guerrillas.
POLITICAL HEADQUARTERS		
COSVN	Located in War Zone C	Political and military headquarters directing all military and political elements of the Viet Cong effort in the majority of South Vietnam.

8

TABLE I (continued)

POLITICAL HEADQUARTERS	AREA OF OPERATIONS	REMARKS
Military Region I	Located in War Zone D	Subordinate to COSVN. Controls and directs VC activity in all of the III Corps area except SAIGON, BINH LONG, BINH TUY, and PHUOC LONG areas.
Military Region IV	Located in Southeastern BINH DUONG	Controls VC activity, political and military, in SAIGON and its surrounding district.
Military Region 10	Probably located in PHUOC LONG	New region in two northernmost provinces of III Corps area—BINH LONG and PHUOC LONG training and recuperation base for infiltrating units.

9

BIG RED ONE BATTLE PRINCIPLES

1. Infantry, armor, and Army aviation find the enemy.

2. Air and artillery kill the enemy.

3. Battalion commanders must know unit locations within 10
    meters at all times.

4. Keep plans and schemes of maneuver simple.

5. Put your back to a landing zone.

6. Foxholes are deep, properly sited, camouflaged, have full
    overhead cover and a frontal protective berm.

10

DEFENSE

1. <u>TEAMWORK</u>: The 1st Division has earned well a reputation for building sound defenses, and fighting from them magnificently. But reputation will never defeat an attacking Viet Cong force. Perhaps more than any other type of operation, successful defense hinges on sound planning, hard preparatory work, vigorous execution, and aggressive follow-up at every level:

*The rifleman whose shovel, muscle, weapon, and courage are the foundation of the defense.

*The NCO whose know-how shapes and ties together the position, who leads the defenders at the point of decision.

*The company officer who lays out the position, and controls the infantry weapons.

*The battalion commander who selects key weapon positions, arranges artillery concentrations, and pre-planned air, and commands the fight on the ground.

*The brigade commander who supervises preparation, and manages from the air fires and exploiting maneuver.

2. <u>THE US COUNTER TO ENEMY ATTACK</u>: The Viet Cong are a tough and wily foe from whom surprises are to be expected. Nonetheless, their doctrine and training seems to compel them to follow a pattern. Usually their attacks are preceded by reconnaissance and light probes designed to delineate our positions, locate our key weapons, and identify weak spots in our line. They then bring their mortars and recoilless rifle well forward, and lay them directly on specific US weapons whose positions they fix during the reconnaissance. Their attack itself is heralded by intense fires from these heavy weapons,

11

TABLE I   VC ATTACK & US COUNTER

              ENEMY TACTIC   1ST DIVISION DEFENSE

(1) *Reconnaissance: probes, harassment,   (1) *Counter-recon security screen:
     pre-attack targeting   LP & OP's trip flares and clay-
                                                   mores
                                                   *Camouflaged positions
                                                   *Fire discipline

(2) *Indirect fire: mortars, recoilless   (2) *Overhead cover
     rifles, rifle grenades

(3) *Direct fire: recoilless rifles,   (3) *Camouflaged positions
     RPG, MG, claymores   *Low silhouettes
                                                   *Full frontal berms

(4) *Frontal assault: SMG and grenades;   (4) *Wire and other obstacles
     concentrated infantry   *Trip flares
                                                   *Claymores
                                                   *Full frontal berms
                                                   *Flanking, grazing fire
                                                   *Positions in depth
                                                   *Large caliber direct fire

12

261

followed by a frontal assault of the US line. The assault infantry are normally led by submachine gunners firing continuously from the hip as they run, supplemented by grenadiers. 1st Division defenses are designed to frustrate both enemy heavy weapons, and enemy infantry assault. Table I outlines the means by which we counter specific enemy tactics.

    3. FIGHTING POSITIONS: The Big Red One fighting position adheres to the following principles:

        a. A frontal protective berm to deflect direct fire.

        b. Forty-five degree firing ports.

        c. Full overhead cover.

        d. Camouflaged to blend into the background.

        e. Low silhouette.

        f. Permits "Bee Hive" rounds to be fired without endangering occupants.

        g. Is continually improved so long as position is occupied.

    4. SITE SELECTION: Difficulty with an individual position--inability to perform mission or extensive labor--usually starts with poor choice of site. Leaders must look for the ground with best command of long graze in their sector, and emplace their automatic weapons there. They should also look for natural cover and concealment for positions, and use it well. Each machine gun should be protected by at least two rifle positions. Positions should be sited in depth, that is, displaced from front to rear 10-50 meters from one another, as in the following idealized diagrams (Figures 1 and 2). It is not sufficient for a company commander, platoon leader, or squad leader to simply locate his unit upon the general trace of a perimeter and begin to

13

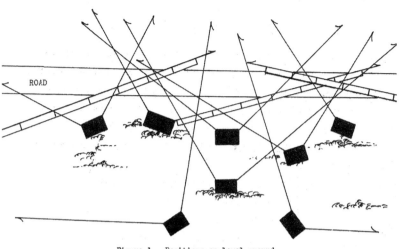

Figure 1. Positions on level ground

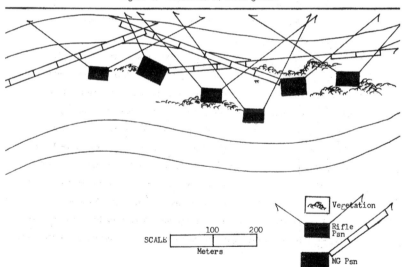

Figure 2. Positions on uneven ground
14

263

dig. These leaders must develop a sensitivity for the defensive possibility
of any piece of ground their unit occupies. They must visualize how the
defense of their assigned sector will develop. They must be alert to the
slightest changes in the lie of the terrain; by moving the tentative location
of a position as little as five feet, a fine field of fire may develop, or
there may be provided a site offering classic cover and concealment. Leaders
must develop the facility to visualize the role each position will play in
the defense, and how the whole sector will interlock into a coordinated system of mutually supporting positions. They must walk the terrain, identify
avenues of approach, and calculate how to defeat enemy assault on those
approaches. In selecting his position the commander will, if possible, avoid
pushing the defensive perimeter out to the tree line at the edge of a clearing.
Well dug-in positions in the open, covered by listening posts in the forest,
take advantage of available fields of fire, and are also less vulnerable to
attack by mortars since tree bursts cannot impact directly upon the unit. The
commander will site his fighting positions to form a perimeter in depth, avoiding a lineal or regular circle configuration, and to interlock positions for
maximum mutual support by flanking and covering fires among individual positions. He will take steps to insure that each soldier will know his own field
of fire and that of supporting positions, and that each of the subordinate
leaders will know the same information for all the positions under his command,
plus the planned mortar and artillery fires (to include planned "bee-hive"
fires) which can support his area of responsibility. Normally, he will establish a unit SOP for the defense and follow it, but any SOP must provide for
siting or checking key positions by the defense commander, and his designating

15

which shall be two, three, or four man positions.

5. SEQUENCE OF WORK: a. Select site. Primary concern is fields of fire, but look also for natural cover and concealment for each position. Walk key machine gun final protective lines to check the selected position, and to identify dead space.

b. Plan camouflage. Calculate how position will be blended into background, and establish paths for approaching site, for pitching tents, and for passing forward to clear fire lanes.

c. Dig a foxhole throwing up spoil to form a berm, which is progressively packed, formed, and apertured.

d. Clear (or preferable selectively thin out) fields of fire, to provide fire lane down each FPL, and observation over the whole assigned sector.

e. Complete walking FPL's and prepare range cards.

f. Emplace claymores, a minimum of one per man.

g. Emplace wire. A frontal perimeter barrier line of trip flares, plus concertina (if available), and obstacles along the friendly side of each FPL.

h. Continue to improve foxhole. Stock hole with ammo, providing storage niches.

i. Put overhead cover on foxholes.

j. Complete camouflage of front.

k. Dig entrance trench, and supplementary hole(s), and camouflage them.

l. Camouflage tents and paths.

m. Dig communications trenches and reserve positions and camouflage. Camouflage will be replaced as needed, berm improved as appropriate, covered

16

sleeping positions prepared, and interconnecting trenches dug. Dummy and alternate positions will also be prepared as time permits.

6. ARMOR IN THE DEFENSE: Armored vehicles will not be positioned in their night defense sites, or along the trace of infantry fighting positions during daylight hours. To do so destroys much of the value of carefully camouflaged fighting positions, and makes enemy reconnaissance easier. Rather, armored vehicles will move to pre-planned, prepared positions after dark. When the mission requires that a perimeter be occupied for several days, the location of armored vehicle positions will be changed periodically, at least once daily. Perimeters composed of armored vehicles will be organized in depth, avoid a lineal or regular circle figuration, and achieve maximum flanking and covering fires for mutual support along the lines prescribed for infantry fighting positions. On vehicle azimuth indicators for range cards, infra-red equipment, and lights will be fully exploited. Mechanized infantry will, of course, fight from holes except for the vehicle driver and the main armament gunner; mechanized infantry APC's will overwatch their squad positions, adding depth to the defense. Armored cavalry fight from their vehicles.

7. CLAYMORES: The claymore mine is an area weapon designed to repel close enemy assault. At a minimum, each defender shall have one claymore aimed to clean out his firing sector at hand grenade range—a claymore set out within sight of his aperture, and protected by his fire. Other claymores may be provided each defender on line to supplement his sector or readily observe. All LP's and OP's should be equipped with claymores, preferably three per patrol for front and both flanks.

8. CONDUCT OF DEFENSE: Our defensive positions are built around the

17

basic positions described above. But principles of fighting these positions in this war are unchanged from those the US Army used during World War II and Korea. There must be defense in depth, interlocking banks of grazing fire, defensive artillery and mortar concentrations, coverage of dead space in final protective lines, tactical and protective wire (as time permits), and trip flares and claymores. When a defensive perimeter is probed, we must not disclose the locations of direct fire weapons, particularly automatic weapons. Rather, LP's fire claymores in the area of the probe, and the line uses indirect fire weapons and M79's initially. Final protective line fires are called for only when the position is under assault. The position must be organized in such strength and depth that it can repel the assault while artillery and air strikes are brought to bear on the attackers. The commander's plan for conducting defense must provide for:

a. Withdrawing his security screen altogether, or selectively by quadrant, ahead of enemy probes to free his indirect weapons. Normally the LP's or OP's fire their claymores to cover their withdrawal.

b. Controlling his fires during probes to avoid revealing his machine guns and other key positions, while delivering 40mm grenades and mortar fires on the enemy scouts.

c. Calling for illumination—mortar, artillery, and air-dropped flares—and positioning it to maximum advantage.

d. Pre-planning use of air firepower by pre-designating radar-controlled bomb targets, and providing for marking lines at night, e.g., vehicle headlights, gasoline flares, or strobe lights.

e. Calling for and stopping final protective fires, for the whole position, or by sector.

18

f. Moving reserves to positions behind portions of the line under assault to block or restore penetration.

g. Firing "bee hive" ammunition over his lines during enemy assault.

h. Conducting resupply. Stocks should be pushed up into the forward holes as available. Prepackaged company issues of small arms ammunition should be prepared for helicopter sling load directly onto position. Battalion packs of medical supplies, and company mortar packs should also be on ready. No resupply should be attempted until enemy direct fire is suppressed. Precipitous evacuation or resupply leads to needless casualties.

9. ROLE OF BATTALION AND COMPANY COMMANDERS. The senior infantry or armor commander present cannot delegate responsibility for organizing the defense. In particular, the senior commander must control artillery and air support—the principal Viet Cong killers—and so much of other key weapons as may be feasible. Thus, a battalion commander should supervise firing in his artillery defense concentrations daily; a company commander should site all his company machine guns, and the battalion commander should at least check his choices.

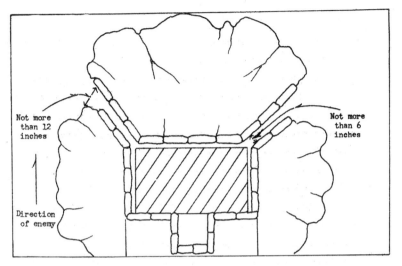

Figure 1. Rifle position, start

1. <u>CONSTRUCTING RIFLE POSITIONS</u>:

a. Large positions are weak positions. Each rifle position should begin with a rectangular hole as long as the shoulder-to-shoulder length of the men who will fight it, as wide as a man plus equipment. Spoil should be thrown forward and to the sides to form a sloped, progressively packed berm.

20

b. The next step at the hole is to cut firing apertures at 45 degrees to the direction of the enemy and deepen the hole, tailoring depth to each man, and carving elbow rests in the parapet for each rifleman to insure solid elbow-under-the piece firing positions. Apertures should be narrow and tapered, just sufficient to command the assigned sector. AR's

Figure 2. Firing aperture

on bipods should have bipod rest slots cut forward of the parapet to allow the bipod to be withdrawn easily and to rest the gun muzzle low.

21

The fitting for firing should be undertaken carefully to counter the natural tendency to shoot high at night. This is accomplished by digging each man down so that standing in his hole in firing position his piece is level at height for graze, firmly seated and supported, and as close to the ground as his mission permits.

    c. Overhead cover is then added:

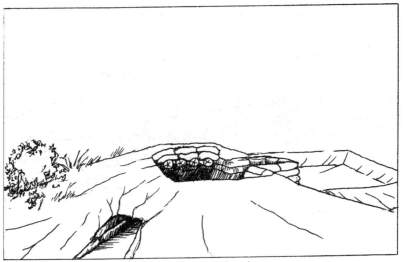

Figure 3. Cross section view
of overhead cover

Cover can be fabricated from large logs plus sandbags or dirt, or sapling/ bamboo mats in three cross-laid laminations plus sandbags or dirt, but should be sturdy enough to take the full weight jumping of a large, combat loaded

22

271

Figure 4. Completed foxhole as viewed from left front with camouflage partially completed.

23

soldier. The unit which habitually carries pioneer tools (including chain saws) is not only ready to defend on order, but possesses the capability to cut emergency LZ's as required. Full overhead cover is constructed over all positions; full cover cuts vulnerability to airbursts and grenades, and lessens prospects of flooding in the event of rain—an important consideration in the monsoon season. Care must be exercised to hold the silhouette of the position as low as possible, and the apertures as small as sector of fire permits. The height of the cover is determined by placing the firers in the hole, and the cover adjusted a full inch above their helmets while they take up night firing positions—head high over the sights. Berms and apertures should be extended and sloped forward to cut vertical surfacing, and to hide muzzle flash from the front.

  d. Camouflage is added. Preferably this should be rooted plants and grass sod, calculated to grow naturally in place on the position, and to blend fully with the surrounding vegetation. While digging the fighting position, maximum care should be taken to prevent the destruction of natural camouflage growing near the hole, scaling off the sod to a depth that will maintain the roots, and setting it aside to be used for camouflage upon completion of the overhead cover. If the position is sited behind thick shrubbery, slightly higher positions than those normally acceptable can be built; positions dug in from behind earth clumps or hummocks offer more headroom and more substantial overhead cover.

  e. Each position is completed before any thought is given to rest. There is only one reasonable sure defense for the soldier against the mortar attack which may come at any moment--be underground. Hence, positions should

24

provide for each soldier a hole in which to stand erect and fight, with adequate overhead clearance, overhead cover, a berm to the front with proper
firing apertures, a berm to the sides, adequate rear protection, and thorough
camouflage.

   f. A rear entrance must be dug. This rear entry should be an auxi-
liary, fully open, individual firing position. This is used for throwing grenades and M79 fires. It should be at minimum designed to allow entry into the
hole from the rear, covered with a poncho or similar screen to cut down back-
lighting the firing apertures. Full consideration will be given to protecting
defenders from friendly direct fire weapons from the rear shooting overhead in
support (including artillery beehive ammunition), and to emergency resupply.
The sleeping position should be directly behind the fighting position. Connecting trenches and spider holes may be constructed.

  2. CONSTRUCTING MACHINE GUN POSITIONS

   The machine gun position is constructed generally following the same
procedure as for the rifle position, except that the hole must be designed
around the gun. The first step is to emplace the gun on its final protective
line, and walk the latter to check the site. The hole is then traced to place
a sturdy firing table with working room for the loader on the left.

25

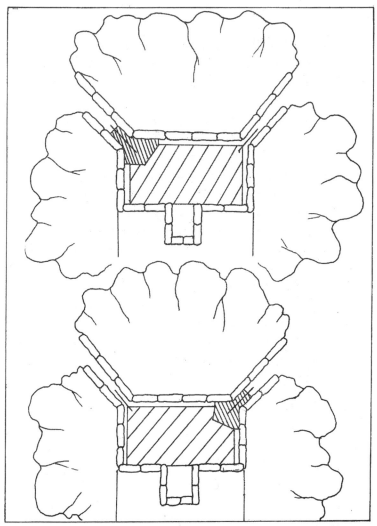

Figure 5. Machine gun positions with machine gun on left and right sides
26

OFFENSE

1. <u>AXIOMS</u>: a. <u>Do not bunch up</u>. No infantry force of any size ever congregates together; close grouping leads to a claymore and multiple casualties. Each leader at every level extends his formations to the maximum consistent with control; distances man-to-man, and element to element, should be in constant tension with the leader's ability to maintain control.

b. <u>Scouts out</u>. No infantry force of any size moves without scouts out. At lead fire team level, this means splitting into scout and overwatch elements; at squad level, leading with a fire team; at higher levels, it means cloverleaf patrolling.

c. <u>Firepower before maneuver</u>. No maneuver is undertaken without covering artillery and/or air. Infantry finds the enemy, but firepower destroys him.

2. <u>ORGANIZATION FOR COMBAT</u>: a. No detail of the individual soldier's equipment should escape command attention. The overladen soldier is prone to overheating, and stays prone under fire. For example, careful planning for individual military loads can be frustrated by the soldier's proclivity to carry ration supplements, cameras, and other impediments. Or, white insect repellent bottles or cigarette packs in his helmet band can violate otherwise good camouflage discipline.

b. Command attention to unit equipment is even more important. For example, the company commander who elects to leave all his mortars behind fails to appreciate that it is always possible to carry one, almost always to get it into action, and often to influence crucially his maneuver. The battalion commander who counts on helicopter resupply for pioneer tools is

27

vulnerable to being trapped in dense jungle without even an emergency LZ.
No battalion or company commander, nor artillery liaison officer, nor forward
observer should advance without carrying a 292 antenna for his radio.

    c. Ammunition load per person, and ammunition packaging is especially
critical. Speed in opening fire is an important consideration, but of overriding concern should be a sustained high volume of fire. Overloaded, poorly
protected rifle magazines invite stoppages. Machine gun belts carried around
necks assure stoppages. Except for a short starter belt (25 rounds) carried
in the gun at half load, all machine gun ammunition should be carried in original, unopened boxes. Seven to ten magazines per rifle, 800 to 1000 rounds
per machine gun, and 35 to 50 rounds per mortar should be a minimum load for
an advance to contact. Emergency resupply in the form of company loads of
ammunition in helicopter sling loads should be in readiness.

    d. The organization and employment of command groups deserves thorough
preplanning. At battalion level, constant FM radio communications with brigade
is of paramount importance; movement of the CP in echelons is normally essential
except for brief periods when the command is airborne. An airborne OP capability
is virtually always essential. At company level, it is normally desirable to
advance with the command group split into two sections, separated for surviva-
bility, with the executive officer or first sergeant in one, and the CO in the
other; both groups should possess radios and the ability to control air and
artillery support, resupply, and medical evacuation.

    e. A well-rehearsed unit SOP will remove from the command net much
cluttered traffic concerning resupply and evacuation, relegating such messages
to the logistic net and to subordinates of the combat leaders. The unit whose

28

commanders must employ command radios for obtaining combat service support is severely handicapped in fire and maneuver.

f. Ground-to-air signal devices—smoke grenades and air panels—are critical to employment of firepower. One smoke grenade per man should be minimum; more should be carried on occasion. Additionally, a company packet of colored smoke grenades should be on hand at the battalion forward command post for lowering or dropping from the LOH if required.

3. MOVEMENT TO CONTACT: a. Infantry maneuvers in the jungle to find the enemy. The underlying purposes in infantry security measures are to prevent the units' thrusting into the killing zone of an enemy defense or ambush more than a fire team; to detect the presence of the enemy before he becomes aware of us; and, above all, to locate the enemy so that our firepower can destroy him. The basic maneuver is the "cloverleaf," so called from the pattern of patrols thrown out in advance of, and to the flanks and rear of advancing units. Every unit moving must use the cloverleaf maneuver applying the over-watch technique in moving to contact.

b. The "overwatch" is one unit always in a position to immediately return fire while the other unit is moving. (Example: One fire team moving, the other one in a firing position "overwatching" the advancing fire team. The advancing team halts and takes up a firing position, the trailing team moves forward until it can take up a position to overwatch.)

c. Cloverleaf. Figure 1. The first unit to move will be the lead squad of the lead platoon. This squad will move out using the bounding over-watch. The bounding overwatch is used when contact is imminent. One fireteam will always be in firing position while the other advances. The front advancing

29

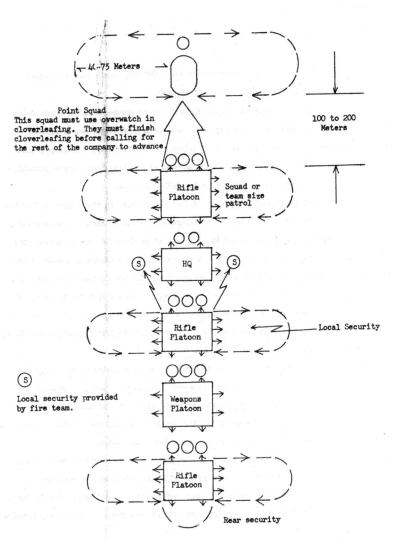

Point Squad
This squad must use overwatch in
cloverleafing. They must finish
cloverleafing before calling for
the rest of the company to advance.

40-75 Meters

100 to 200
Meters

Rifle
Platoon

Squad or
team size
patrol

HQ

Rifle
Platoon

Local Security

Local security provided
by fire team.

Weapons
Platoon

Rifle
Platoon

Rear security

Figure 1. Rifle company cloverleafing in advance to contact

30

279

fireteam will use overwatch within the fireteam (half moving and half over-watching). The forward movement is by bounds. This type of movement again allows the minimum number of men to become engaged by the same source of firepower at once, and someone to return fire immediately. When this squad has moved 100 to 200 meters, depending on terrain, the squad leader will set up a defense position and send his fireteams, one at a time, to the flanks in a cloverleaf. The fireteam (cloverleafing) will advance using the overwatch within the fireteam (half moving and half in a position overwatching). The other fireteam will always be overwatching. When this action is completed, he will call the platoon leader who will displace the platoon forward, fol-lowed by the company until contact is made with the point. As soon as contact is made with the point, it will move out again repeating the same steps. The company will, upon closing on the point squad, set out security immediately and then send patrols out to the flanks. (Each rifle platoon will send a patrol to both flanks.) The patrols will go out, depending on terrain, no less than 40 meters. The rear platoon will, in addition to cloverleafing, send security to the rear. The platoon directly behind the company Hq group should send security to secure the command group. When all clover-leaf pat-rols have returned, the company commander must be notified so that he can move the company forward upon the call from the point element. This type of movement is slow and requires practice, good control and lots of patience; however, time and again, units using the cloverleaf have scouted out the enemy, destroyed him by fire, and then maneuvered in upon his positions without serious casualties. The cloverleaf method is slow. The company depicted (Figure 1) will cover only about 2000 meters in eight hours of advancing. Some

31

commanders who have elected to advance otherwise have taken heavy casualties in their lead platoon and suffered more attempting to extricate them. It is difficult to outline the application of the clover-leaf principle which would correspond to every situation. The preceding example is merely illustrative. Occasions will arise when greater speed of movement will be dictated by mission, terrain, or enemy situation. The clover-leaf principle holds that the rifle company will advance preceded by patrols in all directions. Successful employment of the clover-leaf principle requires intense practice: sand tables or chalk drills at platoon and company level, and practical exercises on terrain, as often as possible. Success also requires patience of commanders at battalion level and above, for they must accept the inherently slower pace of advance which adherence to the clover-leaf principle demands.

32

4. <u>ACTIONS UPON CONTACT</u>. Enemy contact in the jungle usually occurs at point blank range, and more often than not the enemy will enjoy advantages of fortifications, snipers in trees, communication trenches, and minefields to his front and flanks. It is imperative that upon contact, at all echelons, teamwork begins as follows:

    a. Company in contact. High volume of fire in direction of enemy, not neglecting trees. Immediately mark most advanced elements and flanks with smoke. Report direction (magnetic azimuth) to enemy, and range from one marking. Initiate artillery fire mission. Withdraw to place at least 50 meters between most forward element and enemy. Straighten line parallel to enemy line, or to desired air strike runs. Report estimated enemy strength, equipment, and direction withdrawal (if any).

    b. Battalion commander. Immediately request FAC, air strikes, and artillery observer. Locate precisely by map grid point of contact and mark for FAC. Initiate artillery blocking fires, if company FO has not done so. Alert reserves, medical evacuation aviation, and emergency resupply. Control air strikes if company commander not in position to do so.

    c. Commanders at all echelons. Aggressive instincts to flank the enemy position must be curbed. Once the enemy position is established, all commanders must strain their resources to bring available fires to bear on the enemy. Each commander from company on up must be capable of employing air and artillery, practiced in utilizing the channels of communications for each, and quick to initiate action to bring each into play. The most crucial information which the unit in contact must supply is the direction in which the enemy is withdrawing. Based on this sensing, commanders at

33

higher echelons deliver fires to block the avenue of enemy withdrawal or reinforcement. Fires are shifted outward from the point of contact progressively, and are discontinued only when, in the judgment of the battalion or brigade commander, the enemy has escaped. The inception of a heavy volume of artillery fire, and sustained fire can be facilitated by (1) "walking" fires in advance of and to the flanks of the unit as it moves to contact, and (2) keeping the artillery shooting despite use of air in the target area. Upon contact, time should not be wasted on prolonged attempts to fix precise targets. It is imperative that the supporting fires be initiated immediately. They can be initiated at a greater distance and subsequently is worked toward the unit as the situation clarifies. Battalion and brigade commanders must continually keep informed of the location of friendly fire support bases, and periodically war game the simultaneous employment of air and artillery in the event of contact. As a rule, artillery should never be cut off to facilitate delivery of air; rather, it should be shifted to augment the air in a blocking role. Constantly adjusted air-artillery fire control lines can be employed. Experience confirms that once artillery is cut off in favor of air, excessive time is lost in resuming fire. Experience also underscores the importance of the battalion commander choosing correctly among the relative advantages of air and artillery in each given situation. In general, air is the preferred instrument in dense jungle, or against base camps, because it can be delivered dependably very close to troops. Napalm is a fine close support weapon, but should always be delivered parallel to the friendly front. CBU is deadly against enemy outside fortifications, and should also be delivered parallel. Bombs are the answer to VC emplacements. Light artillery

34

is generally ineffective against fortifications, but is a fine, high volume antipersonnel weapon capable of achieving local fire superiority if nothing else. Light artillery and mortars can, of course, be fired in close support, but these too perform more reliably fired parallel to friendly front. Medium and heavy artillery must be echeloned in depth from friendly troops, but can effectively destroy VC fortifications. The mastery of fire control and fire coordination is the most important challenge faced by battalion and brigade commanders in Vietnam. Delegation of fire coordination is impossible; only the commander or the S-3 has the feel for the situation required.

5. FOLLOW-UP TO FIREPOWER: When in the judgment of the commanders concerned fires on the enemy have been effective, the advance will be resumed. Security to front and flanks is restored, and the unit enters the enemy position. At this time the mission of the infantry is thorough police of the battlefield. The Viet Cong are adroit at concealing personnel, arms, documents, and other valuables, and care and imagination are necessary for the searchers to ferret out the fruits of victory. Prisoners are especially valuable in this conflict, and pains should be taken to capture, safeguard, and treat medically any VC who survive our bombardment. Any documents, no matter how unimportant appearing they may be, should be evacuated. It should be a matter of pride to any infantry unit that an area it has searched is left devoid of intelligence.

6. ROAD CLEARING OPERATIONS: Offensive operations frequently entail securing a road for use as an MSR. In undertaking to clear a road, infantry commanders should commence operations by passing troops in V formation down the road, with the opening of the V in the direction of advance. The ends

35

of the wings echeloned forward and outward from the road should be at least
100 meters away from the ditchline, and the soldiers therein should be carefully instructed to search for wires and other signs of command detonated
mines or claymores. At the point of the V, on the road itself, about 200

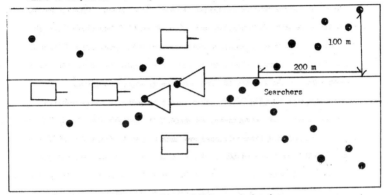

Figure 2. Inverted V for road clearing

meters rearward, should be mine sweep teams.

Experience establishes that the best mine detector we possess is an alert
infantryman with a keen eye, noticing tracks, disturbances in the surface
of the road, or wires. Once the initial clearing patrol moves down the
road, the road must be secured against re-mining and snipers. Troops or
armor assigned the securing mission must penetrate into the vegetation along-
side the road to beyond the limits of visibility, and must patrol actively.
Above all, troops engaged in road clearing must remain alert and dispersed
at all times; in any other posture, they court multiple casualties from
claymores or other command detonated mines.

36

7. <u>TRAINING</u>: a. No unit should move outside a secured, permanent base camp except in tactical formation. Leaders at every level must regard every move as training, and none must hesitate to stop a maneuver if it is being done wrong.

b. Musketry for infantry units should be practiced on every opportunity. As a minimum, riflemen should be required to fire through a basic load at maximum rate to teach them the meaning of volume fire, and to give them a feel for their firepower. Use of tracer ammunition, snap shooting at surprise targets, night firing, and cross training on the machine gun and grenade launcher is also helpful, and cannot be repeated often enough. Fire team and squads must be permitted to conduct field firing as a team.

c. After action critiques are superb training, and help significantly in developing sound SOP.

37

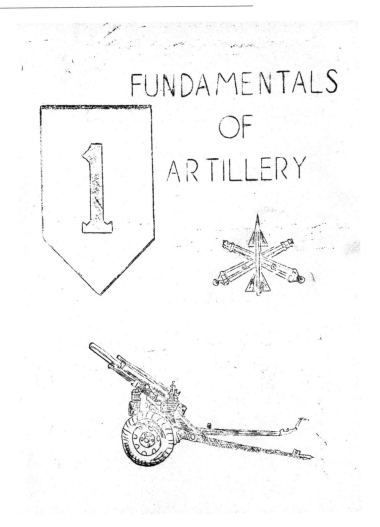

FUNDAMENTALS
OF
ARTILLERY

DEPARTMENT OF THE ARMY
HEADQUARTERS, 1ST INFANTRY DIVISION ARTILLERY
APO San Francisco 96345

AVDB-RA

SUBJECT: Fundamentals of Artillery

Infantry Unit Commanders and Staff Officers

1. In Viet Nam, as in past wars, artillery continues to be the greatest killer on the battlefield. The violent, immediate, and accurate application of artillery firepower in support of maneuver units kills and demoralizes the enemy while saving friendly lives.

2. Artillery can support the maneuver unit in a number of ways: by firing high explosive (HE) ammunition to destroy Viet Cong (VC) personnel and their installations; by illuminating the battlefield at night; by firing "beehive" or HE ammunition in the direct fire role to break human wave attacks; and by many other means.

3. The purpose of this publication is to provide the Big Red One soldier with information that will assist him in utilizing his supporting artillery to obtain maximum destruction of the enemy.

HENRY J. SCHROEDER JR.
Colonel, Artillery
Commanding

CAPABILITY

1. As stated in the Fundamentals of Infantry booklet published by the 1st Infantry Division, "Infantry, Armor, and Army aviation find the enemy; Air and Artillery kill the enemy". To accomplish this end, available to the "Big Red One" is the following organic and attached artillery

    a. 105mm Howitzer: (light artillery)   4 Battalions each with 3 firing batteries for a total of 72 towed howitzers

    b. 155mm Howitzer: (medium artillery)   3 Batteries each with 6 howitzers for a total of 18 howitzers (6 towed and 12 SP)

    c. 8in Howitzer: (heavy artillery)   1 Battery consisting of 4 howitzers (SP)

    d. 4.2" Mortars: (light artillery)   1 "Lighthorse" battery with 4 platoons for a total of 16 mortars

    e. 4.2" Mortars: (light artillery)   4 Base Defense platoons for a total of 16 mortars

2. In addition to the 126 tubes all capable of destroying the VC, the division artillery normally can call on additional firepower of all calibers available through II Field Forces Artillery. This supporting artillery includes the 175mm gun (heavy artillery).

3. The information contained herein is presented to give you a better understanding of the capabilities of each of the weapons available.

4. Projectiles and fuzes.

    a. Various types of projectiles (or shells) are manufactured to support almost any type maneuver unit activity. Some of the more common projectiles are:

2

(1) High Explosive (HE). High explosive projectiles are hollow steel projectiles filled with either composition B or TNT. Shell HE is primarily used to produce enemy casualties and to destroy enemy structures.

(2) Smoke. Shell smoke is a base ejection projectile used for screening enemy observation and for marking positions. Shell smoke is manufactured in 4 colors: White, green, red, and yellow.

(3) Illumination. Shell illumination is a base ejection type projectile that contains a flare suspended by a parachute. Its primary use is for battle-field illumination. It can also be used to mark targets at night. Listed below is the amount of light produced by the illumination projectiles with their burning times:

Caliber	Nomenclature	Candle Power	Burning Time
4.2	M335	500,000	70 sec
105	M314	600,000	70 - 75 sec
155	M118	600,000	45 - 60 sec
155	M485	1,000,000	120 sec

(4) White Phosphorus (WP). Shell white phosphorus is useful for screen-ing, incendiary, and casualty producing actions. It is particularly effective at night. Its use during the day must be closely coordinated with a forward air controller to avoid its being interpreted as a marking rocket for tactical air strikes.

(5) Anti-personnel (beehive). The beehive projectile is a thinskinned projectile that contains small arrow shaped pieces of metal. It is most effective in direct fire against personnel.

(6) Propaganda. Shell propaganda is a base ejection shell used to deliver psychological warfare leaflets.

3

(7) High Explosive Plastic-Tank (HEP-T). Shell HEP-T is provided for the 105mm howitzer for use against armor and mechanized vehicles.

b. Fuzes: The proper fuze must be used with the selected projectiles to cause projectiles to function at the time and place desired. Fuzes are classified according to the method of functioning as listed below:

(1) Quick: Fuze quick or point detonating (PD) functions when it strikes a solid object. In open terrain, fuze quick produces ground bursts; in wooded terrain fuze quick often produces tree bursts. Fuze quick is suitable against:

(a) Personnel in the open.

(b) Personnel in sparsely wooded terrain.

(c) Snipers in trees.

(d) Material when penetration is not required.

(e) Armored vehicles when firing heavy artillery.

(2) Delay: Most point detonating fuzes can be set for a 0.05 second delay. When it is so set, it is referred to as fuze delay. Fuze delay is used as listed:

(a) Destruction mission. Fuze delay is desirable when firing destruction missions at underground bunkers. The fuze allows the projectile to penetrate the structure, then burst underground. Destruction missions are fired only with the 8in howitzer because of its accuracy and large bursting effect. Mixed fuze quick and delay are especially suitable for use against occupied enemy base camps located under jungle canopy.

4

(b) Ricochet fire. Ricochet fire should be used only against personnel dug in or under light cover when VT or time fuzes are not available. Ricochet fire can be employed only when the earth's surface is hard enough and the projectile's angle of impact is small enough to cause the projectile to bounce and achieve an air burst.

(c) Fuze delay can be used to fire through double and triple canopy forests causing the projectile to burst near the ground.

(3) Time: Time fuzes burst the projectile on the operation of a preset time mechanism, or on impact. The height of burst is normally adjusted by the observer; however, it can be set on "safe" to cause it to function as a fuze quick. Fuze time is not effective in jungles where there is heavy overhead growth. It is suitable for use against:

(a) Personnel in the open.

(b) Personnel in entrenchments.

(c) Area targets where neutralization is desired.

(d) Personnel attacking a FSPB in the direct fire role with HE or WP.

(4) Controlled Variable Time (CVT): CVT fuze is a radio activated fuze which bursts the projectile automatically at approximately 20 meters above the earth's surface. Therefore, a height of burst adjustment is not required. During the adjustment, fuze quick is normally employed to obtain greater adjusting speed and to facilitate sensings. Fuze CVT is not effective in jungles where there is heavy overhead growth. It is suitable for use against:

(a) Personnel in the open.

(b) Personnel in entrenchments.

(c) Personnel overrunning a night defensive position which is complete with overhead cover for its defenders. The GVT fused round in this role is fired only upon request of the maneuver force commander of the NDP.

5. The chart below lists the ranges and lethal bursting radii of the various artillery rounds in open terrain. As the density of trees and vegetation increases in an area, generally these radii decrease.

	MAX RANGE	LETHAL BURSTING RADII
4.2"	5,400 meters	30 meters
105mm	11,000 "	30 "
155mm	14,600 "	50 "
8"	16,800 "	80 "
175mm	32,700 "	95 "

6. Maximum rate of fire:

WEAPON	MAXIMUM	SUSTAINED
4.2" Mortar	15 - 20 rnds per minute	15 - 20 rnds per minute
105mm Howitzer	10 rnds first 3 minutes	3 rnds per minute
155mm Howitzer	4 rnds first 3 minutes	1 rnd per minute
175mm gun	2 rnds first 4 minutes	1 rnd per every 2 minutes
8" Howitzer	2 rnds first 4 minutes	1 rnd per every 2 minutes

7. Air Transport. The 4.2 inch mortar, the 105mm Howitzer, and the 155mm Howitzer (towed) batteries are transportable by either fixed or rotary wing aircraft. The 105mm Howitzer battery with 2000 rounds can be transported by approximately 30 CH-47 sorties. One 4.2" mortar platoon can be transported by approximately 26 UH-1D sorties. The 155mm Howitzer battery can be lifted, with 1500 rounds, by 7 CH-54 sorties and 46 CH-47 sorties.

8. Each weapon system has its limits. The direct support artillery battalion commander, S3, LNO's and FO's are all familiar with the capability of each

6

weapon and will select the best weapon to do the job. An example of this is the destruction of enemy base camps. Light and medium artillery are not ef- -- fective against, and hence not used to destroy, VC base camps or bunkers. Normally, these missions are undertaken with 8" howitzers, 175mm guns, or preferably air strikes with heavy bombs.

7

FIELD POSITIONS

1. Artillery batteries are positioned to provide fires in support of infantry and armored operations. Habitually, these operations will be limited to the range of the 105 battery. The mobility of the artillery is exploited to extend the range of such operations. A base camp position offers the following advantages:

    a. The problem of resupply of heavy ammunition is simplified.

    b. Survey data is available to increase the effectiveness of unobserved fires.

    c. No additional infantry units are required to provide adequate security.

2. Infantry units often operate in the field beyond the range of artillery in base camps. To support such an operation an artillery battery is displaced to a fire support patrol base (FSPB) to insure that all units are under the protective umbrella of the 105mm howitzer. FSPB's are selected so that they mutually support one another. This allows defensive fires to be delivered in the event a FSPB or NDP is subject to ground and/or mortar attack.

3. The organization of FSPB's must be a joint effort between the artillery and the security force commanders. The actual positioning of elements within the FSPB's must be accomplished by the commander responsible for the defense of the FSPB. He must, however, closely coordinate with the artillery commander to insure that the artillery can accomplish its primary mission of fire support. The following must be accomplished:

8

a. The artillery battery must be positioned so that it may fire in any direction, a 6400 capability.

b. The crew-served weapons of the artillery battery should be integrated into the perimeter defense.

c. The direct fire capability of the artillery weapons should be considered. The best anti-personnel direct fire ammunition for the 105 howitzer is the beehive round. This round is extremely effective at any range which can be engaged using direct fire technique. The infantry commander must insure that all fighting holes between the artillery and the perimeter wire have a protective berm 2 sandbags thick between the fighting hole and the battery. This will allow the beehive to be fired directly over the fighting hole, if necessary. Sufficient warning must be given prior to firing, because all friendly personnel must be under protective cover. The beehive will be fired under supervision of the senior artilleryman present in the fire support base only after he has obtained authority for its use from the senior maneuver force commander present in the FSPB.

d. The minimum dimensions for space requirements for a 105mm battery are approximately 75m x 100m. The 155mm and 8in Howitzer battery requires at least an area 100 x 100 meters. A type layout of a 105mm battery is shown at figure 1. Individual artillery weapon positions are habitually organized as shown in inclosures 1 through 5.

5. The construction of artillery positions within the FSPB requires extensive sandbagging which can normally be accomplished by the artillery unit. However, when short notice is given for extraction from a position it may be expedient

9

for the infantry commander to provide assistance to close out the position and to bag ammunition.

6. Artillery vehicles required in a FSPB will depend on whether air or road is the primary mode of resupply. In a position where resupply is accomplished by air, the artillery light battery will have 3 wheeled vehicles in the base, one 1/4T truck, and two 3/4T trucks. If the artillery is resupplied by road, an additional 2 vehicles, usually 2½T trucks, remain overnight and are used for back haul. A greater number of vehicles are required in the 155mm and 8in howitzer FSPB to move ammunition and back haul powder canisters and other refuse.

10

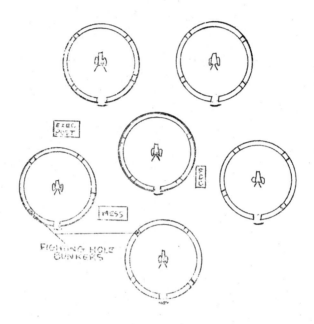

FIGURE 1

298

Inclosure 1 to Fundamentials of Artillery, Standard 105mm Howitzer Position.

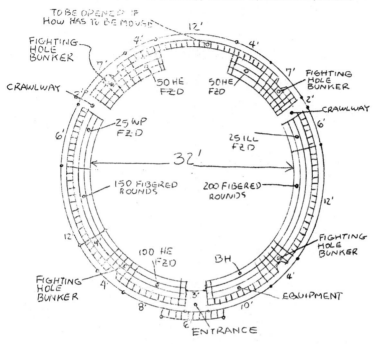

Recapitulation
1. Ammo storage required
   a. HE fuzed - 200 rds
   b. HE in fibers - 100 rds
   c. ILL - as required
   d. P - as required
   e. BH - 6 rds, HEP-T - 2 rds
2. All ammunition and bunkers will have overhead cover. Two thicknesses of sandbags on top and one thickness for sides and fromt are minimum.

Inclosure 2 to Fundamentials of Artillery, Standard 4.2" Mortar Field
Position.

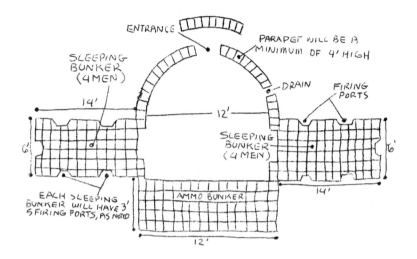

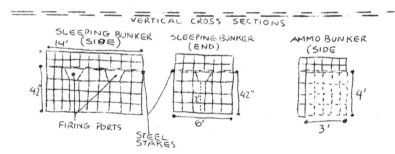

NOTE: All ammunition and sleeping bunkers will have overhead cover. Two
thicknesses of sandbags on top and one thickness for sides and
front are minimum.

Inclosure 3 to Fundamentals of Artillery, standard eight in (SP) Position

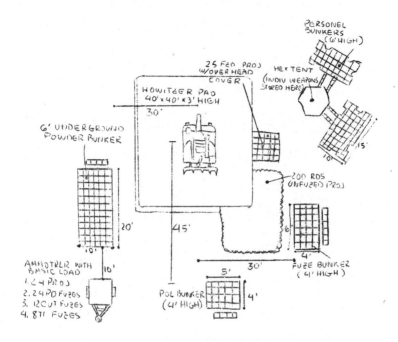

Inclosure 4 to Fundamentals of Artillery Standard and 155 SP Position

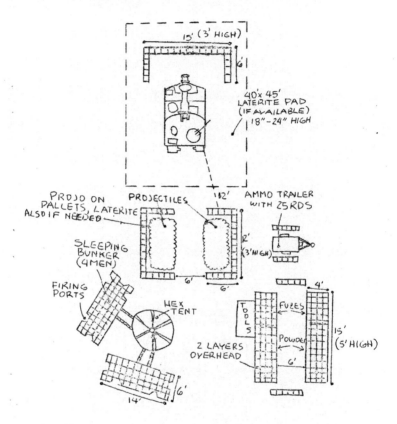

Inclosure 5 to Fundamentals of Artillery Standard 155, Tow Field Position

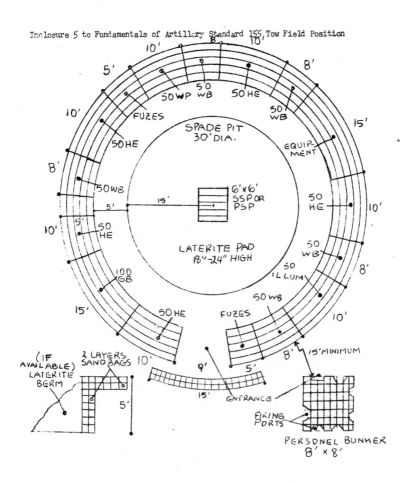

FIRE SUPPORT

1. Fire support and maneuver are complementary. Successfull combat depends on the proper planning and execution of each. Fire planning is a continuous process. It does not cease with the issuance of an order, but continues throughout an operation.

2. To assist and advise you in the planning and utilization of fire support at the brigade level are the direct support battalion commander (LTC), your fire support coordinator, and assistant, your Artillery Liaison Officer (MAJ or CPT). At battalion level, the Artillery Liaison Officer performs as your fire support coordinator. With each maneuver company or troop is an Artillery Forward Observer. In the "Big Red One", once a forward observer or liaison officer joins a maneuver unit he remains with that unit until assigned another duty. You should make him feel that he is a part of your unit which in part he is. The air observers within Division Artillery are located with the Division Artillery Aviation Section and are controlled by the Div Arty S-3. They are assigned to support one of the direct support (DS) battalions on a daily schedule. The forward observer and the air observer are capable of combined adjustment of fires on an enemy in any type terrain or foliage. Due to the nature of the terrain in Vietnam it is often difficult, if not impossible, for the air observer to see his target and the disposition of friendly forces. The infantry commander must assist the air observer by insuring that the disposition of his forces is clearly marked on the ground through the use of smoke. Under no circumstances

11

will the air observer preempt the ground observer firing a mission. The air observer may offer to take over the mission if he has full cognizance of the situation, but must leave the decision to the forward observer on the ground.
3. In order to best utilize the fires available, you must have an understanding of the types of fires and their purpose. The more common types utilized within the Big Red One are as follows:

a. Preparations: Preparations are intense prearranged fires scheduled normally to include all artillery within range and to serve to neutralize a landing zone or an area into which friendly forces are scheduled to operate. Preparations are normally in three phases as follows:

(1) Air strikes utilizing hard bombs, napalm and CBU around the edges of an LZ.

(2) Artillery fires on and around the edges of an LZ to neutralize enemy mines, booby traps, and personnel in the vicinity.

(3) Armed helicopter strikes immediately prior to touchdown and providing support during touchdown.

b. Blocking fires: Blocking fires are planned and fired on order near landing zones to inhibit the maneuver of the enemy. The amount of fire should be regulated in accordance with anticipated and observed enemy activity.

c. Marching fires: Marching fires are fired when a unit is executing a reconnaissance in force mission, or is on the move through a hazardous area. Generally, one round is fired every five to ten minutes 600 - 800 meters to the front of the unit depending on the terrain. These fires provide the observer a point from which he can rapidly shift and bring additional fires on an enemy. Particular attention must be given to the location of the forward

12

elements of the maneuver force. Rate of movement will vary significantly depending upon terrain and vegetation. These fires are delivered under the control of a ground observer.

    d. <u>Defensive Concentrations ("Def Cons")</u>: "Def Cons" are defensive fires planned and fired around a night defensive position. These fires are adjusted by the ground observer prior to darkness and fired in at a distance of not less than 400 meters from the perimeter for the 105mm howitzer. "Def Cons" should be planned along likely avenues of approach, and all members of the observer party will know their locations. When required, a "Def Con" is fired with a battery or the number of tubes the FO intends to use. After the guns are warmed up by firing several volleys in the "Def Con" the FO will adjust the fires towards the NDP to neutralize the enemy attack. The 155mm howitzers can also be used for "Def Cons"; however, for reasons of troop safety they must be placed a greater distance from the NDP.

    e. <u>Harassing and Interdiction fires (H & I)</u>: H & I programs are planned using the best available intelligence information and an understanding of the enemy's use of terrain. H & I fires are usually fired at night without observation. Normally, an H & I target will be attacked by platoon (two howitzers) one round from light or medium artillery. After initial rounds fall into an H & I target area, continued artillery fire is a waste because enemy personnel will have taken cover. This does not preclude firing on the same target during a later period of the program.

    f. <u>Counter mortar/rocket fires</u>: Counter mortar/rocket fires are placed on

13

suspected enemy firing positions based on aerial reconnaissance, counter mortar
radar plots, shell reps, observation tower intersections and intelligence information. These targets can be fired during the hours of darkness as intelligence
fires. A counter mortar/rocket program is developed well in advance and continually improved based on current intelligence, visual observation, and seasonal
changes in the terrain. Such a program is fired when an NDP or base camp is
attacked by mortar or rocket fire.

    g. Recon by fire: Recon by fire are fires placed ahead of maneuver units
into suspect locations to kill the enemy or spoil his ambush.

4. Prior planning is basic to optimum, timely utilization of all means of fire
support. A comprehensive fire support plan will incorporate procedures for
bringing to bear artillery, mortars, air, and gunships on the designated target
with maximum effectiveness. The fire plan further serves as a mutually understood point of departure when the tactical situation dictates quick reaction
changes in fire support and its coordination.. Finally, contingency planning
will increase the flexibility and timeliness of fire coordination. This planning
must consider, but not be limited to, the following:

    a. Artillery gun-target lines.

    b. Location of friendly troops with respect to GT lines and possible
flight paths of TAC aircraft.

    c. Orbit area and flight paths of lift ships, gunships, and C & C ships.

    d. Adjacent units.

5. Successful reaction by fire support elements to targets of opportunity
is predicated upon centralized control and instantaneous communications.

6. In the event artillery fires are being effectively employed in support of troops in heavy contact, these fires will not be lifted for air strikes. Air strikes employing cannon and guns, CBU and Napalm will be used to augment these close artillery fires. Bombs and rockets are not used against the enemy in close contact because of safety considerations, but should be used as destruction or blocking fires on enemy reserves or known base camps in the area of engagement.

7. As an example, a company has been held up by a bunker complex approximately 200 meters wide across the route of advance. (See figure 2)

    a. The artillery FO requests fire from the DS battalion. The target requires heavier ordnance.

    b. Artillery and mortar fires are immediately brought to bear on the target. Meanwhile, the S3 air is instructed to initiate an immediate air strike for subsequent employment by the brigade or battalion commander. The artillery liaison officer determines the direction (gun target lines), the maximum ordinates, and mean points of impact of the artillery fires. This information, together with similar information on mortar fires, is passed to the FAC who plans the direction and type of attack for the aircraft in order to avoid the surface to surface fires. Ordnance, troop location, and direction from the target are also considered. The plan of the air strike is then coordinated with the artillery LNO and, through him, with the direct support battalion FDC which insures that the planned strike avoids all artillery fires. If required, the brigade or battalion commander will apply temporary restrictive fire measures such as fire coordination lines, quadrant allocation of air space, or

15

rectangular allocation of air space. Such measures will be applied at the latest possible time just prior to the first airstrike pass, and be lifted immediately after the last pass. The restrictions on artillery fire will be lifted when there is a time gap between flights to permit artillery to continue to fire.

c. When the FAC notifies the S3 Air, or the Air Liaison Officer (ALO), that high performance aircraft are in the area, the S3 Air informs the LNO who in turn informs the DS artillery battalion to shift fires (not cease), if required, to allow a safe distance between shell bursts and the attacking aircraft. (See Chart 1 for the minimum safe distances of exposed friendly troops and low flying supporting aircraft from friendly artillery and mortar fires.) Upon departure of the aircraft, the artillery may shift back to the center of mass of the target, if necessary. When the target has been neutralized or destroyed, artillery fires then revert to marching, "on call", or preplanned concentrations. Air remains "on call".

8. Helicopter gunships, with lateral separation, may also be brought to bear simultaneously with TAC air; however, each must be aware of the other's attack heading, breakaway heading, and area of maneuver. The supported commander controls the employment of TAC air and the gunships. Through his staff, he maintains constant communication with TAC air by entering the FAC control net. When helicopter gunships are requested, ACC is informed of the supported unit's frequency and call sign. The gunships enter that net for instructions before reaching the target area.

9. Separation of attacking units and consideration of adjacent ground units

is essential for the safety of all concerned. (See chart 2 for the minimum safe distances of friendly troops and low flying aircraft from aircraft delivered ordnance.)

a. Gunships and TAC air must be separated laterally due to delivery pattern differences and high rates of closure.

b. Artillery and TAC air may be separated laterally, vertically, or both. The smaller the target area, the less separation available; thus, there is a need for rapid and accurate coordination between elements. Troops in close contact receiving effective artillery fires will not have their fires lifted.

c. Fighters delivering low-drag bombs from high angle attack will complete their pullout at least 1000 feet above the surface. With this type of delivery, they can work close to, or even above, low angle artillery (vertical separation).

d. If the fighters are on low angle attack (napalm, strafing runs), release and recovery altitude are reduced. Under these circumstances, or with high angle artillery or mortar fire, horizontal separation must be provided.
10. The above principles also apply to "dust off" and resupply helicopters. Termination of artillery when attempting medical evacuation or resupply by air often increases the vulnerability of the aircraft to enemy fires as well as denying the infantry its support. Fires may be continued with the aircraft, given the gun-target lines, moving to and departing from the pick up or drop point on a course which avoids trajectories of fires. Initial instructions and enroute change of these instructions are the responsibility of ACC. Air Warning Centers further advise the pilot of current overall utilization of air

space and safe routing. Finally, the supported unit instructs the pilot on his approach to its landing zone.

11. Every soldier, who has access to a radio, should be capable of requesting and adjusting artillery fire. There are three items of information necessary to obtain artillery fire, as follows:

a. Target location: Target location is merely the grid read from a map of the intended target or enemy location.

b. Direction: Direction is the azimuth measured from the person requesting to fire to the target. When making the request it should be expressed as a grid azimuth.

c. Target description: Target description is an accurate description of the target provided to the artillery fire direction center, the best weapon and type of ammunition with which to attack the target can be determined.

12. It is absolutely essential that the infantry commander knows the exact location of all his units or elements at all times, and that he keeps his artillery current as to their disposition. This will enable the artillery to provide immediate fire support when requested. If the current disposition is not known fires may be delayed, or inadvertantly placed upon friendly elements. The responsibility to provide this information lies with the force commander. The artillery FO and LNO are available to assist him.

13. Effective and coordinated utilization of all fire support resources available will continue to contribute to the Big Red One's success in combat.

18

MINIMUM SAFE DISTANCE TABLE

UNPROTECTED TROOPS AND AIRCRAFT

	RANGE (1,000's meters), MET plus VE									
	2	4	6	8	10	12	14	16	18	20
4.2 inch mortar	450	475								
105mm howitzer		350	400	433	477					
155mm howitzer			420	420	421	428	433			
8 inch howitzer			350	350	350	350				
175mm gun					595	602	610	615	625	633

The table above depicts minimum safe distances in meters with a
0.99 assurance level (maximum damage radii plus 2.5 PE).

No radii of damage has been established for the 81mm mortar.
However, an acceptable minimum safe distance for this weapon
would be 320 meters.

After observed adjustment of battery center of impact on a
target, minimum safe distances in meters are as follows:

81mm mortar-----230	155mm howitzer---320
4.2 inch mortar-300	8 inch howitzer--240
105mm howitzer--270	175mm gun -------500

CHART 1

MINIMUM SAFE DISTANCE TABLE
(All distances in meters)

	PROTECTED TROOPS (1)	UNPROTECTED TROOPS (2)
BOMB: 1000 lb and larger	240	1,000
BOMB: 750 lb low drag	193	750
BOMB: 750 lb high drag	148	750
BOMB: 500 lb low drag	218	500
BOMB: 500 lb high drag	142	500
BOMB: less than 500 lb	142	500
NAPALM: (Delivery parallel to friendly troops)	75	75
NAPALM: (Delivery perpendicular to friendly troops)	112	112
CBU	105	105
ROCKETS: (All pods)	217	217
CANNON and GUNS: (20mm, .50 cal. 7.62mm)	25	25

Protection indicated in column 1 refers to bunkers, trenchs, foxholes or armored vehicles.

Column 1 is based upon figures extracted from USAF ammunition tables ι . and considers delivery system errors. Column 2 is based upon USAF SOP and may be altered by the FAC concerned.

Consideration must be given to type ordnance used, delivery system, attack procedures used, and local weather conditions. Any of these can significantly alter the MSD for a given target.

CHART 2

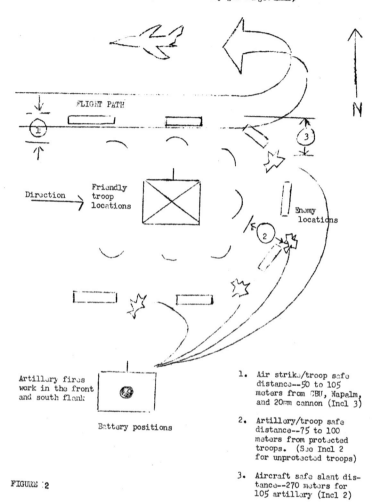

Air w/CBU, Napalm, and 20mm cannon works
flank (away from artillery gun-target line)

FLIGHT PATH

Direction

Friendly
troop
locations

Enemy
locations

Artillery fires
work in the front
and south flank

Battery positions

1. Air strike/troop safe
   distance--50 to 105
   meters from CBU, Napalm,
   and 20mm cannon (Incl 3)

2. Artillery/troop safe
   distance--75 to 100
   meters from protected
   troops. (See Incl 2
   for unprotected troops)

3. Aircraft safe slant dis-
   tance--270 meters for
   105 artillery (Incl 2)

FIGURE 2

Glossary

Glossary

A-22 ammunition A type of ammunition used with howitzers.

AK-47 The standard Russian-made assault rifle. It fires automatic or semiautomatic from a 20-round magazine; 7.62mm.

AR-15 The original version of the standard U.S. assault rifle. The M-16 version fires automatic or semiautomatic from a 20-round magazine; 5.56mm high velocity. It was introduced during the Vietnam War.

Ambush patrols A small group of soldiers sent outside an area or ground held by friendly forces whose function is to ambush enemy patrols or formations.

B-52 strikes Heavy bombers that flew out of Guam and Thailand and delivered carpet-type bombing into the jungle, a.k.a. "Arc Light."

BAR Browning Automatic Rifle.

BG Brigadier general; one star rank.

BN Battalion. A unit of approximately seven hundred men that is found above the level of companies and below the levels of brigades or regiments; it is usually commanded by a lieutenant colonel.

BDE Brigade. A command and control headquarters that operates between the level of a division and the level of battalions; it is usually commanded by a colonel.

Base camps Major military enclaves that were established by U.S. forces to house and administer the war effort. Although periodically subject to enemy mortar and rocket fire, base camps were relatively secure locations.

Bunker A military fortification, normally built to house two or more men; it uses overhead cover to reduce the effect of shell fragments. It is also used to shoot from in defense.

C-4 A white, pliable, powerful, plastic explosive that is used with a detonator.

C&C A command and control helicopter; outfitted with several banks of radios for use in controlling ground operations while airborne.

Call sign The name designated in a written SOP that an individual or unit uses to identify itself when using radio/telephone procedures.

CAR-15 A submachine gun version of the M-16.

Cat Hole A one-time hole dug in the ground in which a soldier would defecate.

CBU Cluster bomb unit. Canisters were often used against enemy personnel because they released large numbers of small bomblets over an area-type target.

CDR Commander.

CH-47 Chinook A large cargo helicopter.

Checkfire The artillery command to stop firing.

Chieu Hoi The name for former VC personnel who turned themselves in to the South Vietnamese government.

Chopper A helicopter (not a motorcycle).

Christmas Tree A formation that helicopters would normally use to land at an LZ or PZ; also known as a staggered trail.

CIDG Civilian Irregular Defense Group; a South Vietnamese paramilitary force.

Claymore An explosive, directional mine. Shaped like a car's brake shoe, it fires ball bearings along the ground with devastating effect, especially when individuals are in the blast path.

Cloverleaf A close-in security patrol that utilizes a circular out-and-in pattern ahead of a unit.

CMD Command.

Company A unit of approximately two hundred soldiers; usually commanded by a captain.

Compass azimuth Direction shown on a compass.

Coordinates A ground location identified by a lettered and numbered grid system that has been superimposed on a map (for example: XT 686576).

C rations Canned food and packaged accessories in a small cardboard box; one meal per box.

DEFCON Defensive Concentrations. A preplanned and registered location for placement of artillery fire in defense.

Dongs Medals and awards hung on the uniform.

DSC Distinguished Service Cross; the second highest U.S. award for valor.

Division A military organization of approximately 17,000 men, normally organized into three brigades and a support command. Each brigade normally has three battalions.

DTOC Division tactical operations center. The brain center of the division that usually housed all the elements necessary for command and control of a division.

Dustoff A medical evacuation helicopter.

Extraction The process of picking up soldiers by helicopters during tactical operations.

FAC Forward air controller. A U.S. Air Force officer who controls air force tactical air strikes from small fixed-wing aircraft.

Field grade officers All officers above the rank of captain.

Flight More than one slick; normally five helicopters.

FM radio Frequency modulated radios; standard military radio used to receive and transmit communications. FM radios use line-of-sight transmission.

FNG Unofficial abbreviation: everyone in Vietnam was a FNG until he was accepted by the group.

Frag order An abbreviation for fragmentary order. An order that only covers absolutely essential elements; normally frag orders were issued verbally.

G3 The staff operations, plans, and training officer, or his office, which has a general officer in command.

GT line Gun target line. A line drawn on a map between a weapon and a target.

Gunships Armed helicopters designed to suppress enemy fire and attack enemy targets by machine guns, grenades, and rocket fire.

H&I Harassing and interdictory fires. Indirect fires or H&I were placed on known or suspected targets of enemy activity. H&I is fired at random without immediate observation of the results.

Helicopter assault, heliborne assault, airmobile assault, and air assault All synonymous terms for the use of helicopters to place troops into a tactical environment.

Hex tent A small tent with six equal sides; normally used to house two to four men.

Hooch A place of residence of soldiers outside the U.S., normally in Asia.

Huey Any of the family of UH-1 Bell helicopters.

INF Infantry.

K-Bar knife A leather-handled knife with a six-inch blade that was normally issued to marines.

KIA or kilos Killed in combat action.

Kudzu A vine-like green plant of many leaves that grows like hell in Vietnam.

Latrine A designated location, normally a hole dug in the ground, used for community defecation.

L-19 birddog The military equivalent of the Piper Cub aircraft.

LNO Liaison officer.

LOH Light observation helicopter (H-13).

Long Toms 175mm M107SP artillery guns. These are long-barreled artillery that have a range of thirty kilometers.

LP Listening post. LPs were primarily used at night. They were placed fifty to one hundred meters outside an NDP to give early warning of the approach of enemy troops. After giving a warning of an enemy presence, the one or two men in the LP would withdraw to the NDP.

LTC Lieutenant colonel. In a division it is the rank of a battalion commander or a senior staff officer.

LZ Landing zone.

M-1 Garand The .30-caliber World War II U.S. rifle.

M-14 The 7.62mm U.S. semiautomatic rifle.

M-16 See AR-15.

M-60 machine gun The standard U.S. 7.62mm machine gun.

M-79 A grenade launcher. The M-79 is a shotgun-like weapon that is loaded with a 40mm grenade cartridge by cracking open the weapon at the breach. It fires grenades accurately up to three hundred meters. Another name for this weapon is "thump gun."

MACV Military Assistance Command, Vietnam.

Main Force Former guerrillas formed into a regular VC division early in the war.

Medevac The abbreviation for medical evacuation. In Vietnam this was usually done by a dustoff.

Mermite cans Insulated food containers.

MG Major general; two stars.

MIA Missing in combat action.

mm Millimeter.

Napalm Jellied gasoline. Napalm is a munition that is normally dropped from air force aircraft or employed by flamethrowers.

NDP Night defensive position. All 1st Infantry Division units established NDPs when they were outside their base camps overnight.

NVA North Vietnamese Army. These were regular North Vietnamese soldiers as opposed to the VC, who were communist guerrilla troops in South Vietnam. The formal name for the NVA was the People's Army of Vietnam (PAVN).

North Vietnam The area in Indochina that was north of the demilitarized zone (DMZ) along the 17th parallel of north latitude.

Ole Abbreviation for "old." It is used in jest by the author and never to a superior officer's face.

OPS Abbreviation for operations.

Platoon A unit of forty soldiers that is usually commanded by a lieutenant. Three platoons typically comprised a company.

PRC-25 A portable FM tactical radio that is normally referred to as a "prick 25."

PRU Province Reconnaissance Unit. A South Vietnamese provincial military element that was normally used to gather intelligence for the province chief.

PT Physical training.

PZ Pick up zone.

RC 292 A large portable radio antenna used to extend the range of radios carried in the field.

Reconnaissance platoon The "eyes and ears" of an infantry battalion that normally consisted of about forty highly trained soldiers.

Regiment A regiment is similar to a brigade, but it is not an operational unit. Infantry regiments are used in the U.S. Army for historical purposes.

RPD 12.7mm Degtyarev light machine gun A drum-fed, bipod-supported, Russian-made machine gun.

RPG Rocket-propelled grenade. The letters actually stand for some Slavic words because RPGs were often Soviet/East Bloc-made weapons.

RTO Radio telephone operator, who was normally called a "romeo." A RTO was typically a designated soldier who carried and operated PRC-25 radios. He was an important man who had to know his stuff.

RVN Republic of Vietnam (South Vietnam).

S3 The operations, plans, and training officer, or his office, at the infantry brigade or battalion level.

S3 Air The assistant to the S3. This officer did all the planning and directing of air operations, both army and air force, at the battalion or brigade level.

SACEUR Supreme Allied Commander Europe.

Seal A tactical maneuver that places friendly troops around a potentially hostile position, usually a village. This maneuver is normally conducted by stealth.

Secret Zone A translation of a Vietnamese term for an enemy stronghold.

Shard A fragment of an artillery shell, usually jagged and dangerous. A piece of shrapnel.

Shoulder patch The distinctive insignia of a division worn on the left shoulder (combat veterans may wear it on the right shoulder).

Silver Star The third highest U.S. award for valor.

Sitrep Situation report. A brief description of a unit's situation or disposition.

Slick A Huey helicopter that was stripped of doors and seats to carry eight to ten U.S. soldiers on assaults and extractions.

Sniper Normally this was a specially trained soldier who tries to shoot selected targets, such as commanders and RTOs, from a concealed position.

SOP Standard operating procedure.

South Vietnam The area of Indochina south of the demilitarized zone (DMZ) along the 17th parallel of north latitude.

Staggered trail An offset flying formation used by helicopters.

TA-1 sound-powered phones Hand-held telephones connected by wire that were powered only by sound waves and thus could not be intercepted by the enemy.

TAOI Tactical area of interest. Usually a large area designated by higher headquarters for oversight by a unit.

TAOR Tactical area of responsibility. Typically a TAOR was smaller than a TAOI and lay within a TAOI. A unit commander has direct responsibility for a TAOR.

Tet Offensive The full-scale battle in South Vietnam, particularly in the cities of Hué and Saigon, that started on January 31, 1968. The VC and NVA forces launched the offensive on the night of the celebration of the Lunar New Year (TET).

TOC Tactical operations center.

Trip flare A munition that burns with a bright light, illuminating the battlefield. The inadvertent pulling of a concealed wire, known as a trip wire, normally sets off a trip flare.

VIC Vicinity.

Viet Cong (VC) The name used for communist guerrillas who fought against the South Vietnamese and U.S. forces in South Vietnam. The formal name for the VC was the National Front for the Liberation of South Vietnam. Its military arm was the People's Liberation Armed Forces (PLAF).

VTR Vehicle, tracked, recovery. An army maintenance vehicle

WIA Wounded in combat action.

War Zone C An area approximately thirty to forty kilometers northwest of Saigon that was a known sanctuary for VC and NVA forces.

War Zone D An area to the northeast of Saigon that was also a known sanctuary for VC and NVA forces.

XO Executive officer; the second-ranking officer in a unit.

Sources

Books

Associates, The Department of Behavioral Sciences and Leadership, U.S. Military Academy, West Point, N.Y. *Leadership in Organizations.* Garden City, N.Y.: Avery Publishing Group, 1988.

Bradley, Omar N. *A Soldier's Story.* New York: Holt, Rinehart and Winston, 1951.

Connell, Evan S. *Son of the Morning Star.* San Francisco, Calif.: North Point Press, 1984.

Crane, Stephen. *The Red Badge of Courage.* New York: Bantam Books, 1895; 1985.

Davidson, Phillip B. *Vietnam at War: The History, 1946–1975.* Novato, Calif.: Presidio Press, 1988.

Doyle, Sir Arthur Conan. *The Conan Doyle Stories.* Leicester, Eng.: Galley Press, 1956.

Field Manual 101-5-1. *Operational Terms and Symbols.* Washington, D.C.: Department of the Army, 1985.

Garland, Albert N., ed. *Infantry in Vietnam.* Fort Benning, Ga.: Infantry magazine; reprinted Nashville, Tenn.: Battery Press, 1967.

Hemphill, Robert. *Platoon: Bravo Company.* Fredericksburg, Va.: Sergeant Kirkland's Museum and Historical Society, 1998; New York: St. Martin's, 2001.

Karnow, Stanley. *Vietnam: A History.* New York: Viking Press, 1983.

L'Amour, Louis. *The Last of the Breed*. New York: Bantam Books, 1986.

MacGarrigle, George L. *Combat Operations: Taking the Offensive, October 1966 to October 1967*. United States Army in Vietnam. Washington, D.C.: U.S. Army Center of Military History, 1998.

Mahler, Michael D. *Ringed in Steel: Armored Cavalry, Vietnam 1967–68*. Novato, Calif.: Presidio Press, 1986.

Malone, Dandridge M. *Small Unit Leadership: A Commonsense Approach*. Novato, Calif.: Presidio Press, 1983.

Mangold, Tom and John Penycate. *The Tunnels of Cu Chi*. New York: Random House, 1985.

McDonough, James R. *Platoon Leader*. Novato, Calif.: Presidio Press, 1985.

Melville, Herman. *Moby-Dick*. Pleasantville, N.Y.: reprint ed., Reader's Digest Association, 1851; 1989.

Moore, Harold G. and Joseph L. Galloway. *We Were Soldiers Once… And Young:Ia Drang, the Battle that Changed the War in Vietnam*. New York: Random House, 1992; HarperPerennial, 1993.

Morris, Donald R. *The Washing of the Spears: A History of the Rise of the Zulu Nation Under Shaka and Its Fall in the Zulu War of 1879*. New York: Simon and Schuster, 1965.

Palmer, Bruce, Jr. *The 25-Year War: America's Military Role in Vietnam*. Lexington, Ky.: University Press of Kentucky, 1984.

Palmer, Dave Richard. *Summons of the Trumpet: U.S.-Vietnam in Perspective*. Novato, Calif.: Presidio Press, 1978.

Register of Graduates and Former Cadets of the United States Military Academy. Association of Graduates. West Point, N. Y., U.S. Military Academy, 1987.

Service, Robert. *Rhymes of a Red Cross Man*. New York: Barse & Hopkins, 1916.

Summers, Harry G., Jr. *On Strategy: A Critical Analysis of the Vietnam War.* Novato, Calif.: Presidio Press, 1982.

Trotter, William R. *Bushwackers!: The Mountains.* Winston-Salem, N.C.: J. F. Blair, 1991.

Utley, Robert M. *Frontier Regulars: The United States Army and the Indian, 1866–1891.* New York: Macmillan Publishing Company, 1973.

Weigley, Russell F. *History of the United States Army.* New York: Macmillan Publishing Company, 1967.

Yearbooks. 1st Infantry Division in Vietnam. Vols. I and II, 1965–1966; 1967–1968. 1st Infantry Division Public Information Office.

Periodicals

Assembly. Association of Graduates of the U.S. Military Academy, West Point, N. Y., 34, no. 3 (December 1975): 123-124.

DANGER Forward. The Magazine of the Big Red One. Vietnam. 1, no. 3 (August 1967).

DANGER Forward. The Magazine of the Big Red One. Vietnam. 1, no. 4 (December 1967).

DANGER Forward. The Magazine of the Big Red One. Vietnam. 2, no. 1 (February 1968).

Flanagan, Richard W. "Shenandoah II." *DANGER Forward. The Magazine of the Big Red One. Vietnam.* 2, no. 2 (June 1968): 2–8.

Shelton, James E. "The Battle of Ong Thanh." *Vietnam* 6 (August 1994): 26–32.

Welcome to the Big Red One. Orientation booklet prepared by the editors of Danger Forward. 1st Division Information Office. No date.

Sources

Interviews

Clarence Barrrow, 1st Sergeant, D Company, 2-28 Infantry

John Cash, U.S. Army Center for Military History

Richard Cavazos, commander, 1-18 Infantry

Joseph Costello, A Company, 2-28 Infantry

Michael Dinkins, C Company, 2-28 Infantry

Fred Gantzler, commander, B Battery, 6-15 Artillery

James D. George, commander, A Company, 2-28 Infantry

Robert Gillard, executive officer, 2-28 Infantry

Thomas Grady, executive officer, A Company, 2-28 Infantry

Michael Gribble, brother of Ray Neal Gribble

Thomas Hinger, A Company, 2-28 Infantry

James Kasik, commander, B Company, 2-28 Infantry

George L. MacGarrigle, U.S. Army Center of Military History

George E. Newman, commander, 1st Brigade, 1st Infantry Division

Thomas Reese, commander, C Company, 2-28 Infantry

David H. Stroup, platoon leader, 3rd platoon, D Company, 2-28 Infantry

Albert Clark Welch, commander, D Company, 2-28 Infantry

Index

Name Index

F

Fallaci, Oriana, 116-17
Familiare, Spec.4 Anthony, 221
Farrell, Spec.4 Michael J., 221
Fehrenbach, T. R., 24
Fitzgerald, Pfc. Paul L., 159, 194, 222
Flanagan, Capt. Richard W., 135
Fortenberry, Lt. Bobby, 154
Frederick William II the Great, 17
Fuqua, Pfc. Robert L., Jr., 221

G

Gallagher, Spec.4 Mike (Pee Wee), 148, 221
Gantzler, Capt. Fred, 182, 185
Garcia, Spec.4 Arturo, 221
Garcia, Pfc. Melesso, 221
Genghis Kahn, 214
George, Capt. James D., 50-51, 75, 88, 104, 107, 126, 127, 128, 130, 155, 156, 157, 158, 161, 162, 175, 189, 207-09, 227, **237**, 244
Gilbert, Spec.4 Stanley D., 221
Gilbertson, Spec.5 Verland A., 124, 125, 221, 241
Gillard, Maj. Bob, 45, 70, 90, 187, 189, 209, 210, **236**
Grady, Lt. Tom (Eltee or LT), xi, 188, 189, 191, **244**
Gribble, Spec.4 Ray N., v, xvii, 104, 105, 219, 220, 221, 228, **243**
Grider, Pvt. Edward, 171

H

Halley, Capt. Nick, 34, 63, 64
Hargrove, Pvt. Olin, Jr., 159, 194, 222
Hay, Maj. Gen. John H., 17, 18, 19, 25, 26, 28, 41, 58, 70, 80, 104, 106, 108, 138, 197-200, 214, 227, **233**
Heller, Joseph, xi
Hinger, Spec.4 Tom (Doc), xi, 141, 151, 158, 160, 188, 190, 191, **244**
Ho Chi Minh, 5
Holleder Maj. Don, xiii, **xxiv**, 82, 124, 125, 126, 173, 174, 176, 186-188, 221, **241, 242**
Hollingsworth, Brig. Gen. James F. (Holly), 16, 18, 198
Huebner, Maj. Gen. Clarence R., 13

J

Jagielo, Pfc. Allen D., 221
Johnson, Sfc Willie C. J., 221

Subject Index

D

About the Author

James E. Shelton was born and raised in the zinc-mining town of Franklin in northwestern New Jersey. He played football at the University of Delaware and entered the U.S. Army as a second lieutenant, infantry, upon graduation in 1957. During his career he served in eight army divisions and the Berlin Brigade. He commanded three rifle platoons, two rifle companies, an airborne infantry battalion, and a mechanized infantry brigade. He also served in the Pentagon in the Office of the Joint Chiefs of Staff. He retired from the army in 1983 as a brigadier general, combat infantryman, and master parachutist. He presently resides in Florida and serves as the Honorary Colonel of the 28th Infantry Regiment. He and his wife, Joan, have five daughters and three sons, and fourteen grandchildren.